Language in Social Groups

Language in Social Groups

Essays by John J. Gumperz

• • •

Selected and Introduced
by Anwar S. Dil

Stanford University Press, Stanford, California 1971

Language Science and National Development

A Series Sponsored by the
Linguistic Research Group of Pakistan

General Editor: Anwar S. Dil

Stanford University Press
Stanford, California
© 1971 by John J. Gumperz
Printed in the United States of America
ISBN 0-8047-0798-7
LC 75-170982

Contents

II. LANGUAGE USAGE AND SOCIAL INTERACTION

Acknowledgments

The Linguistic Research Group of Pakistan and the Editor of the Language Science and National Development Series are deeply grateful to Professor John J. Gumperz, Life Member of the Group, for giving us the privilege of presenting his selected writings as the third volume in our series established in 1970 to commemorate the International Education Year.

We are indebted to the editors and publishers of the following publications. The ready permission on the part of the holders of the copyrights, acknowledged in each case, is a proof of the existing international cooperation and goodwill that gives hope for better collaboration among scholars of all nations for international exchange of knowledge.

Some Remarks on Regional and Social Language Differences in India. Introduction to the Civilization of India: Changing Dimensions in Indian Society and Culture, ed. by Milton Singer (Chicago: The College, University of Chicago Syllabus Division, 1957), pp. 31-38.

Language Problems in the Rural Development of North India. Journal of Asian Studies 16. 251-59 (1957), with permission of the publisher. © 1957 by the Association for Asian Studies, Inc.

Dialect Differences and Social Stratification in a North Indian Village. American Anthropologist 60. 668-81 (1958).

Formal and Informal Standards in Hindi Regional Language Area; with C. M. Naim. International Journal of American Linguis-

Mouton & Company, 1964), pp. 1115-24, with permission of the publisher.

The Relation of Linguistic to Social Categories. A Field Manual for Cross-Cultural Study of the Acquisition of Communicative Competence, ed. by D. I. Slobin (Berkeley: ASUC Bookstore, University of California, 1967), pp. 84-92.

Communication in Multilingual Societies. Cognitive Anthropology, ed. by Stephen A. Tyler (New York: Holt, Rinehart and Winston, 1969), pp. 435-448, with permission of the publisher. © 1969 by Holt, Rinehart and Winston, Inc.

Convergence and Creolization: A Case from the Indo-Aryan/ Dravidian Border in India; with Robert Wilson. Pidginization and Creolization, ed. by Dell H. Hymes (London: Cambridge University Press, 1971), pp. 151-67, with permission of the publisher.

Social Meaning in Linguistic Structures: Code-Switching in Norway; with Jan-Petter Blom. Directions in Sociolinguistics, ed. by John J. Gumperz and Dell H. Hymes (New York: Holt, Rinehart and Winston, in press).

Bilingualism, Bidialectalism, and Classroom Interaction; with Eduardo Hernández Ch. Functions of Language in the Classroom, ed. by Courtney B. Cazden, V.P. John, and D. Hymes (New York: Teachers College Press, in press).

The Editor completed work on this volume during 1969-71, while he was in residence as Visiting Scholar at Stanford University. The financial assistance from the Institute of International Studies, University of California, Berkeley, to cover typing expenses of the manuscript is gratefully acknowledged. He is personally grateful to the Committee on Linguistics and the Stanford International Development Education Center of Stanford University for providing him with office accommodation.

The Editor also wishes to record his thanks to Professors Einar Haugen of Harvard University, Wallace E. Lambert of McGill University, Joshua A. Fishman of Yeshiva University, Susan Ervin-Tripp of the University of California, and other language scholars who have sent us materials for our forthcoming volumes. Afia Dil of the Committee on Linguistics, Stanford University, Nasim Dil of the Department of Special Education, University of Texas, Albert Legrand and Emily Vargas-Baron of Unesco, Dell Hymes and William Labov of the University of Pennsylvania, Jennifer Cook of the University of London, Michael Agar of the Department of Anthropology, University of Hawaii, Sarah Russell and Melanie Tayeb of the University of California, and J. G. Bell of Stanford University Press, deserve our gratitude for help in many ways. Patricia Fisk and Martha Kirtley have done most of the typing of camera-ready manuscript and they certainly deserve a word of appreciation.

EDITOR'S NOTE

These essays have been reprinted from the originals with only minor changes made in the interest of uniformity of style and appearance. A few changes in wording have been made in consultation with the author. In some cases notes and bibliographical entries have been corrected and updated. Footnotes marked by asterisks have been added by the Editor. Chapters within each section have been arranged chronologically (publication of chapter 10 was delayed).

Introduction

John J. Gumperz was born in 1922 in Germany, and came to the United States in 1939. After getting his bachelor's degree in science at the University of Cincinnati in 1947, he did some graduate work in chemistry at the University of Michigan, where he became interested in attending lectures at the Linguistic Institute. He soon switched over to full-time linguistic studies, and in 1954, after two years as a research associate and instructor in linguistics at Cornell University, he was awarded a Ph.D. degree in German linguistics by the University of Michigan. There followed two years of field work in India and an appointment at the University of California, Berkeley, where he became Professor of Anthropology in 1965.

Gumperz is the organizer of the South Asian program at Berkeley and has served as chairman of the Center for South and South East Asia Studies (1968-71). He is one of the senior members of the research team at the Language-Behavior Research Laboratory at Berkeley, which is known for its work in cognitive anthropology, psycholinguistics, and sociolinguistics. Since 1966 he has been active in the Committee on Sociolinguistics of the Social Science Research Council. In collaboration with Susan Ervin-Tripp and Dan I. Slobin, Gumperz has played an important role in planning and organizing cross-cultural research on the acquisition of language, both by training a number of students to do such work and by participating in the preparation of A Field Manual for Cross-Cultural Study of the Acquisition of Communicative Competence (1967). A high point of this activity, supported by the Committee, was a summer training program held at Berkeley in 1968 in which a number of students and scholars from a variety of fields became involved in sociolinguistic work. He is a member of the editorial board of the new international journal Language in Society and has been a life member of the Linguistic Research Group of Pakistan since 1968.

Gumperz first developed an interest in sociolinguistic problems while working on his doctoral dissertation, a study of the Swabian dialect of a group of third-generation farmers in Washtenaw County, Michigan. The discovery that the linguistic leveling processes observable among these people, whose German immigrant ancestors had come from at least two dialect groups, could be accounted for, in large part, by the linguistic and social groupings formed after settlement in the United States, became the basis for his subsequent research on the relationship of speech alternation to social groups.

At Cornell University Gumperz was invited to take over the Hindi language training program. Subsequently he served as a member of a Cornell University team of social scientists carrying out a community study project in a North Indian village. As the only linguist in a team of anthropologists, sociologists, economists, and other specialists, he was forced to come to grips with problems other than linguistic and also to approach linguistic problems from different perspectives. His two years in India provided a rigorous training in interdisciplinary social science research that has proved of great value in his subsequent work. Above all his experience convinced him of the essential part that empirical field work and cultural background knowledge play in the development of good theory.

After his return from India, Gumperz was invited to set up a Hindi-Urdu program at the University of California, Berkeley. While the work of preparing language materials kept him occupied for the first few years at Berkeley, as can be seen from his well-known series of language handbooks and readers, he found his professional interests increasingly centering around the description of sociolinguistic problems in the data on speech behavior he had brought with him from India. He published at this time the first of a series of insightful essays on the relationships of social differences to linguistic differences. In the summer of 1956 Gumperz and Charles A. Ferguson were together as visiting faculty members at the Deccan College,

where they began to share notes on problems of linguistic diversity
and language development in general. They continued this exchange
and organized a symposium on the subject at the 1958 annual meeting
of the American Anthropological Association. The resulting volume,
Linguistic Diversity in South Asia (1960), has since become a standard
work in the field. Its introductory chapter, written jointly by Ferguson and Gumperz, is generally regarded as one of the first concise
statements of sociolinguistic problems and remains unequaled in its
clear grasp of the broad issues.

In 1963, with the help of Dell Hymes and Susan Ervin-Tripp,
he organized symposiums at the spring meeting of the Kroeber Anthropological Society and the annual meeting in November of the American
Anthropological Association. Among the participants in these symposiums were Edward T. Hall, Erving Goffman, Charles O Frake, and
William Labov. The resulting volume, The Ethnography of Communication (1964), edited by Hymes and Gumperz, is another landmark in
the field.

Gumperz spent part of 1963 at the Institute of Sociology at
Oslo University. While in Norway, he collaborated with Jan-Petter
Blom of the Institute of Social Anthropology at Bergen in studying a
community where social differentiation is far less important than in
India. His work there bore out his earlier findings on the importance
of social relationships in determining speech behavior in social groups.
He subsequently extended his field work to Central India, Austria, and
Yugoslavia, collecting data that have further refined his understanding
of bilingualism in relation to social boundaries and overall sociolinguistic structure. More recently, he has also worked with Mexican-
American bilinguals for the Bilingualism and Ethnic Boundaries
Project at the Institute of International Studies at Berkeley. A volume
of readings reflecting some of these interests, Directions in Sociolinguistics, co-edited with Dell Hymes, is scheduled to appear in 1972.

Perhaps the most notable feature of Gumperz's work so far
is the growth of his concept of language as interaction. He is interested less in language per se than in language as it is used by people
belonging to different social groups through particular networks of

relationships, and above all with how these relationships are reflected in verbal behavior. Especially because of his experience with bilingual and language contact situations, he finds it difficult to maintain the separateness of language systems; he prefers to look at languages, dialects, or styles as subsystems within an overall "speech repertoire" of an individual or a social group. "Repertoire," as opposed to the more limited notion of "a language," is a basic concept in his work; he finds the concept of linguistic repertoire necessary, for example, in describing code-switching in the verbal behavior of a bilingual person or community. In proposing such new concepts, Gumperz is in no way taking issue with the study of language in the abstract; his view is simply that sociolinguistic work requires a different set of concepts and methods.

As I see it, Gumperz is moving toward a type of sociolinguistic description that will make possible the processing of linguistic and social information in terms of a more coordinated theoretical framework. In this effort his most valuable contribution to date, as William Labov has observed, is his ability to locate what Merton calls "strategic research sites." His series of articles on language in social groups has been of pioneering value in explaining some sociolinguistic phenomena; but more important, his observations have raised a number of critical questions regarding the nature and function of language, the relationship of linguistic analysis to the speech behavior of people, and the principles and methods of sociolinguistic research. It is with confidence in the stimulating value of his work that I have compiled this volume of his representative essays for the Language Science and National Development Series. It should prove of interest to all students of sociolinguistics, especially those in areas where social processes in multilingual contexts present a challenge to national development and progress.

Anwar S. Dil

Committee on Linguistics
Stanford University
October 1971

Language in Social Groups

Part I. Language and Dialect Diversity

1 Some Remarks on Regional and Social Language Differences in India

A great deal of attention has been devoted in recent years to the problem of linguistic diversity in India and its relation to the development of regionalism. There is disagreement on almost every aspect of the problem. Some writers believe that the growing use of regional languages will hamper communication between the various sectors of the population and impair the proper functioning of the central government. Others are confident that the difficulty will be overcome and that the development of Hindi as a national language will counteract the regional tendencies.

The disagreements are not confined to matters of interpretation and policy making; they touch on almost every aspect of the basic data, such as existing languages and dialects, the areas in which they are used, number of speakers and even connotations given to the basic terminology.

Here are some examples. The word language is used in a number of different meanings. Sometimes it refers to linguistic groups, as in the statement: "India is divided into several regional blocks of languages, each of which would like separate political entity."[1] On other occasions it seems to have something to do with script, as in: "opponents of Hindi stress script and other differences between Hindi and Urdu."[2] Some linguists use it to indicate a group of related dialects, sharing certain common characteristics.[3] Similarly the term dialect is usually left undefined.

Some forms of speech are called languages by certain writers, dialects by others. The introductory notes to the Census of India,[4] for example, raise questions such as: is Konkani a dialect of Marathi or is it a separate language; do Bihari and Rajasthani exist as separate languages or not. Regarding the numbers of languages and dialects spoken in India, Grierson gives two different sets of figures, those of the 1921 census, and those of the Linguistic Survey of India. Writers also differ greatly on the number of speakers of individual languages, for example, figures for Hindi vary anywhere from 100-150 millions.

In a number of cases border controversies have arisen seemingly over the question of whether a certain dialect is part of one language or another. This has happened, for example, in the case of certain Bhili dialects along the Gujarati-Marathi border area. There are of course other political and economic causes for the conflicting claims, but the linguistic arguments figure most prominently in the discussion.

Disagreements of the above kinds are so numerous that they raise doubt as to the adequacy of traditional concepts used in the description of language distribution and the ways of defining linguistic areas. It might therefore be useful to review the situation in the light of what is known on the subject from the work of linguists and make an effort to develop new concepts for interpretation of the available data.

There are two methods of collecting information about language distribution. One may, as is done in the census, ask direct questions of informants as to what languages they speak, or, one may collect samples of speech and analyse them linguistically. In the United States, where the great majority of the population speaks English and those that do not speak well known literary languages, the results obtained by the two methods usually agree. In India this is by no means so. There has always been a big gulf between the speech of the masses and the literary idioms used by the relatively small educated minority. Whatever preoccupation there has been with language so far has been concerned with written

forms. The educated public has paid little attention to the various
forms of popular speech and the average uneducated person, on the
other hand, rarely has occasion to refer to his speech by name.
As a result, names for many of the local forms of speech vary
greatly. Grierson gives the following illustration of this:

> "Another difficulty was the finding of the local name
> of a dialect. Just as M. Jourdain did not know that he had
> been speaking prose all his life, so the average Indian
> villager does not know that he has been speaking anything
> with a name attached to it. He can always put a name to
> the dialect spoken by somebody fifty miles off, but, — as
> for his own dialect, —'O, that has no name. It is simple
> correct language.' It thus happens that most dialect
> names are not those given by the speakers, but those
> given by their neighbours, and are not always complimentary.
> For instance, there is a well-known form of speech in
> the south of the Punjab called 'Jangali,' from its being
> spoken in the 'Jungle,' or unirrigated country bordering
> on Bikaner. But 'Jangali,' also means 'boorish' and local
> inquiries failed to find a single person who admitted that
> he spoke that language. 'O yes, we know Jungali very
> well, — you will find it a little further on, —not here.'
> You go a little further on and get the same reply, and
> pursue your will-o'-the-wisp till he lands you in the
> Rajputana desert, where there is no one to speak any
> language at all. These illustrations show the difficulties
> encountered by local officers in identifying dialects and
> naming them."

Another problem may arise in cases when the dialect of
certain informants is of low prestige and they prefer to list themselves as speakers of a high prestige dialect. This has occurred
with many speakers of tribal languages whose languages are
disappearing and who are identifying themselves with the dominant
Hindu society. It also happened in the case of many Dravidian
speakers in those bilingual areas of Bombay State where the control
of government is (or was) largely in the hands of Maharashtrians.

When direct linguistic field work is done, it is possible to avoid most of the above difficulties. The raw datum is the actual speech, and it may be classified solely by internal criteria, without reference to dialect or language names. The LSI, which is the basic source book for data on language distribution in India, was done at a time when the methodology of linguistic field work and dialect classification had not yet been worked out, and it is some-what deficient with respect to the type of phonological data that are basic for the grouping of dialects. It has been supplemented by a number of more modern studies on individual dialects and although data are still scanty, they seem adequate for a preliminary summary of the facts of linguistic distribution.

1. Types of dialects and languages [5]

We will start at the village level. In certain parts of the Himalayan foothills the dialect of each valley is said to be mutually incomprehensible with that of the neighboring valley. In the plains these variations are not so great, but villagers from one part of the country frequently state that they are unable to understand the local dialect of their relatives by marriage less than a hundred miles away.

Because of the great number of local variations in speech, when a villager visits the bazaar of the nearby trading center and talks with merchants and villagers from other areas he must, in order to communicate effectively, drop his more obvious localisms and use other forms having less restricted distribution. In this manner over the years new trade dialects have developed, which we will refer to as regional dialects, to distinguish them from local dialects. The regional dialect is the native language of small town residents. There are some variations between one town and another, but these are minor in comparison to the differences on a local level. The distinction between local and regional dialect has not been sufficiently emphasized in dialect research in India. Most of the samples in the LSI seem to be closer to the regional rather than to the local village form of dialect.

Some of these regional dialects, such as Braj Bhasa, spoken around Agra, Avadhi spoken around Lucknow, the Konkani spoken around Goa, have in the past been used as vehicles for literature and have become well known. At the present time this literary activity has virtually died out. The number of regional dialects is large. In the census some of the better known ones are listed as separate languages, others as dialects; a great many others are not mentioned at all.

In addition to local and regional dialects, there are the idioms recognized by the Indian constitution, which we will call regional languages. Most political regional agitation has promoted one or another of these languages. Historically, all of them have developed from one of the regional dialects, but now they are spread over areas much beyond the original confines. All regional languages have two styles, the colloquial and the literary. The latter is used in formal speech-making and in writing and is taught in schools. [6] It is often quite different from the colloquial. Only educated people are familiar with it. Uneducated villagers may learn the colloquial style of the regional language through contact with outsiders or residence in the city, but they are rarely fluent in it. Residents of the smaller provincial towns have many occasions to use the regional language and control it quite well, although they speak the regional dialect at home.

In some parts of the country, such as for example the area around Delhi, the regional dialect is almost identical with the regional language. In these areas we may safely say that the regional language is also the native language of the urban population. There are however many other areas where the regional dialect and the regional language differ greatly or are even mutually unintelligible. In those areas only a small minority uses the regional language as their native tongue; for all others it functions as a second language. No matter what the differences between regional dialect and regional language, the latter is the only vehicle for literature and serves as the speech of the educated throughout the area.

In addition to village dialect, regional dialect and regional language, there are the tongues spoken by the tribal groups which have as yet not been integrated within the framework of Hindu society. These we will call tribal languages. This category will include only tongues which are genetically different from the speech of the surrounding populations and mutually incomprehensible with it. Some of them, such as Santhali, Mundari, Bodo, have recently acquired alphabets, and have the beginnings of a literature; others have not been written down. The census lists as tribal languages certain Indo-Aryan dialects which do not differ very much from the speech of the surrounding population. According to our criteria these should be included among the regional dialects.

The speech variations described up to now were distributed geographically. There are also a number of social variations in speech. These are especially common in urban centers, where a large proportion of the population consists of immigrants from different regions. In the United States, cities also frequently have large foreign immigrant groups. These groups usually lose all traces of their native speech after one or two generations. In India, however, this is not so. Minority groups have been known to keep their native tongue for two hundred years or more. This conservatism accounts for the multiplicity of languages in most of the Indian cities, such as Bombay, Madras, Bangalore, and Calcutta.

Social variations in speech exist also in rural areas; this is especially true in tribal areas where different tribal groups have recently settled in the same village. They have become integrated into the village society as separate castes and since they do not mix socially with other villagers, they continue to use their own language. A similar situation arises along the border between the Dravidian and Indo-Aryan speech areas as a result of migrations of certain castes from one area to another.

There are, furthermore, differences between the speech of touchable and untouchable castes and Hindus and Muslims in monolingual areas. Very little work has been done in this field, however, and no general statements can be made. [7]

2. Delimitation of Linguistic Areas

Transitions from one dialect area to another may be of two types. The first occurs with genetically related dialects. Indo-Aryan dialects of North India, for example, form a continuous chain from Sind to Assam. The speech of each area shades off into that of the adjoining one. The individual dialect differences can be plotted on maps in the form of isoglosses, but in no two areas adjacent to one or a group of isoglosses are the differences so great that there is no mutual intelligibility. Lack of mutual intelligibility is found only between areas that are relatively far apart. The regional languages such as Sindhi, Gujarati, Marathi, and Hindi, and also the regional standards, have been, so to speak, superimposed on this chain of local dialects as a result of political or historical accident and, as was said above, they are used primarily as second or third languages.

The transition between dialect areas in which the speech is of different genetic origin, such as that between Indo-Aryan and Dravidian language areas in the South or regional and tribal language areas, is of a different kind. There is a broad belt of border districts in which native speakers of both dialect types live side by side. The distribution is social; certain castes speak one, others speak the other. Most people however are bilingual.

It is possible to classify genetically related dialects into major groups and sub-groups. Grierson has done this. He divides the Indo-Aryan tongues into three branches, each of which contains a number of languages, which in turn are divided into dialects. The term language in his terminology refers to a group of hetero-geneous regional dialects, a usage which is quite different from that employed here. In some instances, as for Bengali, Marathi, Oriya, etc., Grierson's language names are the same as those of regional languages; in others he makes up his own, e.g., Rajasthani, Bihari, etc. There is good evidence for the fact that most of Grierson's languages do represent separate linguistic entities. Their boundaries however are by no means as clearly defined as would appear from a map. Grierson himself states:

"When such boundaries are spoken of or are shown on
a map, they must always be understood as conventional
methods of showing definitely a state of things which is
in its essence indefinite. It must be remembered that
on each side of the conventional line there is a border
tract of greater or less extent, the language of which may
be classed at will with one or the other."

The use of modern methods of dialect classification, based
on phonological, rather than grammatical criteria, might make it
possible to have much clearer boundary lines. However, a great
deal more field research is necessary before there is sufficient
data for this. The geographical area covered by Grierson's linguistically defined languages does not coincide with that of the
regional languages. In the area in which Hindi is the regional
language, for example, Grierson finds a number of different
languages. The western-most of these, Rajasthani, is more different from Hindi than Punjabi, which is a regional language in its
own right, similarly Maithili in Bihar, shows more similarities to
Bengali than to Hindi, the regional language of Bihar.

In contrast to the gradual transition between dialect areas,
transitions from one to another of the regional languages, as
defined in this paper, are sharp. As was mentioned before, these
regional languages are used in writing and taught in school, but
bear no direct relation to the local speech. The area in which they
are used is therefore defined by political and cultural factors, not
linguistic ones, and the borders are quite clearly drawn. In order
to illustrate the situation let us take a hypothetical case of two
villages, A and B, on either side of say the Bengal-Bihar border.
The two local dialects will differ by very little. In village A, however, the regional language will be Hindi while in B it will be
Bengali. A villager from A can easily talk to a friend from B in
the local dialect, however the two will not be able to exchange
letters unless one knows both languages. Government officials
stationed in A and B, who know only their respective regional
languages, can communicate neither orally nor in writing, unless
they know the local dialect.

3. Conclusion

If we use the information presented in section 1 to interpret the census tables, [4] the resulting picture will be quite different from what would appear if we were to take the tables at their face value. The figures in Table I for example indicate speakers who accept, or claim, one of the languages recognized by the constitution as their regional language, and not native speakers of these languages. Some of those included in the figures doubtlessly speak only their own local dialect, others are bilingual with respect to the regional standard, others again control all three linguistic levels. The relative size of each of these three groups is difficult to estimate. It is fairly safe to say that those who are literate speak the regional language; any estimate beyond that would require a great deal more field data than are available now.

With the exception of Nepali and Sindhi, which we may count as regional languages, and Bhumij, which according to Grierson is a form of Mundari and should be listed under tribal languages, all forms of speech listed in Table III represent regional standards. The introductory note to the census indicates that decisions regarding items included in this table were largely arbitrary. The list is far from complete. Well known regional dialects such as Maithali and Bhojpuri in Bihar, Avadhi in U. P. are missing, in addition to scores of less known ones. A comparison with the data in volume one of the LSI shows that it is valueless as a source of linguistic information. There is no reason why the figures for the individual regional dialects should not be added to those of the appropriate regional languages in table one.

In future census surveys it might be more fruitful to replace the question regarding mother tongue by something like the following — a) Which regional language do you accept (or recognize)? b) How do you call the dialect of this language which you speak? The answers to b) will of course diverge widely, but they might be interpreted in terms of available linguistic field data.

The data on bilingualism given in the appendix also needs reinterpretation. The figures listing styles or dialects of the same regional language, as those for Hindi, Urdu, and Hindustani in Uttar Pradesh, for example, have little or no linguistic significance. The same is true for Hindi and Chattisgari in Madhya Pradesh, Hindi and Malwi in Madhya Bharat, and for all figures for Rajasthan. Figures representing differing languages, such as Hindi, Gondi, and Marathi in Madhya Pradesh. Marathi, Telegu and Urdu (Hindi) in Hyderabad, Hindi and Bengali in Bihar have however real significance.

The data in section two will explain some of the border questions that have arisen in connection with the linguistic states controversy in recent times. The borders of the linguistic states coincide with regional language areas and not dialect areas. Border-line problems have arisen in two types of situations. The first is the case mentioned in the introduction, where a dialect area is claimed by two rival regional language groups. A great deal of time has been spent in the past in suggesting solutions based on linguistic affinity of the dialect. This is due to confusion of the concepts of regional dialect and regional language. A more realistic way of settling the matter might be through a survey to determine which regional language the inhabitants would like to adopt.

The other type of problem arises in areas such as the Indo-Aryan Dravidian border areas where speakers of both languages live together. The solution here is more difficult since no matter where the borderline is drawn there will always be substantial minorities which are cut off from their regional language areas.

The preceding discussion, while useful in interpreting the data on language distribution and the difficulties of defining regional language areas, particularly serves to bring out an aspect of the language problem which has so far received little public attention. This problem stems from the difference between local dialects and regional languages. Attempts at spreading the knowledge of Hindi, so far, for example, have been concentrated in areas where Hindi is not the regional language. Similar efforts should be directed towards rural districts within the regional language area.

NOTES

1. From David Sopher, "India's Languages and Religions," Focus, Vol. VI, No. 6, February 1956.

2. From Selig S. Harrison, "The Challenge to Indian Nationalism," Foreign Affairs, July 1956, pp. 620-36.

3. See Sir George Abraham Grierson, Linguistic Survey of India, Vol. I, Part I, 1927, referred to as LSI.

4. Census of India Paper No. I of 1954, reprinted in Introduction to the Civilization of India: Changing Dimensions in Indian Society and Culture, ed. by Milton Singer (Chicago: The College, University of Chicago Syllabus Division, 1957), referred to as Census.

5. Data are derived from the LSI and are supplemented by the author's own field work experience and oral communication from other linguists.

6. For an explanation of the Hindi-Urdu problem see John J. Gumperz, "Language Problems in Rural Development of Northern India," Journal of Asian Studies, Vol. XVI, pp. 251-259 (1957). [In this volume, pp. 12-24.]

7. John J. Gumperz, "Dialect Differences and Social Stratification in a North Indian Village," American Anthropologist, Vol. VX, pp. 668-81. [In this volume, pp. 25-47.]

2 | Language Problems in the Rural Development of North India

       Most of the discussion regarding the language issue in India so far has revolved about two problems. One of these concerns the spread of Hindi knowledge in those areas or fields of endeavor where other regional languages or English are now used; the other, the enrichment of Hindi vocabulary so as to make it possible to use Hindi for dealing with topics related to modern science and technology. The Central Government and several of the state governments have devoted much effort towards the solution of these problems by setting up special departments for the creation of vocabulary lists to deal with new subjects, encouraging attempts to introduce Hindi in universities and legislative bodies, and fostering the growth of societies for the propagation of Hindi learning. These activities have aroused a great deal of controversy, and so much has been written about the pros and cons of the issues involved that the above two problems seem to be the only ones associated with language in the public mind.

       There is, however, another language problem of a slightly different nature which has received little attention so far. This concerns the difference between the everyday spoken language of the people and the literary language used on formal occasions and especially in writing. It applies to all parts of India, including even those areas in which Hindi is now the regional language. It is common knowledge that in addition to Hindi and the various regional languages recognized by the Indian Constitution, a number of dialects are spoken on the village level, but very little is known to nonlinguists about the difference between these dialects and the standard spoken and written language and the extent to which the three are mutually intelligible.

       The present paper is an attempt to illustrate this problem on the basis of observations made during eighteen months of linguistic research in various parts of rural North India.[1] The area chosen for illustration is the area in which Hindi is now the regional language. The problems discussed, however, apply to a greater or lesser degree to all parts of the country. The paper consists of two parts. Part one is a short descriptive statement of some of the facts of geographic and social language distribution in the so-called Hindi-speaking area; the other is an account of some of the linguistic difficulties in communication that have come up between extension workers and government officials and villagers in a North Indian village.

The gap between popular speech and written language has been in existence during the greater part of Indian history.[2] Sanskrit had long ceased to be a spoken language in the times of Kalidasa, the greatest of its writers, and even the Prakrits, which are used by lower-class characters in Sanskrit plays, do not seem to have been accurate reflections of popular speech. In the present discussion, an attempt will be made to draw a clear distinction between literary or written idiom and spoken language.

Before going into the matter of language distribution, an attempt will be made to explain the various uses of the terms Hindi and Urdu, regarding which there seems to exist a great deal of confusion in non-linguistic literature. The word Urdu was originally used to designate the literary idiom which had gained currency in the Dravidian-speaking country of Golconda on the Deccan Peninsula in the late sixteenth century and which was based on the spoken lingua franca used around the Moghul army camps and administrative centers.[3] This language in turn had had its roots in the local dialects spoken in the Gangetic Doab, that is, the area around Delhi and Merut. Urdu literature was written in an adaptation of the Persian script and had taken over a great number of words from Persian. During the eighteenth century it spread to such North Indian urban centers as Delhi and Lucknow. In the beginning of the nineteenth century, a number of Hindi writers began using the Devanagari alphabet for their writings and started replacing many of the Persian borrowings with loan words taken from Sanskrit. The new idiom which thus developed was given the name of Hindi. Literary Hindi and Urdu are thus two styles of the same language; they are used in writing and, on a spoken level, for formal lectures and discussion. Both have the same inflectional

system and a common core of basic vocabulary; they differ in the
learned or abstract words used and in word order. Spoken literary
Urdu also has taken over a number of sounds from Persian, such as
those represented by q and g͟h which have fallen together with those of
k and g in spoken Hindi. [4] The sounds equivalent to k͟h, z, and f, which
also come from Persian, are commonly used in both styles. Literary
Hindi, on the other hand, uses a number of initial and final consonant
clusters which are not common to Urdu.

Side by side with the above two literary idioms, the spoken
lingua franca from which they had sprung continued to spread in the
bazaar towns and urban administrative centers. Its spread was
favored by the fact that it had become the official medium of the
British administration and also by the great improvement in communication facilities during the nineteenth century. Outside the area where
Hindi is the regional language, it is now widely used in such urban center
as Karachi, Bombay, Calcutta, Hyderabad, and others. In British
India it had usually been referred to by the name Hindustani. After
Indian Independence this latter term was dropped and the word Hindi
was adopted for the national language of India. This change in terms,
however, has not resulted in a corresponding change in language.

In spite of the fact that there is a large relatively active group
of people who favor the elimination of many colloquial words in favor
of Sanskrit borrowings, the gap between the spoken language (hereafter
referred to as standard spoken Hindi) and the literary idiom remains.
This fact is usually ignored in the nonlinguistic literature on language
problems. The confusion in terminology is further increased by the
popular use of the terms Hindi and Urdu. Hindus of every class are
now apt to refer to their own speech as Hindi, whether they speak a
village dialect or the standard language. Muslims, on the other hand,
refer to their speech as Urdu, although from the point of view of the
hearer there might be little difference between their speech and that of
their Hindu neighbors. The author has had several experiences in
which Hindus in complimenting him on his efforts to speak the local
idiom would say, "You speak Hindi well," whereas Muslims would
react to the same or similar words with, "You speak Urdu well." A
formal analysis of at least one village dialect has shown that the

differences between the speech of touchable and untouchable castes
are much greater than those between that of Muslims and Hindus.[5]

The area in which Hindi is the regional language extends from
Rajastan and the eastern part of Punjab in the west to the eastern
borders of Bihar and Madya Pradesh. The standard spoken Hindi,
which is current in the urban areas of this region, is relatively uniform.
The literary Hindi idiom is taught in the schools. The introduction of
Hindi literature has displaced a number of older literary idioms in
which there had been literatures since the late Middle Ages. The
best known of these are Braj Bhasa, Avadhi, and Maithili. At the
present time literary activity in these idioms has died out, but the
spoken forms on which this activity was based continue to be used by
educated as well as uneducated city residents in the home and when
among friends. Most city speakers of these dialects are equally at
home in Hindi, however, and actual conversations are characterized
by frequent switching from the dialect to Hindi and vice versa. These
dialects occupy a somewhat intermediate stage between standard
spoken Hindi and the local village speech, since they are spoken in
relatively uniform form over a large area. They will be referred to
hereafter as regional standards.[6] In addition to those mentioned above,
there are a number of regional standards which have had no literature,
e.g., Marwari and Jaipuri spoken in Rajastan, Surguja in Madya
Pradesh, Magadhi in Bihar. Some of these regional standards differ
only slightly from Hindi; others must be classified as different
languages from a linguistic point of view. Thus for example, Braj
Bhasa, the language spoken around Agra, differs little from standard
Hindi. The Jaipuri and Marwari dialects of Rajastan, on the other
hand, show many more differences. They have a much greater variety
of inflectional noun and verb forms. The differences between their
inflectional system and that of Hindi are so great that linguists
generally classify them as part of a separate language, Rajastani,
which as Grierson states, is more different from standard Hindi than
Punjabi, one of the regional languages recognized by the Indian
Constitution. The greatest amount of linguistic difference within the
Hindi-speaking area is found between Maithili and Hindi. Maithili
has a vowel system which is akin to that of Bengali and a system of
verbal inflection in which the verb is inflected for person and according

to the social status of both the subject and the object, and not according
to person and number as in Hindi. [7]

On the level of village speech, the amount of linguistic variation
is even greater. The saying goes in rural India that each village has
its own dialect. This is of course an exaggeration. In the Gangetic
Doab, however, the region where standard Hindi first developed,
differences are so great that villagers from Moradabad District state
that they have difficulty in understanding the speech of their own
relatives by marriage from Karnal District, slightly more than a
hundred miles away. These local dialects have been studied very little
by linguists so far. Grierson's survey is based on written answers to
questionnaires administered through British official channels and not
on direct field work; most of the other publications on Indian dialects
deal with regional standards. [8]

From a linguistic point of view the local dialects form a
continuous chain from Sind to Assam, the speech of each area shading
off into that of the adjoining one. The individual speech differences
can be plotted on a map in the form of linguistic isoglosses, but in
no two areas adjacent to one or a group of isoglosses are the difference
so great that there is no mutual intelligibility. Lack of mutual intelligibility is found only between areas that are relatively far apart. The
regional languages such as Sindhi, Gujerati, Marathi, and Hindi, and
also the above-mentioned regional standards have been, so to speak,
superimposed on this chain of dialects as a result of political and
historical factors. If therefore we take two villages, say on the
borderline between Rajastan and Gujerat, we will find that villagers
will have no difficulty in understanding each other, whereas government officials who speak only the standard languages might have to
resort to interpreters in order to communicate effectively. If the
official from Rajastan knows the regional standard, communication
will be easier. Learning a literary idiom for a villager, on the other
hand, often requires much more than mere acquisition of literacy—
it may be equivalent to learning a foreign language.

The greatest amount of conservatism and inflexibility with
respect to local dialects is found among those groups in the village
that have little opportunity for contact with outsiders, such as women

and certain members of the lower castes. Outside the village, when
talking to traders and officials in the bazaar towns and administrative
centers, villagers are forced to drop some of their most divergent
localisms and adapt their speech to the regional standard. It is also
in centers of this type that standard Hindi is becoming more and more
current. Many of them contain settlements of traders from different
areas, e.g. , Marvaris from Rajastan, Sikhs from Punjab, Muslims
from Lucknow or Delhi, who use Hindi to communicate with the local
population. Other factors which aid in the spread of Hindi are the
improvement of communications, which has made long travel rather
painless, the schools and the movies, which may be found in the
smallest of towns. Data from one village in the Bhojpuri-speaking
area of U. P. shows that a large proportion of the local men understand
and speak some Hindi; the women and many of the low-caste people,
on the other hand, have trouble in following it. It must be remembered,
however, that the language which is spreading is the spoken standard
Hindi are not the literary idiom. Except in the schools, the average
villager has very little opportunity for coming in contact with the
literary language, since the amount of printed material that reaches
him is still very small. It is also true that the conversations in
standard Hindi that the ordinary villager has occasion to engage in
revolve about such everyday matters as common greetings, commercial
transaction, etc.; conversations about philosophical problems or the
more intimate problems of family life and religion would be more
difficult to carry out in Hindi. Anthropologists working in the Gangetic
Doab have found difficulties in discussing such matters without resorting
to the local dialect.

     The studies of written communication were made in a village
in Saharanpur District of Uttar Pradesh. The dialect of the area is
referred to by Grierson as Vernacular Hindustani and it is one of the
group of local dialects which show closest affinity to standard Hindi.
The standard speech is universally understood, although the village
speech itself is not easily understandable to outsiders from different
regions.

     The village is located in a fertile agricultural area, which has
in recent years become one of the centers of Indian sugar-cane production. Cane is the principal village crop. There are two large sugar

mills at a few miles distance, and between the months of November
and May, during the sugar-cane season, cultivators make several
trips a week to the mill to deliver cane. The tahsil (sub-district)
headquarters, a town with a population of about 25,000, is located
about six miles away on the main railroad fromDelhi to Saharanpur.
Local roads are quite good and rail and bus connections with Delhi to
the south and Ambala and the Punjab to the north and west are excellent.
Villagers have marriage relations as far away as Ambala in the Punjab
and Bulanshaher and Moradabad towards the east. Many of them have
had several occasions during their lifetime to travel within this entire
area in connection with family or business affairs. The primary
school in the village dates back to the 1920's. An inter-college
(equivalent to a senior high school) has been in existence for seven
years. It is supported primarily by village funds and many of the
local boys attend. The C. D. P. (Community Development Project)
has been active in the village since 1953. All in all, the village seems
exceptionally well provided, as Indian villages go, with educational
facilities and opportunities for contact with the outside world.

From the point of view of literacy, the adult population, i.e.,
people between the ages of twenty-five and fifty who carry the major
responsibility of village life, can be divided into three groups. The
literates are those that can read well and regularly read newspapers,
novels, or other literature. The majority of them have had five or
more years of schooling. Their first instruction was in Urdu, since
until Independence Urdu was taught in the primary schools of the area.
They have had to learn the Hindi script and literary idiom for themselves. There is another group of semi-literates which includes those
who at one time or other have had some schooling but read with
difficulty, or those who have taught themselves to recognize the letters
of the alphabet. Many people in this group have had up to five years of
schooling; some of them say that at one time they read well but have
forgotten now. This group is numerically much larger than the first.
It is constantly growing since many people have begun to learn to read,
either on their own or with the help of neighbors. The last group, that
of the illiterates, includes those that do not have a knowledge of the
alphabet and is approximately equal in numbers to the other two groups
combined.

The intelligibility tests were conducted with a pamphlet, distributed by the C.D.P., announcing a development fair. This pamphlet contains forty-five lines of text announcing the various features of the fair. It was tested with a panel of informants drawn from the three above-mentioned groups of literates, semi-literates, and illiterates. The methods used for testing were patterned on the traditional way in which written materials are made known to illiterate villagers. This is usually done by reading the pamphlet out loud to the audience, paraphrasing the text in the village dialect and commenting on it. In the present tests the text was read to the illiterates; semi-literates and literates read the text themselves; all informants were asked to explain the meaning as if they were telling somebody else about the pamphlet.

The illiterates were able to obtain only the vaguest notion of the contents of the material read to them. They made mistakes in understanding in ten to fifteen of the forty-five lines of text. The semi-literates did slightly better; they averaged about ten mistakes. The literates understood the main part of the message; however, even they did not know some of the terms used. In passages which dealt with something familiar, such as those features that are usually associated with a fair in the experience of villagers (e.g., wrestling contests, shows, cinema), the informants were able to guess at the contents of a passage from a few words. The purpose of the fair, however, was to stimulate interest in new ideas, such as crop competitions, public health, domestic industries, the participation of women in community life. The greatest number of misunderstandings occurred in the passages relating to these last features.

From a linguistic point of view the difficulties encountered were largely lexical. Here are some examples. The announcement referring to a baby show read: tīn sāl tak kī āyū kē chōṭe bālkõ kē svasty kī pratiyōgitā hōgī, 'there will be a show of healthy babies up to the age of three.' This was interpreted by several people as: 'There will be a wrestling match of three-year-old children.' The difficulty lies in the use of the terms pratiyōgitā 'show' and svasty 'health' instead of the common words numāysh and hālat. Another example of the type of misunderstanding that occurred is the following: mahilāõ kē līye ēk din vishēš prakār sē rakkhā jāyēgā 'a special day will be set aside for women.' The word for women mahilā is somewhat similar in phonetic shape to the local form mahōllā 'neighborhood,' and the words vishēš 'special' and prakār 'manner' were not understood. The common interpretation of the passage was, 'people from every neighborhood are invited.' Only the literates understood the passage. Examples of other words that were not understood are: virāt 'big,' ev 'and,' avsar 'occasion,' unnatī 'improved,' kr̥si 'agriculture, gr̥h udyōg 'domestic industry,' lōk gīt 'folk song,' sammēlan 'assembly.' Many of these indicate exactly those concepts that the C. D. P. has been attempting to introduce. It was rather surprising to see that the official name of the C. D. P. center, samudāyik vikās yōjnā kēndr, which was placed above the title of the pamphlet, was known to only one among all the informants interviewed. The common word in the village is the word parōjak 'project.' The village-level worker is usually referred to by the term dabalū 'double u' (from V. L. W.) or naspattar 'inspector' (the name given to agricultural officials during the British regime), instead of the official term grām sēvak.

Some of the other difficulties in understanding were due to the use of words in a meaning different from the meaning they commonly have in the village; e.g., the use of the word dangal to mean 'contest' in one case caused great difficulty for several informants who knew only the village meaning 'wrestling match.' Difficulties in syntax were rare; a few informants had some trouble with word order, but they were able to make it out after going over the pertinent passages a few times. It should be expected that syntactic difficulties would be greater with speakers of languages more different from Hindi such as Rajastani or Maithili.

Difficulties in comprehension similar to those mentioned above were found to a greater or lesser degree in most of the literature that reaches the village, such as in farm magazines, newspapers, and the few extension leaflets that are passed out. In one leaflet, which was distributed by the local school authorities on the occasion of a visit to the village by the President of India to lay the foundation stone of a hospital, the word for hospital and foundation stone were not known to any of the informants. Illiterate and semi-literate informants also had great difficulty in understanding an article on better methods of cotton cultivation in an agricultural magazine which regularly reaches the village.

Lectures on technical subjects by outside officials are also likely to present difficulty. The village level worker and the officials from the local development center who have been in the area for awhile have no trouble in making themselves understood. There have been some lectures, however, by outside technical experts, notably one on artificial insemination, which were understood by only a few of the literate villagers. There are five or six radios in the village, but people do not ordinarily listen to the All India Radio News broadcasts because they say the language is too difficult for them.

In the relations of villagers with traders from the bazaar towns and with the courts, another type of difficulty arises. Urdu is still used by many businessmen for keeping accounts and for posting written notices. The account sheets issued by the sugar mills, listing the deliveries of cane, are printed in Hindi, but the local clerks often write in the figures in Urdu. Urdu is also still used in some of the land records. There are, furthermore, a few cases where instructions in English have been issued to the sarpanch, the head of the village tribunal, by the superior court official. The person in question happens to be literate in both Urdu and Hindi, but since he knows little or no English, the instructions have so far been disregarded. In some cases persons involved in a trial are furnished only English transcripts of the judgment in their case. There are two railroad crossings near the village, on dirt roads travelled primarily by bullock carts, where the only warning signs are in English.

If a villager therefore wants to be able to read the sort of literature that reaches him in the village and thus remain in direct touch with the outside community, it is not enough that he know the Devanagari alphabet. In order to read Hindi he has to learn a great deal of new terminology and new syntactic constructions. In order to transact business he has to master the Urdu script and Urdu literary style and it would also be useful if he knew at least some English. In the absence of this knowledge he is forced to depend on middlemen, whose reliability he has no way of judging.

From the point of view of rural development, the local language situation imposes severe limitations on the methods that may be used for spreading new ideas. The only reliable means of communicating with villagers is personal contact by the village level worker or a local project officer. Written communications at best reach only the relatively small group of literate villagers, and the probability of misinterpretation by readers who are unable to comprehend the contents and pass on their misapprehensions to their illiterate neighbors are quite high. The present language situation further serves to preserve the traditional barrier between the villager and the outside world, a barrier which the C. D. P. is trying to remove.

The effectiveness of development might be greatly increased if the diversity in style and language used by local government agencies could be eliminated and all persons concerned could be trained to use a style intelligible to villagers, at least in those writings that are destined for village consumption. It would then be possible to reach the ever increasing group of semi-literates, many of whom might otherwise revert back to illiteracy. There have been some attempts made to train writers in the production of literature for new literates, but the writings produced have so far not reached the village in which this study was made.[9] In any case, what is needed is a co-ordinated effort on the part of all agencies concerned, not just the distribution of a few booklets.

The data presented in the foregoing is based on only one village, but the impressions gained have been confirmed by other researchers with experience in Indian villages.[10] Furthermore, the linguistic diversity described in the first part of the paper seems to indicate that similar conditions exist also in other areas. The problem seems real enough to suggest further study, based on a more detailed regional survey of language problems at the village level.

NOTES

1. The field observations resulting in this study were made under a fellowship granted by The Ford Foundation. The conclusions, opinions, and other statements in this publication, however, are those of the author and not necessarily those of The Ford Foundation. The author is further indebted to Professor Morris Opler and the staff of the Cornell University India Project for furnishing living quarters in the village and providing much helpful background information for the study. Special thanks are due to Dr. S. C. Dube for his help in formulating the problem.

2. India is of course not unique in this respect. Similar differences existed throughout medieval Europe and still exist, for example, in Greece, where they have become the subject of a great deal of political controversy.

3. Sir George Abraham Grierson, Linguistic Survey of India (Calcutta: 1927). For an account of the rise of spoken and literary Hindi see Vol. I. Another account of the development of modern Indo-Aryan vernaculars, which also discusses the gap between spoken language and literary idiom, is given in S. K. Chatterji, Indo-Aryan and Hindi (Ahmedabad: Gujarat Vernacular Society, 1942).

4. The Library of Congress transcription of Devanagari as adapted to Hindi is used throughout.

5. John J. Gumperz, "Dialect Differences and Social Stratification in a North Indian Village." [In this volume, pp. 25-47.]

6. Grierson does not draw this distinction explicitly; however, it is implicit in his comments.

7. See Grierson, IX, Pt. 2, p. 1 for Rajasthani, and V, Pt. 2, p. 13 for Maithili.

8. Some excellent examples of studies of this type are:
Baburam Saxena, Evolution of Avadhi (Allahabad: 1937); Dhirendra
Varma, La langue Braj (Paris: Librairie d'Amerique et d'Orient,
1935).

9. Workshops on writing for new literates were held in Delhi
in 1953 and in Mysore, Poona, and West Bengal. The Indian Council
of Agricultural Research publishes a journal, Dharti ke lal, intended
for new literates, which has a circulation of about 8,000; cf. The
Ford Foundation and Foundation Supported Activities in India (New York:
The Ford Foundation, 1955). The Uttar Pradesh Development
Commissioner at Lucknow has also published a series of pamphlets
on agricultural topics for new literates.

10. Mr. Philip Barker, a linguist who has spent about eighteen
months in rural areas of Sarguja, Madya Pradesh, tells me that
villagers in his area were not able to understand the terminology of
official announcements posted in the village. See also Chatterji,
pp. 140f.

3 | Dialect Differences and Social Stratification in a North Indian Village

It is generally recognized that dialect differences exist in every large speech community. When these differences are minor and do not appreciably affect mutual intelligibility, they are disregarded for most purposes of linguistic description. Areas in which there are no significant linguistic barriers are thus ordinarily said to contain speakers of a single language or dialect. However, detailed studies by dialectologists of the distribution of minor speech variants have shown that these are not idiosyncratic, as had been assumed by some, but are patterned and socially determined.

Leonard Bloomfield postulates a direct relationship between linguistic diversity and the amount of verbal interaction among individual members of a community.[1] The model he provides is quite similar to the sociogram of the modern social psychologist. He states:

> The most important differences of speech within a community are due to differences in the density of communication . . . . Imagine a huge chart with a dot for every speaker in the community and imagine that every time any speaker uttered a sentence, an arrow were drawn into the chart pointing from his dot to the dot representing each one of his hearers. At the end of a given period of time, say 70 years, that chart would show us the density of communication in the community. . . . We believe that the differences in communication are not only personal and individual but that the community is divided into various systems of subgroups, such that the persons within a subgroup speak much more to each other than to persons outside their subgroup. . . . Subgroups are separated by lines

of weakness in this net of oral communication. These lines are local, due to mere geographical distribution and non-local or as we say social.

If this method is valid, then investigations into the relations of speech differences to other types of social interaction should be of great interest to students of social structure. Work in this field, however, is still in its beginnings. [2]

The first systematic attempts to formulate relationships along the above lines were made by McDavid (1946, 1948, 1951). His data were drawn from the field records of the Linguistic Atlas of the United States, a geographical survey aimed primarily at collecting data for historical studies, but which used a sample drawn from the upper, middle, and lower strata of American society. The distribution of the dialect differences discovered was found to be determined by social as well as geographical factors. McDavid suggests that these social speech styles reflect what he calls "social tensions" such as those existing between Negroes and whites, Catholics and non-Catholics, and others in northern industrial communities. The field methods and sampling of the Linguistic Atlas have recently been severely criticized on grounds of reliability and validity (Pickford 1956), but this does not destroy their usefulness in providing leads for more detailed studies.

A recent study of the relations of dialect differences to social structure in Mexico City makes an effort to avoid some of the methodological shortcomings of the Atlas (Sapon 1953). The community is divided into ten status groups, using Warner's Index of Status Characteristics, and the linguistic sample was drawn from each of the groups. The results have not yet been published.

The present study was done, in cooperation with a team of social scientists, in Khalapur, a relatively small, highly stratified North Indian village community. [3] Linguistic differences were determined from a sample of the most important caste groups in the village and the results are compared with anthropological information collected through day-by-day observation over a period of two and a half years.

In discussing language distribution in the Hindi speaking
area of Northern India, it is convenient to distinguish three forms
of speech (Gumperz 1957). At the local level there are the village
dialects, which vary from village to village. In the small market
centers, a form of speech is current which avoids many of the
divergent local features and is relatively uniform over a large area;
this is the regional dialect. The third form, Standard Hindi, is used
most widely in larger cities such as Delhi, Agra, and Lucknow. It
is native only to certain groups which have traditionally been city
residents; others speak some regional dialect. The amount of difference
between the above three forms varies. There are many regions where
at least two of the three are mutually unintelligible, but in others the
three are relatively close.

The speech of the region around Khalapur is Khari Boli, a
subdialect of Western Hindi. It is a transition dialect between the
Bangaru of Karnal and the Khari Boli of Meerut (Grierson 1916;
Gumperz 1958), relatively close to Standard Hindi and mutually
intelligible with it. The Khalapur village dialect is readily understood
by speakers of the regional dialect. However, persons who control
only Standard Hindi often have difficulty in following the local village
idiom.

Most male residents, especially those who travel considerably,
speak both the village and the regional dialect. The former is used
in the home and with other local residents, and the latter is employed
with people from the outside. Educated people and some who have
spent much time in larger cities speak Standard Hindi, although they
employ the local idiom at home.

The present analysis deals with the village dialect only.
Differences occur on the phonological and lexical level, but only
phonological variants are used in the grouping of subdialects. This
has not been the practice in the past. Previous studies employ lexical
as well as phonological and morphological criteria and do little in the
way of structural analysis. There are a number of reasons in favor
of the present approach. Phonological features lend themselves to
classification according to the degree of structural relevance and thus
provide a reliable tool for estimating the importance of a particular

difference.[4] They are automatic and more closely embedded in our
habit pattern than lexical items, and are therefore less subject to
change when in contact with variant dialect forms. Furthermore
they present less difficulty in obtaining reliable responses, since
forms can be elicited without the informant being aware of which
features interest the linguist. With lexical data, on the other hand,
each item is of the same importance as the other. There is a further
problem in eliciting, since it is often difficult to determine which of
two alternate forms is most frequently used.

Khalapur is located in Saharanpur District of Uttar Pradesh,
in the Gangetic plain between the Ganges and Jumna rivers, about
80 miles north of Delhi and three miles west of the Saharanpur-Delhi
road. The inhabitants are divided into thirty-one endogamous caste
or jati groups,[5] ninety percent Hindu and ten percent Muslim, which
may be ranked hierarchically along a scale according to ritual status.
Each group ranks either high or low with respect to any of the others;
no two have equal status. At the top of this ritual caste hierarchy are
the Brahmans, Rajputs (Warrior-Rulers) and Vaishyas (Merchants),
the twice-born castes according to the traditional varna system. They
are followed by a large group of middle castes, mostly artisans and
laborers. The three lowest ranking groups are the Chamars, a group
of landless laborers, Jatia Chamars or Leatherworkers and Bhangis
or Sweepers. These will be referred to as untouchables to distinguish
them from the majority or touchable group. The Muslims also belong
to several castes, all of which rank fairly low ritually. The most
important of these are Muslim Rajputs and Oil Pressers.

The village population is about five thousand. Forty-two percent of the population is Rajput; Chamars are next with twelve percent,
and after that come Brahmans with five percent. The remaining
twenty-eight caste groups make up the rest. Of the other castes mentioned in this study, Sweepers have four percent, Leatherworkers two
percent, Chamar Julahas (one of the three weaving castes) two percent,
Muslim Rajputs two percent, Teli three percent.

The Rajputs, both Muslim and Hindu, are the dominant caste.[6]
They own more than ninety percent of the land and wield most of the
political power. Brahmans are accorded first rank with respect to

ritual status, but are second to the Rajputs and some of the Merchants with respect to wealth and actual prestige.

The residential area of the village is divided into seven geographical subdivisions, or paṭṭis, [7] related to lineage groups among Rajputs. Most Rajput residents of a paṭṭi hold land in the same area. Members of non-Rajput castes are said to belong to the paṭṭi of the families who own or used to own the land on which they live.

In selecting informants for the study, care was taken to choose only people who were willing to use the village and not the regional dialect. All informants were male. They were either illiterate or could read only with great difficulty. Students of the Inter-College, which is located in the village, and people who regularly read newspapers or books, were not interviewed. Two or more informants were used from each of the eighteen castes having more than one percent of the village population. [8] In the case of Rajputs and other large groups with settlements in several parts of the village, informants from each of the settlements were used.

The following methodology was employed for the collection of linguistic data. As a first step, the phonemic structure of the village dialect was determined from the speech of one informant. The statements were checked for completeness with several other informants, and notes were kept on any dialect differences found. These notes were expanded by observations made in informal conversations with a wide variety of villagers on topics not connected with the linguistic study. A questionnaire was then prepared on the basis of the notes. The information obtained from this questionnaire was analyzed and a series of hypotheses was drawn up regarding dialect distribution. These hypotheses were again tested over a period of several months through informal observation of the speech of all caste groups concerned. A number of tape recordings of village speech were also made.

The linguistic data were supplemented by a series of interviews with a cross-section of informants for the purpose of determining the extent to which villagers are aware of the caste differences in speech and the function of the differences in determining caste status.

Information from these interviews is presented along with the list
of differences.

The dialect has the following inventory of phonemes:[9]

Consonants:	labial	dental	alveolar	retroflex	palatal	velar	glottal
stops	p b	t d		t d	c j	k g	
spirants			s				h
sonorants:							
nasals	m	n		n			
laterals		l		ḷ			
		r(trill)		r̥(flap)			

Vowels:	front		central		back
high	i				u
		ɪ		ʊ	
mid	e		ə	o	
		æ		ɔ	
low			a		

Diphthongs: aɪ, uɪ, oɪ, uə   Nasalization: ~
Word juncture: (space)   Stress: [10]

The system used for classification of dialect differences was
outlined in an earlier article (Gumperz 1958). Differences in the
village are of three types: (1) differences in phonemic distribution
statable in terms of phonological environment; (2) etymological
differences, i.e., those differences in distribution that hold true
only for certain lists of cognate items; and (3) phonetic differences,
i.e., those that do not affect distribution of phonemes. The term
Standard is used to indicate the majority speech; other forms are
referred to as variants. The following differences occur:

1. Differences in phonemic distribution

The Standard has contrasts between simple vowels /a/, /u/,
/o/ and diphthongs /aɪ/, /uɪ/, /oɪ/ before consonants. Members of the
Sweeper caste do not have this contrast:

Standard	Variant	
1. /bail/	/bal/	ear of corn
2. /lal/	-	red
3. /jhuɪl/	/jhul/	cattle blanket
4. /phul/	-	flower
5. /khoɪr/	/khor/	cattle trough
6. /mor/	-	peacock

In word final position, however, the above diphthongs may occur in the speech of all villagers: Standard and Sweepers /khaɪ/ eat (inflected stem).

2. Etymological differences

(a) Occurrence of /ə/ and /ʊ/ before stressed vowel in the next syllable in certain forms:

Standard	Variant	
1. /kʊrélṇa/	/kərélṇa/	(to) shovel
2. /dʊtéi/	/dətéi/	blanket
3. /mʊṇdássa/	/məṇdássa/	head cloth
4. /khʊréra/	/khəréra/	cattle brush
5. /nʊláṇa/	/nəláṇa/	(to) weed
6. /pʊcháṇa/	/pəcháṇa/	(to) send
7. /dʊpéṭṭa/ ~ /dəpə́ṭṭa/	-	turban
8. /dʊphǽra/ ~ / dəphǽra/	-	noon
9. /kʊpás/ ~ /kəpás/	-	cotton
10. /ləgám/	/lʊgám/	bridle
11. /dəláṇ/	/dʊláṇ/	a type of village building
12. /bətáu/	/bʊtáu/	a condition of the soil

In examples one to six, the Standard has /ʊ/. In seven and eight, all informants show free variation between /ə/ and /ʊ/ forms; both are therefore part of the Standard. In ten to twelve, the Standard has only /ə/.

Many Chamars and most of the Shoemakers have /ə/ in all
the above forms. Among the Chamars, however, the /ə / pronunciation is considered "old fashioned" and has low prestige. Many
members of the caste use /ʊ/ throughout, even in forms ten to
twelve where the Standard has /ə / . Their speech therefore remains
distinct in spite of their apparent efforts to adapt to the Standard.

The nonstandard use of /ʊ/ and /ə / in these and similar
examples is recognized by villagers as one of the distinguishing marks
of Chamar speech. Most of the informants interviewed in regard
to attitudes toward language forms, when asked who uses forms like
/dətəi/ , blanket, laughed and said, "That is Chamar speech." Two
Chamar leaders evidenced a great deal of emotion on hearing the
form. They did not answer the question, but entered into long
explanations to the effect that Chamars have hitherto been denied
educational opportunities by the higher castes.

(b) /ɪ / and /ə/ in certain forms before nonfinal single consonant
or consonant cluster plus stressed vowel:

Standard	Variant	
1. /rɪpə́ṭ/	/rəpə́ṭ/	(to) slip (stem)
2. /bɪchṇóa/	/bəchóṇa/	blanket
3. /sɪluár/	/səluár/	pajama for women
4. /rɪjéi/	/rəjéi/	comforter
5. /bɪtóra/	/bətóra/	stack of dung cakes
6. /sɪkhána/	/səkhána/	(to) teach
7. /pɪchórna/	/pəchórna/	(to) sift grain
8. /bɪṇóla/	/bəṇóla/	cotton seed

Many people have free variation between /ɪ/ and /ə / in the
above forms. The / ə/ forms have low prestige, especially in the
last three examples. The frequency of these forms is highest among
the untouchable castes. The use of /ə/ is generally regarded as a
sign of "old fashioned" or "ignorant people's" speech, although it is
not necessarily characteristic of low caste status. The particular
informants who used these old fashioned pronunciations regularly
were characterized as "backward" and "ignorant" also with respect

to other nonlinguistic matters. Other informants used them occasionally in extremely informal situations, but when asked to repeat they gave /ɪ/ forms.

Field records from another village twenty miles to the north indicate that there /ə/ is used by most Rajputs in the above items. Thus it seems that the /ə/ pronunciations have lost prestige and are going out of use in Khalapur, while they remain as the prestige forms in other areas. There is no similar evidence for /ʊ/ and /ə/.

(c) Accented /æ/ and /ə/ in certain words of the type CVCCV and CVCV:

Standard	Variant	
1. /ǽsa/	/ə́sa/	like this
2. /kǽsa/	/kə́sa/	how
3. /bǽngaṇ/	/bə́ngaṇ/	brinjal
4. /bǽṭṭho/	/bə́ṭṭho/	visit

Chamars, Shoemakers and Sweepers have /ə/ in these forms.

(d) Nasalized and oral vowels:

Standard	Variant	
1. /ik/	/ĩk/	sugar cane
2. /júa/	/jũa/	joke
3. /khat/	/khãt/	cot

Untouchables of all three castes have nasalized /ĩ/ /ã/ /ũ/.

Higher castes consider features (c) and (d) as indications of untouchable speech. Some of the more educated Chamars have begun to use /æ/ in the words given in (c); however, they tend to relapse into their old habits in unguarded moments.

(e) /m/ and /ũ/ in words of the type CəũVC where V stands for /a/ or /aɪ/:

Standard	Variant	
1. /dəũáɳ/	/damáɳ/	head of a cot
2. /jəũáɳ/	/jamáɳ/	a spice

Chamars and Shoemakers have /m/ in these words, all others use the Standard forms. Field records for a village in Karnal District, Punjab, show the /m/ pronunciations in a number of forms where Khalapur village has only ˜ . This seems to indicate that the situation is similar to that of /ə/ in 2b; /m/ is being replaced by / ṹ/ .

(f) Alternation between medial nasal plus consonant clusters and single consonants, double consonants or consonant clusters:

Standard	Variant	
1. /ɖhɪdáɳ/	/ɖhindáɳ/	a grass
2. /kɪkkər/	/kɪnkər/	a tree
3. / əkkás/	/ənkás/	sky
4.. /sátti/	/sánti/	a type of rice
5. /gánna/	/gánda/	cane
6. /lóbri/	/lómri/	fox

There is a great deal of free variation between the two sets in all castes. The variants are regarded as signs of uneducated speech and are more frequent among old fashioned and untouchable speakers.

(g) Relative position of consonants in certain words. The following are the alternants:

Standard	Variant	
1. /mə́tləb/	/mə́tbəl/	meaning
2. /rəjbháɪa/	/rəbjhaɪa/	irrigation canal
3. /bəxhóra/	/əbkhóra/	torch
4. /jəuáɪɳ/	/əjuáɳ/	a spice

Variants are considered uneducated speech and are used largely by the old fashioned and untouchable groups. An interesting

hypercorrect form, / nisán/ for standard /ɪnsáŋ/, man, appears
in one of the Chamar field records.

3. Phonetic differences

   (a) The allophone of /æ/ in word final position in utterances
such as /kərǽ/ he does; /ghər tæ/ from home, /hæ / is, is
[æ] in the Standard. The variant [əˇ] is used by the Shoemakers. It
was also heard in free conversation from one old Chamar. The
[əˇ] pronunciation is the prevalent pronunciation in several neighboring villages where the dominant castes are Jat and Tyagi.

   The [əˇ] could also be analyzed as an allophone of the phoneme
/ ə / . This would change the difference between the Shoemaker speech
and the Standard to one in phonemic distribution. In comparative
studies of this kind, however, just as in comparative historical studies,
it is useful to talk o phonemic differences only when there is no other
possible analysis.

   (b) Allophones of / ə /, /a/ , /o/ and /u/ . Before the consonants
/ h, r, ḷ, ṛ, d, n, ṇ, ḍ/ followed by /i/ or /e/ , allophones of / ə/
appear in three degrees of tongue height: low, medium, and high.
Allophones of /a/ , /o/ , and /u / in this same environment show
three degrees of phonetic diphthongization. Members of the Sweeper
caste have the low allophone of /ə / and undiphthongized [a] [o] [u]
in these environments. With residents of C and G paṭṭi /ə/ has the
high allophone [ɪ] and /a/ /u/ and /o/ are fronted and are followed
by strong upglides [a<e], [u<i], [o<e]. All other villagers have [ɛ]
with medium tongue height as the allophone of /ə/ and the offglides
of the /a/ , /o/ and /u/ allophones are lower and less pronounced.
In each case, tongue height and offglide are slightly lower before /e/
than before /i/ . Some examples of items in which these allophonic
variations occur are:

1. / də́ri/   rug   5. / cúḍhe/ sweepers
2. /ghə́ni/   much   6. /suṇhi/ broom
3. /peṭṭi/   village subdivision 7. /bóri/   sack
4. /mháre/   my (pl.)

The Sweeper pronunciation in these items is closest to Standard Hindi and is characterized as saap, "refined," by villagers. The pronunciation of C and G patti villagers is considered somewhat uncouth, and Rajputs from other parts of the village cite it as evidence for the fact that these people are somewhat backward. The field notes show that a few other Rajputs used pronunciations similar to those of C and G in very informal situations. However, all these informants reverted to the Standard when asked to repeat the utterance.

On the basis of the preceding list of phonological speech differences, we may distinguish six linguistic groups or subgroups in the village:

A. The majority group of speakers of the Standard, consisting of all Hindu and Muslim touchable castes, except for "old fashioned" persons and Rajput residents of pattis C and G.

B. Rajput residents of C and G pattis, distinguished from Group A by the phonetic features of 3b.

C. "Old fashioned" individuals of all touchable castes, characterized by the etymological differences of 2b, 2d, 2g.

D. Chamars, who share most of the characteristics of group C and in addition show the etymological differences of 2a, 2c, 2e, and 2f.

E. Shoemakers, with characteristics similar to those of the Chamars except for the features mentioned in 2a. In addition they have the phonetic features of 3a and 3b.

F. Sweepers. This group is distinguished from all the rest by the difference in phonemic distribution of 1 and the phonetic difference of 2b. It further shares differences 2b, 2c, 2d, 2f, and 2g with groups D and E.

There are also a number of lexical differences. Each of the larger castes has a special vocabulary referring to items of its subculture not shared by others. The vocabulary of Hindus and Muslims also differs, especially in regard to items of clothing, cooking utensils, and food. A detailed consideration of these differences is beyond the scope of this paper. However, it is interesting to point out that Hindu-Muslim speech differences in Khalapur are of the same order as those between individual touchable castes and certainly much less important than the variation between touchables and untouchables. In other areas of India the gap between Hindu and Muslim speech is said to be much larger.

Of the above phonological groups, F is the most divergent, since it is set apart by a phonemic difference. It is most similar to the regional dialect, which also has no contrast between simple vowels and diphthongs before consonants and shares the allophonic features of 3a. The differences between A, B, and C are relatively minor and the same is true for those between D and E.

Villagers show awareness of some but not all of the dialect differences listed. Certain forms are labelled as Chamar speech and the Sweeper idiom is said to be "refined," but the divergences between Chamar and Shoemaker speech are not usually recognized. Rajputs occasionally refer to a caste brother by the expression "he speaks like a Chamar." By this they refer to the fact that the person curses considerably and uses uncouth words, rather than to his pronunciation.

Dialect A functions as the prestige dialect. The replacement of /ə/ by /ʊ/ in 2a, /ə/ by /ɪ/ in 2b, and /ə/ by /æ/ in 2c shows the efforts of minority groups to imitate it. The field records also show one instance of a Sweeper using the Standard allophone [a$^{<e}$] for /a/ in the word /bari/, cotton (see 3b). The normal Sweeper pronunciation [a] was recorded for the same speaker in a conversation with a caste brother. It is of interest to note here that a form which is closer to the regional dialect is given up in favor of a divergent form. Dialect studies made in other countries usually show displacement of local forms by the regional dialect.

Speech differences like those found in Khalapur may arise
in the course of normal linguistic development. Language habits are
constantly in a state of flux. Just as fashions come and go, new
linguistic forms are acquired and old ones are dropped. Under the
conditions of communication prevalent in most Western rural
communities, where, to use Bloomfield's term, the "density of
communication" is relatively uniform, one would expect a form
adopted in one sector either to disappear within a relatively short
time or to be adopted by the entire group. If, however, there is a
break in communication, the spreading of forms from one sector
to the other will be delayed, thus giving rise to subdialects. The
speech differences between groups A and D might have arisen in
this way. The fact that Chamars and Shoemakers share all the
features of old fashioned speech and show traces of forms still
prevalent in other parts of the area, seems to indicate that they are
more conservative than the other subdialects. Dialect A would then
be the innovating dialect.

The Sweeper speech does not seem to fit into this pattern,
as there is no indication that the village dialect ever had the features
of 1 and 3b. Since the majority of Sweeper men have spent much
of their life in the cities and army camps, one possible explanation
is that they brought in the new forms after their absence from the
village. If this were so, it would be difficult to explain the retention
of other divergent low-caste forms such as those of 2b, 2c, 2d, 2f,
and 2g which are not found in the regional dialect. Replacement of
the diphthongs in the items of 1 would involve the loss of a phonemic
contrast. Historical linguistic studies indicate that this is much
more difficult to achieve than the process of replacing a phoneme
in certain words by another already in the system, which is all that
would be required for the elimination of variants in category two.
The Sweepers, furthermore, are not the only group that finds
employment outside. Many of the Shoemakers spend several years
of apprenticeship in neighboring bazaar towns. Children of higher
castes are often educated outside. Merchants make weekly trips
to the bazaar and sometimes spend weeks and months outside the
village. The common practice is for villagers returning from
outside to revert to village speech, no matter what their level of

education. There are interview data to show that people are ridiculed and accused of "taking on airs" if they use the regional dialect at home. A more likely explanation for the Sweeper dialect is that it was brought in when the group settled in the village. Evidence from genealogies indicates that the present Sweeper group immigrated from elsewhere a little more than a hundred years ago.

An accurate determination of the origin of the various variants requires a great deal more comparative data about dialects in the entire area than are available now. From a sociological point of view, however, the origin of the dialect differences is less important than the fact that they have maintained themselves in this relatively small community for such a long time. Genealogical evidence indicates that the village population has been fairly stable for more than a hundred years. Aside from a slow turnover among the lower castes, there has been no large scale immigration. The common marriage pattern is village exogamy, but this applies equally to all castes. It might therefore be useful to look for other factors in the social system which might tend to create or preserve speech differences. The following are considered: residential patterns, ritual purity, work or economic contact, informal adult friendship, and children's play-groups.

The map gives a schematic representation of the residential patterns. Touchable castes occupy the main part of the village. Members of a particular caste tend to be grouped together in housing clusters. Most of the larger castes occupy a number of such clusters in different sections, but their quarters are not really segregated. In the last fifty years the village has expanded greatly beyond its former boundaries; new Rajput residences have sprung up in what formerly were cattle compounds or grazing grounds, and habitations of other service castes have grown up around them. The untouchable quarters formerly were some distance away, but because of the recent expansion they have begun to merge with the village itself. However, untouchable housing is still largely confined to separate sections. The Sweepers and Chamars each have two quarters at opposite ends of the village. The Shoemaker settlement is in M patti near the Sweeper quarter.

Differences in ritual purity are evidenced by prohibitions concerning the following practices: touching the other person or his children, touching or approaching his cooking hearth, his cooking utensils or charpoy, and accepting either fried, boiled, or uncooked food from him. Each caste has a slightly different set of prohibitions, which is more or less extreme depending on the level of the other caste in the hierarchy. The lower the position of a particular caste, the greater is the number of castes from whom boiled food is accepted.

A tentative ranking, based on social-distance interviews with members of twenty-two castes concerning prohibitions of the above type, shows the following rough groupings: High castes are those from whom all others take boiled food and allow touching of clay utensils. Middle castes may touch brass utensils and offer fried food and water. Lower middle castes are those from whom one does not take food but whose touch is not polluting. In the case of the untouchables, the

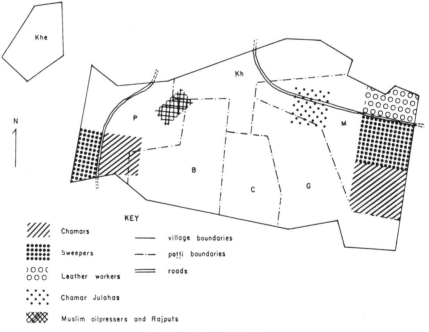

Outline Map of Khalapur

entire set of prohibitions holds. The Chamars, Shoemakers, and Sweepers, i.e., those castes referred to as untouchables in this paper, are clearly at the bottom of the hierarchy. The status of Muslims, including Muslim Rajputs and of Chamar Julahas (one of the three weaving castes) is somewhat intermediate between untouchable and lower middle. Many villagers state that they do mind their touch and would not let them use the village wells. In practice, however, they are known to use these wells. They live among other castes (see map) and are integrated into the regular neighborhood patterns of borrowing of implements and social intercourse. The distinction between high and middle castes is also somewhat vague. Brahmans and Rajputs are clearly at the top, but the status of Merchants, Goldsmiths, and Bhaats, a lower group of Brahmans, is intermediate between that of high and middle castes.

The ritual prohibitions also operate among the untouchable castes. Chamars do not accept food from Sweepers and Shoemakers. Some Sweepers are less strict and accept food from Chamars, especially those who perform services for them, but this practice is looked down upon by other members of the Sweeper group.

There are some interview data to suggest that in the past the separateness of the untouchables has been forcefully maintained by the higher castes. Shoemaker women, for example, report having been prevented by Rajputs from wearing ornaments and clothes similar to those of the Rajput women. Attempts to imitate Rajput speech might also have been discouraged for fear of incurring the displeasure of the higher castes. This explanation, however, would not account for the linguistic diversity among the three untouchable groups.

Work or economic contacts may be of the employer-employee or of the vendor-customer type. The former involve close day-to-day contacts and require a great deal of verbal communication, while in the latter contact is limited to occasional short periods. The majority of employers are Rajputs, Brahmans, and Merchants. Among the artisan castes, including Shoemakers,

some members work at their profession in their own homes or
rent land and thus have little contact with outsiders; others serve
as farm laborers. The great majority of the Chamars either work
as farm hands or as day laborers in construction work, where
they are constantly together with members of other castes. Among
Sweepers, women devote most of the day to cleaning the houses
and cattle compounds of the village, and much of that time is
consumed in gossiping with and listening to the conversations of
their employers. Men used to work in the cities. At present, most
of them earn their living as occasional agricultural laborers, and
few also do cleaning work similar to that of the women. Chamars
and Sweepers thus seem to have the greatest amount of work
contacts with other castes.

        Informal contacts occur in children's play groups and in
adult intercaste friendships. Among the touchable children, play
groups are formed on a neighborhood rather than a caste basis. If
the neighborhood is exclusively Rajput, play groups will be limited
to Rajputs; in intercaste neighborhoods, however, children from
all resident castes may play together. Some groups observed
playing in the streets or on certain ceremonial occasions were
found to include Rajputs, Brahmins, Carpenters, Muslim Oil
Pressers, Watercarriers, Potters, and others, but untouchable
children were not observed in any of the groups.

        Studies of informal friendships among adults show that
while friendships tend to be primarily within the caste, intercaste
friendships are by no means rare. There are a number of instances
of close personal relationships between Rajputs and Brahmins,
Rajputs and Merchants, Goldsmiths and Rajputs, Muslim and Hindu
Rajputs. Among the middle castes, where each group has relatively
few members, this type of intercaste contact is even more frequent.
Since only caste fellows can share the same hukka (waterpipe),
many people keep special hukkas for their friends from other
castes. A number of stores, artisan's shops, and cattle compounds
serve as regular centers for informal intercaste neighborhood
gatherings. In these gatherings it is common to smoke the chilam,
a clay pipe which can be shared with other castes. Women of

different castes also visit each other frequently. There is one active religious sect in the village, the Kabir Panti sect, which has members belonging to Muslim, Rajput, Weaver, Carpenter, Potter, and Merchant castes; the leader of this group is a Potter.

Among the three untouchable castes, each group forms a more or less self-contained unit with its own well or water pumps. Each of the residential quarters is shut off not only from the touchable castes but also from the adjoining quarters of other untouchable groups. In M paṭṭi, for example, the Chamar and Sweeper quarters adjoin, but they are separated by walls. To go from one to another it is necessary to make a detour through the main village lane. While among the touchables, mens' quarters are open to view from the lane and hukka groups often congregate on the road or in the square, similar groups among untouchables meet inside the quarter, where they are not exposed to view from other sections of the population. Contacts with members of other untouchable castes tend to be formal rather than informal. There are no informal neighborhood gatherings. Intercaste friendships exist but are much rarer than among touchables. Children keep to themselves and do not form intercaste playgroups; they either stay within their quarter or accompany their parents to work. Sweeper boys and girls guard the pigs which scavenge in the village lanes and around refuse piles, but wherever they are, they keep to themselves.

The anthropological data provide some interesting information on relations with Rajputs from other paṭṭis of Rajput residents of Kh paṭṭi, who enjoy great prestige and have more contact with the outside officials. A questionnaire which was administered to half the family heads in Kh paṭṭi included the following questions: (a) what persons do you sit with most often? (b) of these, which is your best friend? (c) with whom do you exchange labor or bullocks or agricultural implements? A sociogram constructed from the answers to this questionnaire shows a smaller number of friendship choices in C and G than in any of the other paṭṭis, including Kh which is farthest away. C and G Rajputs are also set off from the others by the dialect difference of 3b.

The above data should be sufficient for some preliminary conclusions. It is clear that the linguistic differences represent social and not geographical groupings, since members of the same caste living in different sections of the village speak the same dialect. There is some correlation between the linguistic groupings and ritual status. Both agree in setting off the untouchables from the majority group and from each other. The distinction between high and middle castes, however, is not reflected in village speech, and on the other hand the differences between C and G paṭṭi, old fashioned speech and the Standard, have no relation to ritual status.

In examining intercaste communication, we find that linguistic differences have no correlation with work contacts. Bloomfields's concept of "density of communication" therefore needs some refinement. It becomes necessary to distinguish between several forms of communication. Not all of them have the same effect on linguistic diversity. In the present study, the determining factor seems to be informal friendship contacts. We may assume that the population is divided into a number of small friendship groups of the type described by Katz and Lazarsfeld (1955). Each of these creates its own norms and exerts pressures for uniformity. A linguistic form adopted in one group may spread to the other, through individuals having membership in both groups, and is then adopted. Since there are a number of intergroup and intercaste friendships among touchables, there is no barrier to the spread of innovations from one sector to the other. However, these friendships do not extend across the touchable-untouchable line or from one untouchable group to another, and thus account for the linguistic isolation of the untouchables. The linguistic peculiarities of the C and G Rajputs can be explained in a similar way.

The exact relationship between linguistic and social groupings needs a great deal of further clarification. We need to know more about what types of contact favor the spread of linguistic innovations and what processes are involved. For example, it is not clear from the present study whether children's play groups or adult friendships are more important in language habit formation. Hockett has suggested that age-grading plays a decisive role, but this has never been tested (Hockett 1950). If it is true, then the present linguistic diversity reflects the situation of some years ago, rather than the present one. Another problem of interest is the relationship between the amount of linguistic difference and the social distance between two groups. Lexical variants in Khalapur occur between individual castes, phonological differences correlate with larger groupings. The distinction between Chamar and Sweeper speech is phonemic, while that between Chamar and Shoemaker is relatively minor. Does this also indicate that in the case of the former the social distance is greater? It would be of interest to learn more about correlations of differences at each of the various levels of language structure with other aspects of the culture. Detailed interdisciplinary study is required, based on research designs suitable for isolating all social factors that have a bearing on the formation of speech habits.

NOTES

The data for this study were collected during a two year stay in India under a Ford Foundation fellowship. Morris E. Opler and the staff of the Cornell University Field Project provided quarters in the village. The author is especially indebted to John T. Hitchcock for data on friendships among Rajputs, Pauline Mahar for information on Sweepers and on ritual caste ranking, and Michael Mahar for data on Chamars and Shoemakers. Thanks are also due to David G. Mandelbaum and Sarah Ann Robinson for many helpful comments.

1. Leonard Bloomfield 1933:46.

2. For a more detailed listing of the literature on the subject see Putnam and O'Hern 1955.

3. Other literature dealing with the village is found in Gumperz 1955, 1957, and Hitchcock 1956.

4. For a discussion of the difference between data on language structure and other social science data, see Lévi-Strauss 1951:156.

5. In the transcription of caste and other names, traditional transliteration is used.

6. For a discussion of the difference between ritual and other caste rankings, see Srinivas 1957. The concept of the dominant caste is discussed in Srinivas 1955:17. The distinction between the ritually highest caste and dominant caste is important for dialect studies in India, since the dialect of the "highest caste" cannot always be presumed to be the prestige dialect.

7. Paṭṭis will be referred to by initials as in the outline map.

8. There are insufficient data for the Watercarriers (3 percent of the population).

9. For a detailed description of the phonology of the dialect, see Gumperz 1955.

10. Stress is marked only in words of more than one syllable.

REFERENCES

Bloomfield, Leonard. 1933. Language. Henry Holt, New York.

Grierson, Sir George Abraham. 1916. Linguistic survey of India, Volume 9:1. Government of India, Calcutta.

Gumperz, John J. 1955. The phonology of a North Indian village dialect. S. K. Chatterji Jubilee volume, Indian Linguistics, Calcutta.
_____ 1957. Language problems in the rural development of North India. Journal of Asian Studies 16.251-59. [In this volume, pp. 12-24.]
_____ 1958. Phonological differences in three Hindi dialects. Language 34.212-24.

Hockett, Charles F. 1950. Age grading and linguistic continuity.
    Language 26.449-57.

Katz, Elihu and Paul F. Lazarsfeld. 1955. Personal influence. The
    Free Press, Glencoe, Illinois.

Lévi-Strauss, Claude. 1951. Language and the analysis of social laws.
    American Anthropologist 53.155-63.

McDavid, Raven I. 1946. Dialect geography and social science prob-
    lems. Social Forces 25.168-72.
    _____ 1948. Post vocalic /-r/ in South Carolina: a social analysis.
    American Speech 23.194-203.
    _____ 1951. Review of The Australian language, by Sidney J. Baker.
    Studies in Linguistics 9.13-16.
    _____ 1951. Dialect differences and inter-group tensions. Studies
    in Linguistics 9.27-33.

Pickford, Glenna R. 1957. American linguistic geography: a socio-
    logical appraisal. Word 12.211-33.

Putnam, George N. and Edna M. O'Hern. 1955. The status significance
    of an isolated urban dialect. Language Supplement, Language
    Dissertation No. 53.

Sapon, Stanley M. 1953. A methodology for the study of socio-economic
    differentials in linguistic phenomena. Studies in Linguistics
    11.57-68.

Srinivas, M.N. 1955. The social system of a Mysore village. In Village
    India, McKim Marriott ed. American Anthropological Associa-
    tion Memoir No. 83.
    _____ 1957. Varna and caste. In Introduction to the Civilization of
    India: Changing Dimensions in Indian Society and Culture, Milton
    Singer, ed. The College, University of Chicago Syllabus
    Division, Chicago.

4 | Formal and Informal Standards in Hindi Regional Language Area

In Collaboration with C. M. Naim

The Hindi regional language area is the part of North India, where Hindi serves as the official medium of local government and administration. This area, which includes the present states of Rajasthan, Delhi, Himachal Pradesh, Uttar Pradesh, Madhya Pradesh, Bihar and parts of Punjab, is not only the largest of the linguistic units on the subcontinent, but also stands apart in other respects. In other sections of the country regional languages are limited to compact, geographically well defined areas, a fact which has made possible the recent organization of linguistic states. Furthermore there is in each area a well recognized standard, known by a single name, which although often linguistically distinct from local dialects, has served as the prestige form for some time. Literature in this standard is generally read and accepted by the educated, including those who know English well. All this is not the case with the Hindi area. Some forms of the modern standard language have been current since the early days of Muslim rule, but many distinct varieties exist. These varieties are spoken in geographically widely separated areas, used in different social situations, under differing prestige conditions and are called by many different names.

We find a multitude of conversational styles— apart from the local dialects — variously called Hindustani, Khari Boli, Dakkhini Hindi, Dakkhini Urdu, Bazaar Hindustani, or also Urdu and Hindi.[1] They are spoken not only within the regional language area itself but throughout urban North India in centers as far apart as Karachi, Bombay, Lahore, Calcutta, Ahmedabad, Hyderabad and many others. The exact spread of all these forms of speech has never really been surveyed and there is furthermore little agreement on the application of the above names. Different individuals may give different names to the same variety while others use identical terms to refer to linguistically distinct varieties. On the literary level two distinct styles are usually recognized: Urdu, which takes its learned vocabulary largely from Persian and is written in an adaptation of the Perso-Arabic script and Hindi, which draws on Sanskrit for its loans and employs the Devanagari script. There is however much stylistic diversity, even within these two named entities. One school of Hindi writers has introduced so many Sanskrit borrowings that its writings are incomprehensible to a speaker of the colloquial language trained only in Urdu. A second group writes in a way which is very close to the colloquial and which could become Urdu merely by changing script and substituting a few key terms. Other writers have introduced a number of local dialect features into their works thereby causing difficulties for readers from distant areas. [2] There is furthermore some controversy about the application of the term Hindi to the various medieval and post medieval literatures. The tendency in recent years has been to use Hindi for all texts produced in the present regional language area. But, many object to this practice and continue to employ the old dialect names. Literary Urdu is a little more uniform than Hindi but writers still vary greatly in the extent to which they borrow from Persian.

The bulk of the linguistic studies so far have concentrated on one or another of the above named entities and have as a rule treated it as a separate unit with little reference to the speech community in which it was used or to related forms of the language. We have grammars of Hindi based on writings in the Devanagari script which often include a number of the sub-regional dialects. [3] Analyses of Urdu may deal either with the literary style or with one or another of the spoken varieties current among the educated groups. [4] Of the grammars which carry the title Hindustani, some cover the style current in the Indian Army — others the so called Bazaar Hindustani or a somewhat Urduized urban speech style. [5] Even

Grierson's Linguistic Survey of India, which contains the most
detailed information on speech distribution operates with unit
dialects or styles. [6] It is moreover not based on direct field work,
but rather on written information elicited by a somewhat circular
procedure in which informants were asked to furnish translations
of a standard text into one or another named speech form as known
from local sources. These dialects were then again treated as
separate units. Studies like the above, while useful for those whose
interest is confined to literature or to the structure of a single
variety, nevertheless represent rather arbitrary abstractions from
actual linguistic behavior, which are of little aid in clarifying the
bewildering range of varieties of Hindi-Urdu found in North India.
If we are to understand speech distribution, we must describe it in
terms of the society in which it operates. [7]

    The present study therefore takes as its unit of analysis
not a particular style, but all forms of the standard language in
the regional language area as defined in the first paragraph. We
will disregard the traditional language names and will feel free to
deal with any standard varieties used in this area, excluding however others not found there such as the Urdu of Pakistan, or the
Bazaar Hindustani of Bombay and Calcutta. The paper is divided
into two parts, part one describes the social environment of the
standard, its relation to local dialects, its development and function
within the speech community. Part two presents a linguistic
analysis of speech variation and its relation to other factors in the
social system.

    1. The total range of speech varieties found among urban
and rural, educated and uneducated, high class and low class
residents of the Hindi regional language area may be described in
terms of three strata, each corresponding to its own network of
communication and having different functions in the social system.
The dialects spoken at the local or village level form part of a chain
of mutually intelligible varieties of Indo-Aryan stock, extending
through all of North India from the Arabian Sea in the West to

Assam in the East. They vary geographically from village to village
and socially from caste group to caste group. [8]

Superposed above this chain we find the sub-regional dialects,
varieties which avoid the most divergent localisms and are understood over somewhat wider areas. They are the native speech of
the traditional service and trading castes, residing in small bazaar
towns as well as in the larger urban centers, who cater to the needs
of the rural population. Villagers employ these dialects as a second
speech style for inter-group or inter-village communication.
Grierson's classification based on historical similarity sets up for
the present Hindi area five groups of varieties called 'languages'
each of which in turn contains several dialects. These groupings
are: Western Hindi, Eastern Hindi, Rajasthani, Bihari and
Pahari (further subdivided into Eastern, Central and Western
Pahari). [9] Only the first two of these groups show a direct relationship to Hindi, others are linguistically closer to neighboring
regional languages. Furthermore, as with the local dialects,
language distance increases with geographical distance, so that
there is mutual unintelligibility among speech forms at opposite
extremes of the region.

Before the advent of the British, in Muslim times, many
of the sub-regional dialects had great importance as the literary
media for the then dominant devotional and court poetry. The
social function of these literatures was quite limited, however,
and different from that of a modern standard. We have no evidence
for the existence of a single prestige style or range of styles which
served for all types of writing and formal discourse as is the case
in modern western societies, but rather there was a series of
quite distinct styles, each used for a particular purpose. Administration was carried on in Persian or Sanskrit, Vedic was used for
traditional Brahminical rituals, trading communities had their own
special medium of communication and there seem to have been almost
as many co-existing different literary styles as there were distinct
religious cults or literary traditions. Each of these literary styles

in a way served as the symbol or trade mark of a particular group. Compositions were intended primarily for oral presentation and were spread beyond the original dialect area through the religious establishments, migrant preachers, ascetics and performers belonging to that group. Thus Braj Bhasha was the literary vehicle for the poets of the Krishna cult of which Surdas and Mirabai are the best known, Avadhi was the language of Tulsi Das's Ramayan, and Maithili is famous for the Vaishnavite poetry of Vidyapati. Literary activity of this type now lives on only in oral folk tradition and has all but lost its former social importance. The medieval literary dialects however still receive a great deal of scholarly attention. Moreover some of the better known, e. g. Maithili, Avadhi, or even Grierson's historical constructs, Rajasthani and Bihari, continue to be listed among the major languages of India. [10]

The third stratum is that of the standard, which we shall refer to by the collective term Hindi-Urdu. The varieties of this stratum are in turn superposed above the local and sub-regional dialects. They are the native speech of only a minority of urban residents; for most people they serve as a second or third speech style. Modern Hindi-Urdu had its origin in the speech of the Gangetic Doab, just north and northeast of Delhi, in the districts of Meerut and Moradabad. Soon after the Muslim conquest, a trade language, based on this speech, became accepted as the lingua franca of the courts, army camps and trading centers of the new ruling groups. The use of this language for trade purposes spread through much of North India, into many districts where the native dialects were quite different, as far as the coastal district of Bengal and Gujarat and Maharashtra. Some hundred years later we find records of several literary styles bearing various degrees of similarity to the spoken trade idiom. Among these are the Khari Boli of Amir Khusrau and later of Kabir, the Rekhta of Delhi, the Dakini of the Muslim courts of the Bahmani kingdoms in the Deccan, where the local population spoke a Dravidian tongue, and several others. Throughout this early period these styles were similar in function and distribution to the sub-regional dialects described above.

Compositions were confined to a particular form of religious or
court poetry, which was not the only, but one of many coexisting
literary traditions in the area. As a matter of fact, during the
seventeenth and eighteenth century Khari Boli poetry was largely
replaced by Braj Bhasha. The development of the modern standard
language did not really begin until the second quarter of the nineteenth century, after the consolidation of British rule, when literary
Urdu replaced Persian as the official language for the purpose of
local administration. After that time a new Urdu prose style
developed; the language came to be taught in schools and greatly
gained in prestige. Because of its association with Islam, however,
the new style was not universally accepted. While many Hindus
were on the whole willing to use Urdu for the purpose of business
and administration, few accepted it as a literary language. A second
prose style was created by discarding the Persian alphabet in favor
of the Devanagari script and substituting Sanskrit borrowings for
the Persian loan words. The new Hindi for some time became the
symbol of the rising forces of reform Hinduism as represented by the
religious centers of Benaras and Allahabad, the Arya Samaj, and the
Brahmo Samaj movements. Religious reform and Hindi education
went hand and hand and a wide-spread system of Hindi vernacular
schools and colleges was set up paralleling the Urdu school system.
By the end of the nineteenth century the two new standards had all
but replaced the sub-regional dialect literatures throughout the
present Hindi area. But they did not spread into all regions where
the Hindustani bazaar language was employed. In Gujarat, Bengal
and Bombay other literary styles were already well established while
spoken varieties of Hindi continued to function as trade idioms with
little prestige. [11] After independence in 1947, Hindi replaced Urdu
throughout the present regional language area as the sole official
medium of administration and education and is now learned by all.
Urdu literature however continues to flourish.

With the increasing tempo of urbanization and the recent
improvements in communication, the varieties of the standard
stratum are beginning to make greater inroads among the local
dialects. Native speakers of Hindi-Urdu still represent a minority,

although an ever increasing one. They are found primarily among
the westernized, urban groups, who have moved away from their
home region and have lost connection with their rural past. For a
much larger number of individuals the standard continues to function
as a second or third speech style, used only in certain social
situations, e. g. on formal occasions, with individuals of different
social background, in the office, in school, on the college campus,
etc. But the number of situations which call for the use of the standard is growing, and sub-regional dialect forms are being more and
more confined to the family circle.

        The existence of the standard as a common prestige form
has a profound effect on the region as a whole. It makes it possible
to overcome local variations in speech and culture. A person who
knows Hindi or Urdu not only has little trouble in making himself
understood wherever he travels in the area, regardless of local
dialect, but he is also certain to find many other individuals who
read the same literature and in general share his intellectual
interests. Even among those who barely know it the standard has a
certain prestige position. We find it used for example in public
meetings with audiences made up entirely of uneducated monolingual
villagers. In the traditional Muslim 'Milad' the Maulvi is required
to preach in a highly Persianized Urdu and in certain Hindu meetings
of the 'Kirtan' type the audience expects a very Sanskritized form
of Hindi. The function of the standard on these occasions is
primarily ritual since very little concrete information is conveyed.

        The relation between the standard and the sub-regional and
local dialects may be likened to that between Redfield's great and
little tradition. [12] The former serves both as a model for prestige
imitation and as a channel of communication through which new
concepts are funneled into the other two levels. Linguistically
these innovations are reflected in loan words and phonological and
morphological borrowings, leading to the reinforcement of those
local dialect features which are similar to the standard and to the
creation of differential rates of linguistic change on two sides of
a regional language boundary. Traditional dialect surveys which tend
to concentrate on old or antiquated speech, disregarding newly

borrowed features show little evidence of the above processes. But
if we were to make a modern study of every day speech, say at
three equidistant points, A, B, C, along our North Indian chain
of mutually intelligible local dialects, where A is separated from
B and C by a regional language boundary, we might expect the over-
all language distance between A and B — measured in terms of the
totality of grammatical, lexical and semantic differences — to be
greater than that between B and C. Speakers in the latter two
locations should share a number of learned and elegant features,
borrowed from the regional language, which we would not find in
A. The standard thus acts as a unifying force linguistically as
well as culturally, a common mold which counteracts diversity at
the local level and separates the regional language from other
neighboring districts.

If we consider the group of standard speakers from the
point of view of communication, we find that it has a number of
characteristics which set it off from the rest of the population. [13]
Those who know only the dialects still live, so to speak, in relatively separate isolated and traditionally oriented speech communities. Their contacts with the outside world — if we leave aside
the intra-local networks — tend to cluster around neighboring
towns or urban centers, and even when they do visit these centers
they do not usually come in touch with persons of different regional
and social origin. Participation of these dialect groups in political
life is limited.

Conditions at the regional language level are different.
The large Indian cities derive their population from widely divergent
sources, including speakers of different sub-regional dialects as
well as persons from other regional language areas. The Marwaris
of Rajasthan, Sikhs of Punjab and other such communities have
large colonies in almost every urban center between Bombay and
Calcutta and these colonies maintain regular contacts. Recent
anthropological research shows that even among the laboring
classes we find groups which migrate thousands of miles in search
of work. There is also an increasing group of professionals and
government employees who shift from city to city. These are the

people among whom we find the greatest percentage of native
speakers of the standard. Politically they constitute the active and
innovating groups of the population, those among whom new ideas
of national independence and religious reform arose and took root.
Since Hindi and Urdu act as symbols of these reform movements,
villagers and small town residents who aspire to participate in
them have gone out of their way to learn the new styles. Although
there are no statistics to prove this, it seems reasonable to assume
that a high proportion of speakers of the standard are literate.
Literacy provides direct access to newspapers and related means
of mass communication. Radio and the cinema are available to
urban literates and non-literates. All these media help to lend
unity to the urban speech stratum and set it apart from the countryside which is as yet little affected. [14] If we were to compare the
communication density —— measured in terms of personal contact
and mass media —— between distant urban centers as Patna and
Delhi, or Kanpur and Jubbalpur, we might find that it is equal to
or even greater than that between geographically less distant areas,
say a village in the Awadhi region around Lucknow and another in
the Braj area near Aligarh in U. P. There is therefore some
justification for speaking of a single urban speech community
connected by a super-regional network of communication which
extends from one urban center to another, without directly touching
the intervening rural areas.

The average individual living within this community does
not confine himself to a single style, but has at least some knowledge of all. Literary Hindi and literary Urdu in their extreme
forms are cultivated by separate social groups and are considered
separate courses of study. Among the educated there are some
who read only writings in the Devanagari script; a second group
knows only the Perso-Arabic alphabet; a third reads both and
others again are comfortable with neither style and do most of
their reading in English. Since independence Hindi has become
compulsory in schools, but Urdu continues to be used extensively
in commerce, and the Ghazal, the best known form of Urdu poetry,
is universally popular. If we look at the modern realist Hindi
writers, we find that they utilize both Sanskrit and Persian borrowings.

The juxtaposition of the two styles serves to express subtle shades of meaning and to lend reality to their writings. Similarly on the conversational level the use of Hindi and Urdu forms is not simply a matter of birth and education. But, just as it is customary for individuals to alternate between dialect and standard depending on the social occasion, so when using the standard itself the speaker may select from a range of alternatives. Hindi and Urdu therefore might best be characterized not in terms of actual speech, but as norms or ideal behavior in the sociologist's sense. [15] The extent to which a speaker's performance in a particular communication situation approximates the norm is a function of a combination of factors such as family background, regional origin, education and social attitude and the like.

In our linguistic description we will try to observe the distinction between ideal and actual behavior by comparing our texts collected by ordinary linguistic field methods with normative styles, those features which are regarded as suitable for formal communication and serve as models for actual speech. The fact that we draw this distinction does not mean that we intend to revert to an uncritical acceptance of the traditional prescriptive grammar, but rather we include only those features which seem to us to have a real prestige function. Modern linguists have shied away from the study of prescriptive grammar in recent years on the basis of their experience with Western languages where these grammars too often represent grammatical fictions adhered to by certain groups of grammarians and having no real currency in the community at large. In India this is not the case. Literary styles are learned through many years of oral mimicry memorization —— both at home and in the class room —— and many of the phonemic distinctions not part of the common core are acquired in this way.

A detailed study along the above lines would of course require extensive field work. Normative styles would have to be validated for each region with questionnaire techniques of the type used by social psychologists and would then have to be compared with an adequate sample of language texts collected under carefully controlled interview conditions. The present paper is a preliminary statement, based on a limited amount of data, which might help to

define some of the research problems involved and isolate variables
that could be tested in a more detailed study. Information on
normative styles was collected by consulting traditional grammars
and in consultation with those among our informants who could
qualify as experts. The main body of the texts was collected
from seven native informants, from different parts of the Hindi
regional language area. Informant A is a native speaker of Punjabi
who has lived most of his life in Delhi. Informant B is from the
Meerut district of U. P. , C is from Lucknow, F and G from the
Bhojpuri regional dialect area of U. P. D is an additional speaker
of Bhojpuri from Bihar and E is a native speaker of Maithili from
Bihar. All of them are well educated and have had some formal
training in one or both of the two literary styles. C and F are Muslims trained in Urdu. C has an advanced degree in the language
and has also studied some Hindi. G and D are teachers of Hindi and
Sanskrit. A, B, and E are graduate students in other subjects with
some training in the literary styles.

Except for G and E each informant was subjected to three
sets of interview conditions, a) informal conversation with friends,
b) reading a passage of prose in a formal style containing features
associated with the literary Hindi under conditions approximating
those of a lecture to a learned audience, c) reading of a similar
passage in literary Urdu. Whenever possible the literary passage
was given in the original script, but for informants who did not
know the script, passages were put into romanized transcription.

2. The formal and informal styles of Hindi-Urdu differ in
phonology, morphology, syntax and lexicon. In this paper we confine
our discussion to the most important items in the first two of these
categories.

2.1 Maximum Phonemic Inventory:

The table below is a listing of the total range of contrasting
segmental phonemes occurring in the data. There are some speakers whose speech shows all these contrasts. The majority however
does not have all. Segments not found in all idiolects are placed in
parenthesis.

Consonants:

	bilabial	apico- dental	apico post- dental	lamino- palatal	dorso- velar	back dorso- velar
voiceless Stops	p, ph	t, th	ṭ, ṭh	c, ch	k, kh	(ḳ)
voiced	b, bh	d, dh	ḍ, ḍh	j, jh	g, gh	
voiceless Spirants	(f)	s	(ṣ)	(š)	(x)	h
voiced	v	(z)		y	(γ)	
Nasals	m	n	(ṇ)	~(nasalization)		
Laterals		l r (trill)	(ṛ) (flap)			

Vowels:

	Front	Central	Back
High	i		u
	ɪ		ʊ
Mid	e	ə	o
	(ɛ)		
Low	æ		ɔ
		a (unrounded)	

Consonants and vowels may occur initially, medially, and finally with the exception of /ṇ/ and /ṛ/ which do not occur initially. Aspirate stops do not occur as geminates. All other consonants except /h/ , /x/ , /ṛ/ , /γ/ , /š/, / ṣ/ and / n/ appear as geminate or double consonants, e. g. /pəta/ 'address', /pətta/ 'leaf'. /v/ and /y/ which are traditionally treated as semivowels are here included among the consonants since they pattern like consonants.

The approximate phonetic range represented by each symbol is indicated by its position in the chart. Additional information is given in the text whenever relevant. $/\,\widetilde{}\,/$ indicates nasalization and is written above the vowel symbol, e. g. / hæ̃ / 'are', /hæ/ 'is'. Of the vowels, /ɪ/ , /ɛ/ , /ə/ , and /ʊ/ are always short. The others vary in length depending on the environment in which they occur.

Consonant Clusters

The table lists all initial and final two consonant clusters which occur in the Hindi-Urdu texts. Initial clusters are shown at the top of the square, final clusters at the bottom. An asterisk indicates items occurring in Urdu, a small circle those found in Hindi. Distributional details will be discussed in section 2.2.

II I	p	b	t	d	ṭ	ḍ	c	j	k	g	ḳ	f	v	s	z	š	x	g̱	h	m	n	l	r	y
p			*o											*								*o / o	*o	*o
b				o				o						*								*o / *	*o	o
t									f*	v o	s o									o *	o	*o / o	*o / o	o
d																						o	o / o	o
ṭ																						* o		
ḍ																						* o		
c																								o
j			*											*								*o	o	o
k										f *o	s o / o										*o / *	*o	*o / o
g																						*o	o	
ḳ		*										*		*		*				*		* / *o	*o	
f		*												*								*	*	o / o
v														*								o		
s	o / *o		o / *o		o / *o				o			*		o		*				o / *o	o / *	o / *	o / *o	o / *
z		*		*																*	*			*
š	o	*o		o					*o	*		o / o								*o	*o		*o	o / o
x		*										*		*						*		*	*	
g̱			*											*										
h																				*			*	
m	*o	o	*	*								*	*								*	o / *o	o	o
n			*o	*o	*o	*o	*o	*o	*o	*o		*		*o	*	o				o			o	o
l	o	*o	*	*o					*o			*				*				*o			o	o
r	o	*o	*o	*o	*o	*o	*o	*o	*o	*o	*	*o	o	*	*	*o	*	*		*o	o			o
y																								

2.2 Phonological Sub-Systems.

There are a number of speakers whose speech shows all
the contrasts in the maximum inventory; the majority however does
not have all of them. If we subtract the segments with limited
distribution from the maximum inventory, we arrive at what we may
call the common core, representing the minimum number of contrasts
necessary for a native speaker of Hindi.

Historically, segments not in the common core did not form
part of the local dialects from which the modern standards developed.
They came into the system through the influence of other literary
languages. /š/ occurs in loan words from Sanskrit (Sk,), Persian
(Pe.), Arabic (Ar.), English (En.), and other Western European
languages, e. g. /šobha/ Sk. 'beauty', /šadi/ Pe. 'marriage'.
/f/ and / z/ were introduced through Persian, Arabic, English,
etc., e. g. / fɔrən/ Ar. 'immediately', /farm/ En. 'farm',
/ bazar/ Pe. 'market', /rezər/ En. 'razor'. /ḳ/ , /x/ , and
/ɣ/ occur in words of Perso-Arabic sources only,/kərib/ Ar.
'near', /xʊda/ Pe. 'god', /ɣæb/ Ar. 'secret'. /ṇ/ and /ṣ/ are
found exclusively in direct borrowings from Sanskrit, e. g.
/karən/ Sk. 'reason', /kəṣṭ/ Sk. 'trouble'. Two additional items
occur only in English loan words. These are /ɛ/ and /ɔ/ , e. g.
/čɛk/ En. 'check', /bȯl/ En. 'ball'. The position of /ṛ/ is somewhat different. The original local dialects seem to have had two
phonetic segments [ṛ] and [ḍ] which were in complementary distribution, [ṛ] occurring medially between oral vowels and finally, [ḍ]
occurring elsewhere. English borrowings such as /soḍa/ 'soda
water' however introduced contrasts between these two allophones
and as a result the distinction became phonemic.

Although we refer to the above segments as loans it should
be remembered that most of them have been in common use since
quite early in the history of the modern standards and by now are
regularly part of everyday speech. Their occurrence and non-
occurrence however forms a convenient basis for distinguishing
sub-systems within the maximum inventory.

The normative Urdu pronunciation may be defined as the
pronunciation considered suitable for formal speech making or

reading of literary Urdu prose. It consists of the common core plus
the following segments: /f š x z ɣ k̲ r̲/ . Although normative
Urdu is traditionally taught with reference to the writing system it
does not incorporate all the distinctions made in the latter. The
letters svad, se, and sin, originally Arabic /ṣ θ s/ respectively,
are all pronounced alike as /s/ . zvad, ze, zal and zo which in
Arabic represented /ḍ z ƌ ẓ/ are all pronounced /z/ . te and to,
Arabic / t ṭ/ are pronounced / t/ . ain and hamzah which were
Arabic / ʕ ʔ / respectively are no longer pronounced as consonants.

A glottal stop [ʔ] is occasionally heard in the speech of
older traditionally trained individuals, e. g. [bə ʔ id] for /bəid/
'far' (spelled with ain), but this pronunciation seems to carry little
prestige. The pronunciation of Sanskrit loan words is regularly
assimilated to the Urdu system: Sk. /ŋ/ becomes /n/ and Sk.
/ṣ/ becomes /š/ , e. g. / karən/ 'because'/ bhaša/ 'language'.

The normative Hindi system, the pronunciation considered
suitable for formal Hindi, consists of the common core plus: /ŋ/ ,
/š/ , /r̲/ and /ṣ/ . Traditional pandits also teach a high central
vowel pronunciation [ɨ] in the sequence [r ɨ], in words written
with the corresponding syllabic r symbol in Sanskrit. But this
feature seems to have little real prestige function and might be
considered part of a special pandit style. On the level of phonemic
distribution, normative Hindi differs from Urdu by the use of final
short vowels /ɪ/ and /ʊ/ as in /pətɪ/ 'husband' and /kɪntʊ/ 'but'.
Both styles share final short /ə/ as in /nə/ 'not'. Whereas in
normative Urdu consonants in Sanskrit borrowings are generally
assimilated, the position of Persian loan segments within the
normative Hindi system will require some clarification. Traditional
grammars treat these sounds as being outside the system proper
and there are some modern writers of Hindi who object to the use
of special Devanagari symbols to represent them. In practice
/k̲/ /ɣ/ and /x/ are generally assimilated, /f/ and / z/ however
are quite common at least in Western U. P. and those who do not
pronounce them properly are often ridiculed. More detailed
sociolinguistic investigation into the prestige position of these items
should be of great interest.

The vowel segments /ɛ/ and /ɔ/ as in /cɛk/ 'check',
/bɔl/ 'ball' are found primarily in the speech of English speaking
bilinguals. Their position with respect to the two normative systems
is uncertain. Quite possibly more detailed study might isolate a
third, Westernized Hindi-Urdu normative style characterized by
/ɛ,ɔ/ as well as /z, f, š, ṛ/ .

In addition to the differences in phonemic inventory and
distribution, normative Hindi and Urdu show a number of important
distinctions in consonant clusters. For Urdu our cluster chart
lists only a limited number of initial sequences of the type consonant
plus l, r or y. Hindi shows many more items in this category
and in addition has several other cluster types. Among the more
distinctive Hindi initial clusters we might list the following:

kš	kšəma	'forgiveness'
st	stuti	'praise'
sv	svərg	'heaven'
šr	šri	'Mr.' (Urdu /šıri/)
sn	sneh	'affection'
ny	nyay	'justice'

The number of final clusters if larger than that of the
initial ones in both styles. Many of these clusters are shared, but
each has a few distinctive sequences. Aside from combinations
involving loan phonemes, the following clusters might be considered
as distinctively Urdu. a) Combinations of m plus non-homorganic
stop or spirant: mt, md, ms, mn. b) Sequences with final l; Hindi
has only ml in this category, Urdu has bl, tl, kl, sl. c) Clusters
with final s: Hindi has only ts, Urdu has ps, rs, ms. d) h plus
consonant, hr, hm:

mt	sImt	'direction'
ms	ləms	'touch'
kl	šəkl	'shape'
hr	šæhr	'city' (Hindi /šəher/ or /šəhər/

Most important among the distinctive final Hindi clusters
are sequences of consonant plus v and y. These do not occur in
Urdu:

tv	məhətv	'importance'
šv	əšv	'horse'
ny	əny	'other'
ly	muly	'price'
rv	gərv	'pride'
jy	rajy	'rule' (Urdu raj)
ry	sury	'sun'

It is interesting to note that many of the sequences with
final /y/ are re-sanskritizations of borrowings which in earlier
Hindi texts appear with simple consonant endings. Thus Bharatendu
Harischandra, the most important of the early Hindi writers, uses
/raj/ not /rajy/ 'rule'.[16]

The two styles further differ with respect to clusters
involving aspirate stops, which were not listed in the chart. In
Urdu aspirate stops occur only in final clusters after nasals. Hindi
has the following types of additional sequences:

rth	ərth	'meaning'
rbh	gərbh	'embryo'
rkh	murkh	'fool'
khy	mʊkhy	'chief'

2.3 Observed pronunciations.

In this section the normative pronunciations are compared
with field data from India and the formal and informal interview
texts collected for this study. Differences among informants
are classified according to the level of structure at which they
appear, i. e. according to whether they affect the phonemic inventory, phonemic distribution or whether they are phonetic.

Differences in Phonemic Inventory.

The majority of the uneducated illiterate speakers of Hindi and the regional dialects ordinarily replace the borrowed segments / š/ , /f/ , /x/ , /z/ , /ɣ/ , and /ṇ/ by /s/ , / ph/ , /kh/ , /j/ , /g/ , and /n/ respectively, and /ḍ/ and /ṛ/ for them are allophones of the same phoneme. With the educated informants recorded for this study the situation is more complex. All of them regularly distinguish between /š/ and /s/ . The segment /ḳ/ occurs only with informants C and F, both trained in Urdu. All others do not have it. The most common reflexes found in words with an original /k/ were /x/ before voiceless stop and /k/ elsewhere, e. g. /kanun/ for /ḳanun/ 'law', / vəxt/ for /vəḳt/ 'time'.

Informants C and F also regularly observe the contrast between /ɣ/ and /g/ , e. g. /ɣul/ 'noise', /gul/ 'flower'. E uses /g/ in all words of this type, and thus has no phoneme /ɣ/ . With A and B the position is as follows. There are some items in which the pronunciation varies between [ɣ] and [g], e. g. [ɣələt] ~ [gələt] 'wrong'. Others such as [gəŋga] 'Ganges' always have [g]. The phonetic alternation is confined to a limited list of items and is not predictable in terms of the phonological environment. It is necessary therefore to set up /ɣ/ as part of the phonemic inventory of informants A and B, although it is marginal. Items like the word for 'wrong' above are said to have two phonemic forms: we write /ɣələt/ when [ɣ] is heard and /gələt/ when we hear [g].

The segment /x/ regularly occurs with informants A, B, C, and F. D and E show variations similar to the /ɣ/ and /g/ alternation described above, e. g. [xas] ~ [khas] 'special'. /x/ is therefore phonemic in their speech.

Similar alternations between [j] and [z], and [ph] and [f] are found with informants B, D, and E, e. g. [cij] ~ [ciz] 'thing', [kaphi] ~ [kafi] 'enough'. The distinctions between [j] and [z] and [ph] and [f] are therefore phonemic for them.

The contrast between /n/ and /ṇ/ is regularly found only
with E, B, A, and D. Informant C varies between [n] and [ṇ] in
certain words. / ṇ/ is a marginal phoneme in his dialect. F never
shows [ṇ]. The contrast between / š/ and /ṣ/ was heard only with
informant E and his speech shows variation between [š] and [ṣ] in
words with Sk. /ṣ/ .

An interesting feature of the alternations between 'loan' and
'native' phonemes is their apparent irregularity in certain loan
words and their regularity in others. Informant E for example
regularly has /j/ in /jɪla/ 'district' and /jərur/ 'certainly', but
alternates between [z] and [j] in other items like /zyada/ 'more'.
The consistent use of either of these two phonemes in any particular
items suggests that these items were borrowed at a quite early
stage directly into the regional dialects. The /f/ and /ph/ alternation for some informants extends also to certain words which are
Indic in origin and should have /ph/ consistently, e. g. /phɪr/
/fɪr/ 'again', /phəl/ ~ /fəl/ 'fruit'.[17]

Differences in Phonemic Distribution.

The most important difference in this category is in the
distribution of vowels. Informants D, E, have contrasts between
/a/ , /i/ , /u/ and /ə/ , /ɪ/ , /ʊ/ in final position, e. g.
/nə/ 'no' /ka/ 'of' / yədI/ 'if' / nədi/ 'river', /kɪntʊ/ 'but'
/babu/ 'clerk'. Other informants have final /ə/ and /a/ but
only one high front and high back vowel /i/ and /u/ respectively
in this position. D and E further have the final sequence /əh/ in
a number of polysyllabic words including words of both Indo-Aryan
and Perso-Arabic origin, e. g. /barəh/ 'twelve', /terəh/
'thirteen', / jəgəh/ Per. 'place', /tərəh/ Ar. 'kind. The remaining informants seem not to have this final /əh/ . Correspondences vary between /a/ or /ha/ in words of IA origin like
the numerals and further also include /e/ or /he/ in some of the
loan words, /bara/ ~ /barha/ 'twelve', /jəga/ ~ /jəgha/ ~
/ jəge/ ~ /jəghe/ 'place'.

There are other alternations in phonemic distribution of
varying degree of importance which cannot be discussed here in

any detail but which might be worthy of further investigations. One
might mention the variation between single and double consonants
in items like /buḍha/ ~ /buḍḍha/ 'old'. Similarly of interest are
the alternations between /ks/ and /kkh/ , e. g. /dəksɪn/ ~ /dəkkhɪn/
'south', between /v/ and /b/ , e. g. /vən/~ /bən/ 'forest',
between nasalized and non-nasalized vowels, e. g. /ĩṭ/ ~ /iṭ/
'brick', and many more.

Phonetic Differences.

      On the phonetic level the following variations were found.
With informant A the phoneme /ə/ has allophones ranging between
[i] and [ə] before certain retroflex consonants. Other informants
vary between [ə] and [ʌ] in those environments. Allophones of
/ ə/ before /h/ cluster around [æ] or [ɛ] for most informants.
E and D have [ʌ] in this environment. The allophones of /i/ ,
/ɪ/ , / e/ , /u/, /ʊ/, and /o/ are comparatively high and tense
with D, E, and F. They are lower and more lax with A, B, and
C.

      / ɔ/ and /æ/ represent monophthongal low back and front
vowels in the case of informant A. With B and C the pronunciation
is diphthongal with a low vowel onset followed by a very short
upward glide [ɛe] and [ɔo]. The diphthongal glide with a central
vowel onset, [əɛ] and [ə o], is pronounced with informants D, E,
and F.

      /y/ and /v/ are pronounced with relatively strong conso-
nantal friction by A, B, and C. Informants D, E, and F have a
great deal more of vowel color.

      The tongue position of the retroflex consonants /ṭ/ and
/ḍ/ is most retracted and the preceding vowel has most retroflex
color with informant A. Informants B, and C have less retracted
tongue position and D, E, and F have least retroflection. The
progressive loss of phonetic distinctiveness of the dental-retroflex
contrasts if of interest in view of the fact that the dialects of Bihar
are closest to Assamese, which does not have this contrast.

Analysis of the pronunciation differences observed so far shows that the occurrence and non-occurrence of borrowed segments is related both to education or family background and to regional origin. The two Moslems C and F who have had formal training in Urdu agree in the consistent use of Perso-Arabic loan segments. All Hindus and C who has had some Hindi training have /ŋ/. With informants from the West / z/ , / f/ , and /x/ are regular parts of the phonemic inventory, whereas with D and E from Bihar these contrasts are marginal. This seems to reflect the fact that Indo-Islamic influence has been most profound in the West and Urdu literature most widely accepted. Differences on the phonetic level on the other hand are correlated primarily with regional origin. Informant A who has lived in Delhi most of his life is set off from all others by his pronunciation of /ə/ , /æ/ , / ɔ/ , /t̩/ and by forms such as /terha/ 'thirteen', features which seem characteristic of the sub-regional dialects in the Hindi-Punjabi border area. Similarly D, E and F, the two Hindus and the Moslem from Bihar show similarities in the pronunciation of vowels, of /t̩/ and /d̩/ , /y/ and /v/ and of final /h/. All these features are also found in the sub-regional dialects of Bihar.

The data regarding situational variants in pronunciation is meager. Informant C uses /ṇ/ only in situations calling for normative Hindi. The speech of informant D shows a much higher incidence of /z/ and /f/ in conversations with Moslems and Westerners; /j/ and /ph/ are more prevalent when he talks to his fellow Hindu from Bihar. Both authors have observed additional situational variants in India with older Hindus, trained in both styles. These individuals use /k̩/ , and /ɣ/ only in situations which call for normative Urdu. With other informants interviewed for this study variations of this type were less pronounced. More detailed investigation is needed with closer specification and better control of interview conditions.

There is furthermore little correlation between formal and informal interview situations and the pronunciation differences discussed so far. Formal-informal differences are more clearly evident in the pronunciation of consonant clusters. Uneducated low prestige speech shows the smallest number of clusters. In this style only sequences of consonant plus /y/ occur initially, and finally there are only clusters of nasal plus homorganic stop or sibilant plus stop. Clusters in common loan words are replaced as illustrated in the patterns below:

/ glas/	'glass'	/gɪlas /
/skul/	'school'	/ɪskul/ (East) or /səkul/ (West)
/kšəma/	'forgiveness'	/chəma/ or /šəma/
/ xətm/	'end'	/xətəm/
/šrəm/	'labor'	/šərəm/
/šərm/	'shame'	/šərəm/
/nəɣd/	'cash'	/nəkəd/ or /nəgəd/ or /nəgd/
/rəsm/	'tradition'	/rəsəm/
/šʊkr/	'thanks'	/šʊkʊr / or /šʊkər/
/prem/	'love'	/pɪrem/ or /pərem/
/rajy/	'rule'	/raj/
/smərəŋ/	'remembrance'	/sʊmirən/

Educated speakers regularly use initial clusters of the types Cr, Cy, Cl, and Cv, except for occasional variations in individual words such as that between /pleṭ/ and /pəleṭ/ 'plate'. Initial sC sequences however tend to be replaced by VsC in informal contexts, e. g. /skul/ ~ /ɪskul/ 'school', /stešən/ /ɪsṭešən/ 'station'. In final position similar formal-informal alternations are found in /kɪsm/ ~ /kɪsɪm/ 'kind'. /bəks/ ~ /bəkəs/ 'box' /iənm/ ~ /iənəm/ 'birth'. With a number of final clusters, alternations with consonant vowel consonant sequences are possible in some words but not in others. Thus educated speakers may say /bərəf/ or /bərf/ 'snow', but always use /s rf/ 'only'. Similar examples are: /təxt/ ~ /təxət/ 'throne, bench' versus /səxt/ 'hard'; /kɪlk/ ~ /kɪlɪk/ 'reed' versus /mʊlk/ 'country'; /bhəsm/ ~ /bhəsəm/ 'ashes' versus /jɪsm/ 'body'; /muft/ ~ /mʊfət/ 'free' versus /koft/ 'disgust'; /məkr/ ~ /məkkər/ 'deceit' versus /šʊkr/ 'thanks'. A third set of items always shows final clusters: /šəbd/ 'word', /šəxs/ 'person', /svərg/ 'heaven'.

Clusters not shared in both normative styles tend to be replaced in the style in which they do not occur. Some common instances are: U. /šɪri/ for H. /šri/ , U. /raj/ for H. /rajy/ 'rule', U. /krɪšən/ for H. /krɪšn/ 'Krishna', H. /šəher/ for U. /šæhr/ .

2.4 Morphological Differences.

A complete analysis of morphological variants within Hindi-Urdu is beyond the scope of this paper. We will note here only the most striking differences.

One major distinction is found with demonstrative pronouns. Normative Hindi has four different forms, which are kept distinct in spelling and pronunciation:

/yəh/ 'this', /ye/ 'these'   /vəh/ 'that', /ve/ 'those'

Normative Urdu has only two forms, written yəh, vəh but pronounced as below:

/ye/ 'this, these'   /vo/ 'that, those'

Informants A and F always use /ye/ and /vo/ , C employs the first set only in formal Hindi contexts. B, D and E alternate between /yəh/ and /ye/ and B also changes between /vəh/ and /vo/ in the singular. All three keep the plural /ve/ distinct. The Hindi normative set is most closely adhered to in formal situations. It would also seem that the Urdu system is more common in the West, but more information is needed on the details of the alternation and on its social function.

Borrowings from Persian and Sanskrit, in addition to creating differences in lexicon, have also brought in a number of differences in the inventory of derivational morphemes. Thus in Urdu we have :

-ən	/nɪsbətən/ 'relatively'
-in	/rəngin/ 'colorful'
-mənd	/gərəzmənd/ 'desirous'
-ɪya	/məzaḳɪya/ 'funny'
həm-	/həmdərd/ 'friend' (lit. one who shares the pain)
ba-	/baḳaɪda/ 'according to rules'
-nak	/xətərak/ 'dangerous'
pʊr-	/pʊrlʊtf/ 'pleasant'
dər-	/dərmɪan/ 'middle'
-šmas	/fərzšɪnas/ 'conscientious, dutiful'
bəd-	/bədnam/ 'notorious'

Some characteristic Hindi affixes are:

-təh	/ səmbhəvətəh/ 'probably'
-lu	/ šrəddhalu/ 'respectful'
-ək	/ səhayək/ 'helpful'
-akar	/ golakar/ 'circular'
-ɪk	/pərɪvarɪk/ 'domestic, of family'
dʊr-	/dʊrdəša/ 'bad condition'
-ta	/kəʈhorta/ 'brutality'
ən-	/ənərth/ 'useless'
svə-	/ svəbhav/ 'nature'
prə-	/prəkop/ 'extreme anger'
ə-	/əvak/ 'silent'
-man	/bʊddhɪman/ 'wise'
-ɪt	/ jivɪt/ 'alive'
ʊd-	/ʊddhar/ 'release'
-purvək	/bhəktɪpurvək/ 'full of piety, faithfully'
-tv	/ məhətv/ 'responsibility'

It is interesting to note that the bulk of the Sanskrit loan affixes are freely used only with direct Sanskrit borrowings (tatsamas) and the Perso-Arabic loan affixes are used only with Perso-Arabic borrowings. Only a few have come to be used also with indigenous roots (tadbhavas). Among these are:

-dar	/dukandar/ 'shopkeeper', /ʈhekedar/ 'contractor'
be-	/bejan/ 'lifeless', /bedhərək/ 'fearless'
-ana	/buzurgana/ 'elderly', /jogiana/ 'like a jogi'
na-	/nagəvar/ 'unbearable', /nasəməjh/ 'unwise'
-xana	/dəvaxana/ 'hospital', /kuṛaxana/ 'garbage pile'
ən-	/ənpəḍh/ 'illiterate', /ənərth/ 'meaningless'

The first five items in the above list are of Persian origin
and are used with Persian loans and tadbhavas. The last item is
from Sanskrit and is used with tatsamas and tadbhavas. We have no
instance of a Persian loan affix used with tatsamas or a Sanskrit loan
affix used with Persian loan roots.

In normative Hindi a number of roots undergo morphophonemic changes on the analogy of Sanskrit Sandhi, e. g. /ved/
'Veda', /vædɪk/ 'Vedic'. Traditional prescriptive grammars as a
rule describe these changes in terms of the Sanskrit system, using
the same classification and terminology. [18] In practice the Hindi
system is somewhat different from the Sanskrit—we may have for
example both /rajnitɪk/ and /rajnætɪk/ 'political'—but these
differences have not as yet been described.

As with consonant clusters, the speech of the uneducated
shows the smallest number of derivative compounds. When arranged in order of formality the affixes roughly fall into three groups.
The items in the third set of examples given above and few others
such as -ɪya, -bəd are in common use. Others indicate either
relatively formal Urdu, e. g. -mənd, ba-, or relatively formal
Hindi, e. g. -lu, -ək, -akar, -ta. A third group of very formal
items is productive primarily in writing and very rarely in speech,
e. g. Urdu -ən, pur- or Hindi -təh, -ɪk, -purvək-, -tv. In
ordinary speech the relatively formal and very formal affixes are
most usually substituted by phrases. Thus /səmbhəvətəh/
'probably' becomes /səmbhəv hæ/ or /mumkɪn hæ/ or /nɪsbətən/
'relatively' becomes /ʊs ke mukable mẽ/ etc.

Among the lexical borrowings from Persian and Sanskrit
there are also a number of common conjunctions and adverbs which
have considerable structural importance, and might be classed as

function words.[19] These form another important criterion for
stylistic distinctions. The listing below gives items occurring in
normative Hindi, normative Urdu and informal conversation.

Normative Hindi	Informal Conversation	Normative Urdu
/yədɪ/ , /əgər/ 'if'	/əgər/	/əgər/
/yədyəpɪ/ 'although'	/əgər/	/əgərcɪ,' , /halakɪ/
/təthapɪ/ , /to bhi/	/phɪr bhi/ , / to bhi/	/ təb/ bhi/ , /phɪr bhi/
/phɪr bhi/ 'yet', 'nevertheless'	/ təb bhi/	
/evəm/ , /tətha/ , /or/ 'and'	/ ɔr/	/ ɔr/
/karəɳ/ 'reason'	/ karən/ , / vəja se/	/səbəb se/, /vəje se/
	/vəje se/	
/ kɪntu / , /pərəntu /	/məgər/, /lekɪn/	/məgər/, /lekɪn/
/məgər/ 'but'		
/sərvda/ , /səda/, /nɪty/ 'always'	/səda/, /həmeša/	/səda/, /həmeša/
/səhɪt/ , /sath/ 'with'	/ sath/	/sath/
/ətəh/ , /ɪslɪe/ 'therefore'	/ɪslɪe/	/cʊnancɪ/ , /ɪslɪe/

The items in the normative Hindi and Urdu columns can again be
arranged into relatively formal and very formal groups. Items in
the first category are: Urdu /halãkɪ/ 'although', /cʊnancɪ/
'therefore' and Hindi /yədɪ/ 'if' /perentʊ / 'but'. In the latter
group we find Hindi /təthapɪ/ 'yet', /evəm/, /tətha/ 'and'
/kɪntu / 'but /səhɪt/ 'with', /ətəh/ 'therefore'. It is interesting
to note that none of the function words in the normative Urdu
column are in the very formal group. A characteristic feature of
very formal Urdu style is the use of the enclitic -e ' of' and -o
'and' borrowed from Persian, e. g. /sahəbe xana/ for the more
common /ghar ka sahəb/ 'owner of the house', /dərde dɪl/ for
/dɪl ka dərd/ 'pain of the heart', /abo həva/ for /həva aur pani/
'climate' (lit. 'air and water'), /səvalo jəvab/ for /səval aur jəvab/
'question and answer'.

3. Conclusion

The standard speech stratum in the Hindi regional language
area can be described in terms of a single range of styles. Within

this range we may distinguish a common core, shared by all
including the uneducated and two, or possibly three, formal extremes
or normative styles which are set off from each other by features
of phonology, morphology and syntax. In actual texts, spoken as
well as written, the differences between the extremes tend to be
blurred somewhat but we may distinguish various degrees of Hindi,
Urdu and Westernized coloring. The various styles within the
standard stratum tend to be associated with particular communication
roles and the speech of any one individual varies accordingly. Some
individuals are at home in both normative styles, with others the
variations are more limited. Aside from the Hindi-Urdu differences,
we find speech differences such as the contrast between /s/ and /š/
and the use of certain consonant clusters, which correlate with
differences in education. Degree of formality and informality is
signalled by other consonant clusters, by derivative suffixes,
borrowed enclitics and certain types of function words.

The exact nature and social function of the above stylistic
markers varied from region to region. In the West for example
the contrast between /z/ and /j/ is a regular part of the phonemic
inventory of educated speakers; in the East it is marginal for many
and only persons with special training in Urdu have it regularly.
Regional origin is most clearly evidenced on the phonetic level. All
speakers from a particular area tend to have the same allophones
regardless of social background. A person from Bihar trained in
Urdu might have the same phonemic inventory as another Urdu
speaker from Lucknow, however, in items which are part of the
common core, the allophonic content of his speech resembles that
of other speakers from the same area who often have different
phonemic inventories.

NOTES

1. For a somewhat different and more detailed discussion
of the general Hindi or Hindustani problem see S. K. Chatterji,
Indo-Aryan and Hindi (Ahmedabad, 1942).

2. The variations within Hindi are similar to the differences between Colit Bhasha and Sadhu Bhasha in Bengali, described by Dimock and Chowdhury in this volume. [Linguistic Diversity in South Asia ed. by Charles A. Ferguson and John J. Gumperz (Bloomington, 1960)].

3. See for example the following: S. H. Kellog, A Grammar of the Hindi Language (3rd ed. , London, 1938); K. P. Guru, Hindi Vyākaran (Banaras, 1957); A. Sharma, A Basic Grammar of Modern Hindi (Delhi, 1958), this is the most recent official grammar published by the Government of India, Ministry of Education and Scientific Research.

4. The standard reference work is John T. Platts, A Grammar of the Hindustani or Urdu Language (London, 1920).

5. See for example A. H. Harley, Colloquial Hindustani (London, 1944); M. C. Saihgal, Hindustani Grammar (11th ed. , Simla, 1945); T. G. Bailey, Teach Yourself Hindustani (London, 1950). Some of the grammars in our three categories discuss both scripts but do not discuss the relations between the styles.

6. Sir George A. Grierson, Linguistic Survey of India (19 vols. , Calcutta, 1903-28).

7. The most useful of the traditional treatments is S. K. Chatterji, op. cit. , but this contains little concrete linguistic data.

8. Cf. J. J. Gumperz, "Language Problems in the Rural Development of North India," Journal of Asian Studies, 16. 251-9 (1957). For a discussion of similar local dialect chains elsewhere; cf. Trevor Hill, "Institutional Linguistics," Orbis, Volume VII, No. 2, 1958, pp. 441-455. See also the discussion of L complex and L simplex in C. F. Hockett, A Course in Modern Linguistics (New York, 1955) p. 323 ff.

9. Sir George A. Grierson, op. cit.

10. Cf. O. H. K. Spate, India and Pakistan (London, 1954), the standard geography of India which lists Bihari and Western Hindi along with Gujarati, Bengali, etc.

11. S. K. Chatterji, who suggests that Bazaar Hindi be made the national language, does not consider these prestige relationships.

12. Cf. R. Redfield, Peasant Society and Culture (Chicago, 1956), p. 70 ff.

13. For a general discussion of relevant communication problems see K. W. Deutsch, Nationalism and Social Communication (New York, 1953).

14. Cf. Deutsch's concept of mobilized population, ibid., p. 99 ff.

15. Cf. K. Davis, Human Society (New York, 1948), p. 55 ff.

16. Cf. R. C. Shukla, Hindī Sāhitya Kā Itihās (Banaras, 1955), p. 529.

17. Cf. the change from ph to f in 19th century Bengali described in S. K. Chatterji, Origin and Development of the Bangali Language (Calcutta, 1926), Vol. I, p. 442.

18. Cf. K. P. Guru, op. cit.

19. For the use of this term see C. C. Fries, The Structure of English (New York, 1952).

5 | Speech Variation and the Study of Indian Civilization

Although inquiry into the relationship between language and culture has grown considerably in recent years, most modern American work in this field so far operates with unit languages and cultural isolates. The Whorf hypothesis has focused attention on the relationship between linguistic structures and native ways of categorizing cognitive experience and led to important advances in structural semantics. In cross cultural analyses of such structures, however, each system is treated as a homogeneous "linguistic and cultural whole" (Kroeber 1939), regardless of internal social or geographical differences in speech and behavior patterns. Studies of linguistic diffusion similarly emphasize borrowings between distinct and often unrelated languages. Less attention has been devoted to Bloomfield's "dialect borrowing" (1933:476), the spread of features within a speech area. Furthermore, historically oriented structural linguists confine their research to historical linguistics or internal language history, the formal reconstruction of hypothetical parent varieties from a series of distinct languages or dialects, in contrast to external language history, the study of linguistic change in relation to the social currents which affect it. The great body of 19th and 20th century research on speech variation within single speech communities has as yet evoked little interest among either structural linguists or social scientists in the United States. Yet, much of this work is of central relevance for the studies of complex civilizations or "intermediate societies" as they have recently been termed (Casagrande 1959), which are becoming more and more common in modern anthropology.

In contrast to many modern American linguists who, because of their concern with methodology, have often found it difficult to communicate with other students of culture, dialecto-

logists—and especially those trained in the European tradition—
tend to think of themselves primarily as cultural geographers,
folklorists, or social historians. They regard linguistic analysis
not as an end in itself but rather pursue it for the information it
provides about the history and culture of a region. Thus, of the
earlier work, the investigations of the German scholars Fischer,
Haag, and Wrede have produced convincing evidence for the relationship between present-day dialect isoglosses and certain German
territorial boundaries of late medieval and early modern times
(Bach 1950: 81ff.). Gillieron, the author of the Linguistic Atlas
of France (Gillieron et Edmont 1903-10) and his students, although
their primary concern was with phonetic change, have given us
many new insights into the manner in which the rise and spread of
certain words or pronunciations reflect the social forces and
intellectual currents of a period. More recently, the Linguistic
Atlas of Italy and Southern Switzerland by Karl Jaberg and Jacob
Jud (1928-1940) provides maps which show the distribution of
linguistic forms, along with their changes in meaning. It furthermore gives detailed drawings of the objects of material culture
which these forms represent and their regional variations in shape.
The most extreme position on the relation between dialect study
and cultural phenomena is that of the German, Theodore Frings,
who coined the slogan "Sprach-geographie ist Kulturgeographie"
and dropped the term "Sprachraum" (linguistic region) in favor of
"Kulturraum" (cultural region) (Bach 1950: 63 ff.). Frings' cultural
regions were defined in collaboration with teams of social historians,
geographers, and folklorists. These same regions then became
the units for detailed enquiries into the conditions leading to the
rise of new linguistic forms and into the geographical and social
itineraries by which these forms spread both within regions and
from one region into another. In these studies, speech features
were treated as units of social communication and were surveyed
along with such other traits as housing types, dress, ritual, and
folklore. The general orientation of European dialectologists also
carried over into the planning of the linguistic atlas of the United
States, which was done in cooperation with social historians and
anthropologists, and which employs a stratified sample including
upper, middle, and lower class speakers (McDavid 1958). Although
this work is as yet incomplete, the results obtained so far indicate

a close connection between speech and land settlement and migration patterns.

Aside from geographical surveys, we also have a number of studies showing correlations between speech and social groupings. Jaberg and Jud, in the course of their investigations of Italian dialects, found considerable differences between speakers of different social classes in urban Florence (Jaberg 1936). Marcel Cohen's Pour une sociologie du langage (1956) constitutes a detailed but somewhat discursive and uncritical review of the literature in this field. Bach (1950:227 ff.) gives a somewhat better organized account of German work on the subject. In the United States there have been several recent highly suggestive studies on social speech differences and on the function of speech variants as class and status signals (McDavid 1958; Putnam and O'Hern 1955).

The methodological approach of much dialect research so far is open to criticism. Linguistic data were too often collected through mail questionnaires or recorded by means of impressionistic phonetic notations which omit information crucial for phonemic analysis (Bloomfield 1938; Smith 1952). There is, furthermore, little concern, as a rule, with adequate methods of sampling and with problems of reliability and validity (Pickford 1957). In spite of these and many other shortcomings, the general concepts used in the study of speech variation are quite applicable to modern research problems. A combination of the analytic methods of structural linguistics with the sampling and interviewing techniques of modern social scientists should provide new scope for cooperative research in language and culture.

In a recent publication an effort was made to bring together some modern linguistic studies on social and functional intra-language variation in India, along with an introduction discussing the place of such studies in modern linguistic theory (Ferguson and Gumperz 1960). The present paper is a more general effort to relate the analysis of speech variation to current research trends in the study of Indian civilization. An attempt will be made to point out problem areas where linguistic data might help to clarify

relationships and to suggest ways in which linguistic tools can be
utilized for relevant research.

Levels of Social Communication

       We begin with the problem of delineating cultural sub-
divisions. Most early efforts in this direction have employed the
concept of the culture area as developed for tribal cultures of the
North American subcontinent (Wissler 1938; Kroeber 1939), in
which diversity was conceptualized in terms of a series of distinct
cultural wholes. Bacon's attempts to utilize this concept in classify-
ing both tribal cultures and complex civilizations on the entire
Asian continent have met with a number of criticisms (Bacon
1946; Kroeber 1952). There is even less agreement in regard to
the culture areas of the South Asian subcontinent, where the variety
of criteria available for such subdivision is so great as to give
rise to many conflicting classifications (Cohn 1957). As Berreman
states in examining the applicability of the culture area concept to
a highly diversified Himalayan hill area (1960):

> In discussing cultural affiliations of Sirkanda
> residents, one could defend as valid their membership
> in any or all of the following culture areas: North India,
> Pahari, Central Pahari, Garwal, Tehri Garwal, Bhatbair.
> Others could be delimited including some crosscutting
> these. Groups peripheral to some of these areas might
> be located centrally in culture areas defined by different
> criteria. . . . The crude groupings which result from
> culture area studies are subject either to the limitations
> inherent in the study of a few elements or patterns selected
> from the universe of cultural data and divorced to some
> extent from their cultural context or to the limitations
> inherent in the subjective comparison of total configura-
> tions.

       In suggesting an alternative framework of analysis, Cohn
and Marriott (1958) bypass the problem of isolating cultural wholes

and, following the guidelines set down by Redfield and others, focus
on the communicative processes which tie together the diverse
components of Indian civilization. They view these processes in
terms of four levels of communal relations of different geographical
extent. These are: 1) the all-India level, defined by the subcontinent;
2) the region, defined by literary language and distinctive caste
patternings; 3) the subregion, defined by certain spoken dialects,
and showing some peculiar cultural distinctiveness and characteristic
castes; and 4) the local level, which may constitute either a single
village or a group of villages tied by common kinship or other
social ties. The integrative processes which tie together these
levels are two: supra-local networks of relationships, such as
marriage, pilgrimage and trade networks, and relationship with
centers, where various sources of innovations are concentrated.

Stratified distribution models like the above find their
clearest illustration in speech variation. European scholars
regularly differentiate between dialects and the standard speech of
the educated and urban population. Recently, writers have pointed
to additional distinctions between local varieties ("patois" or
"Mundart") and supralocal varieties ("regional dialects," "dialects"
or "Halbmundart") (McIntosh 1952; Moser 1950; Martinet 1954).
It is also commonly understood that these levels are at least partly
independent of each other and correspond to different networks of
social communication. An often cited example is that of the "dialect
continua" (Hill 1958; Ferguson and Gumperz 1960) such as the
chain of similar Germanic dialects running from Switzerland to the
North Sea and including the German, Dutch, and Flemish language
areas, or the various Romance dialects found along the shores of
the Mediterranean in a region including Italy, France, and Spain.
Within a dialect continuum mutual intelligibility is proportional
to geographical distance and not directly related to political and
standard language boundaries. Rural populations on both sides of
such a boundary usually have no difficulty in understanding each
other, while they might be unable to comprehend geographically
distant varieties spoken in their own language area. The relationship between standard language and local speech in such speech
communities has recently been termed one of "superposition"

(Ferguson 1959; Ferguson and Gumperz 1960). They serve as special styles used on formal occasions or for communication with outsiders, and local populations are for all intents and purposes bilingual or, to coin a new term, "bilectal."

In India, Cohn and Marriott's generalized levels parallel distinctions between regional languages, reflecting the urban and national trends of the last hundred years; regional or subregional dialects which serve as the media for the traditional hinge groups; and local varieties spoken around the home and farm (Gumperz 1958a; Gumperz and Naim 1960). The diversity of networks integrating these levels is reflected in further variations such as those between Hindi and Urdu normative styles (Gumperz and Naim 1960), the various forms of standard Bengali, literary and colloquial Tamil (Dimock 1960; Chowdhury 1960; Pillai 1960), the many subregional dialect literatures, trade languages, and in caste dialects on the local scene (Gumperz 1958a; Bright 1960).

Linguistic studies illustrating these networks may take two forms: they may either trace the distribution of a single dialect or variety, or focus on the relations between systems through comparison of two or more dialects or styles. While the linguistic methods used for this purpose will be generally those of dialectology, they will have to be specially adapted and modified for the task at hand. We will first discuss distribution at the local level, since the bulk of anthropological research so far has centered around village communities, and then deal with the relationship of local to other superposed levels.

Local Variation

The problem of isolating distinct speech or culture areas becomes less complex if supra-local features are excluded from consideration. This is accomplished in dialect studies by concentrating on rural districts and emphasizing speech forms used around the home and farm. Although changes in mutual intelligibility in a dialect continuum are gradual, it is possible to draw certain relatively sharp boundary lines by mapping historical or typological isoglosses, thus separating out areas of greater or lesser uniformity. Different isoglosses do not necessarily coincide, however, and dialectologists as a rule do not attempt to assign each single locality to one or another dialect area. They distinguish between "focal areas," that is, zones that are relatively free from major isoglosses, and "transition zones," that is, those that are cut by large bundles of isoglosses. The focal area-transition zone model thus draws a distinction between areas of uniformity and areas of diversity where two or more behavioral alternatives are possible, a distinction which could fruitfully be applied to the study of other cultural phenomena.

Speech communities differ in the ease with which they lend themselves to subdivision. Scholars working in Italy have found little difficulty in defining large relatively homogeneous dialect regions, such as Piedmont and Liguria, which are sharply cut off from others by series of important isoglosses. In central France, on the other hand, speech is much less diverse, and changes are so gradual that some of the early Romance dialectologists have categorically stated that since each word has its own history and distribution, it is impossible to separate out distinct dialect areas (Bach 1950; Jaberg 1936). The opposite is the case in southwest Germany, where diversity is so great that many villages can be said to have dialects of their own. The problem of evaluating dialect boundaries has been solved in part by distinguishing between more or less important bundles of isoglosses, but there is little agreement on criteria to be used for this. Already in 1931 Troubetzkoy (1949) pointed out that the use of phonemic in place of the usual phonetic or lexical isoglosses might lead to a clearer definition of speech boundaries. Since Troubetzkoy's time, structural linguists have developed a number of conceptual schemes suitable for comparing phonemic structures of dialects. Best known among these are the over-all pattern developed for English by Trager and Smith (1951) and the related common core approach which was recently illustrated by J. C. Catford (1958). Another approach is the distinctive feature analysis as developed by Jakobson and others which has recently been applied to the study

of Slavic dialects by Stankievicz (1956). So far, however, these
methods have been used primarily for the comparison of dialect
areas. They have not been applied to the study of particular dialect
boundaries.

A preliminary survey of three village dialects in the Hindi
area of North India, utilizing a technique of grading isoglosses
adapted from that suggested by Troubetzkoy, discovered a number
of isoglosses of varying degrees of structural importance (Gumperz
1958b). The data suggest that transition from one type of phonemic
structure to another is not as abrupt as one might suppose. Phonemic
contrasts tend to show a decrease in functional load and phonetic
distinctiveness as one approaches an isogloss. Thus, for example,
in the case of the retroflex and dental nasals /ṇ/ and /n/ which
contrast in the western portion of the region studied and not in the
eastern section, we find that the number of words with the retroflex nasal decreases as we go east. Furthermore, whereas in the
west the retroflex and the dental are clearly distinguishable
phonetically, when we come closer to the boundary this phonetic
distribution becomes more and more difficult to hear. The phonetic
interval decreases until the distinction is audible only in slow speech.
Similar phenomena were observed by Moulton in his recent study
of Swiss dialects (1960). There is, therefore, little reason to
believe that the use of structural in place of phonetic or lexical
isoglosses will obviate the need for distinguishing between focal
areas and transition zones.

The cultural correlates of local village dialects may be
studied either from the historical point of view or from the point
of view of present day social relationships. The social historian
might ask: what are the connections with territorial boundaries
and settlement and migration patterns? Is it possible to find clear
relationships such as exist in Europe? Grierson's dialect survey
for the Hindi area as a whole shows many north-south isoglosses
and few boundaries going from east to west (1916). This could be
a reflection of the direction of Aryan colonization, or the spread of
Brahminical influences which proceeded east along the Ganges
and then fanned out to the north and south. One recent study seems

to confirm this view (Agraval 1959). There are many aspects of
Indian civilization, however, which should keep us from drawing
overhasty conclusions. Cohn and Marriott point to the diversity
of administrative, economic, and religious centers and of market
and pilgrimage networks which seems much greater than in other
parts of the world. Possibly this diversity is also reflected in
language boundaries.

The present-day social correlates of language isoglosses
are usually described in terms of communication density. Bloomfield's illustration of this concept has a great deal of similarity
with the sociogram of the modern social psychologist (1933:46).
But it does not seem likely that a conventional sociogram compiled
on the basis of research with small groups will coincide with
important speech boundaries. Work in Germany seems to point to
connections with larger networks such as those dominated by
administrative and market centers (Bach 1950). For India it
might be of interest to investigate correlations of local dialects with
marriage networks, such as those described by Rowe (1960),
geographical distribution patterns of dominant caste groups, or
with trading and pilgrimage networks. Since traders and pilgrims
do not ordinarily occupy high positions in the local caste hierarchy,
it is doubtful whether their contacts with the village have as profound an effect as kinship ties. But this is a matter for further
study. Cooperative surveys by anthropologists and linguists
covering both focal areas and transition zones which would sample
highly diversified hill areas, such as that described by Berreman
(1960), as well as the more uniform plains regions, might provide
some important insights into the basic processes of social change.

Local and Superposed Systems

Although most dialect surveys concentrate on the speech
of the home and farm, it is well known that local varieties coexist
with supra-local or superposed styles or dialects. Even small
rural communities are rarely completely uniform, but usually
show a diversity of speech styles. Angus McIntosh (1952:29) in

illustrating this problem in Scotland states, "...there may exist
in any given community a complex linguistic situation, for members
of the community may differ greatly ... in the way they talk. At
one end of the scale, there is in many places the 'broad' local
dialect speaker who is least affected by influence from the outside;
at the other there may be someone whose speech has no perceptible
regional characteristics at all. In between these extremes there
may be intermediate types of speech and some people will have
more than one at their command, each available for appropriate
occasions." He also speaks of "a network of dialects each inevitably
influencing the other." The coexistence of local and supra-local form
within the same locality find its behavioral correlate in the anthropologist's concept of "levels of sociocultural integration" (Steward
1951). The systematic treatment of the linguistic phenomena
involved has so far been considered outside the scope of dialectology,
but as McIntosh suggests, and as we will attempt to show below, it
can be of great importance for the study of civilizational processes.

In a general discussion of the problem of coexistent styles,
Hill (1958) suggests a distinction between two types of varieties:
"vernaculars" transmitted by parents to children, and "koines" such
as trade languages and standard languages. We will adopt Hill's
distinction. The term "vernacular" will be employed for the form
of speech used in the home and in the local peer group. This is
not always the same as that transmitted to children by parents
since it is quite possible that age grading is as important as family
background in shaping basic speech patterns (Hockett 1950). For
all other styles of speech found in the village we will use the term
"argot" and define it as any speech variety distinct from that used
around the home and the local peer group, which serves as the
norm in one or more socially definable communication situations.

Linguistic diversity in rural South Asia is relatively
greater than in Europe. The local dialects discussed above serve
as vernaculars for most villagers. There may also be some
untouchable groups with distinct vernaculars of their own (Gumperz
1958a). In addition to the vernaculars there will be several argots.

One form of the sub-regional dialect is used with traders from
nearby bazaar towns. Other different forms may be employed with
wandering performers or religious ascetics. There is some
evidence to show that in earlier times two or three different sub-
regional literary dialects cultivated by different groups of literati
coexisted in the same region. Thus, wandering ascetics of the
Krishna cult might use Braj Bhasa, while worshipers of Ram
would use Avadhi. Standard Hindi is the norm for intercourse with
educated outsiders. We also find it used in certain religious,
caste, or village uplift meetings. On other occasions, especially
in business transactions or when talking to educated Muslims,
Urdu is called for. Furthermore, a few of the more educated
people know English and there are others who have at least some
knowledge of Sanskrit. These two languages, although not directly
related to the local forms, function as integral parts of the village
stylistic web. Educated speakers tend to switch freely from one
language to another when conversing about urban subjects, often
inserting entire English phrases into their Hindi discourse. Others
who do not have a command of English use a large number of English
loan words in similar situations. Sanskrit is an essential component
of certain Brahminical communication roles. The distinction
between bilingualism and "bilectalism" thus becomes blurred in
social situations of this type.

In the small urban centers the sub-regional dialect serves
as the vernacular of the trading and service castes. Argots aside
from standard Hindi, Sanskrit, and English might also include
one or more of the local dialects. Similarly, standard Hindi is
the vernacular of a few of the highly urbanized big-city residents.
These individuals, however, will usually be familiar with English
as one argot and will also command one or another of the sub-
regional dialects for contacts with the local population.

The ordinary villager or small city dweller of course does
not control all the above argots, but he recognizes their function as
ideal speech behavior: if he does not have command of the stylistic
norm associated with a social situation, he will at least attempt to

modify his speech in the direction of this norm by borrowing features of pronunciations, verb or noun endings, or lexical items associated with it. Similarly, traveling performers learn to modify their literary style so as to adapt to the local speech of their audience. Stylistic variation seems least pronounced in the speech of those individuals who tend to their own farms. It is greater with those who have outside economic interests or are active in religion and greatest with those who seem to have political ambitions. This suggests that, as in the case of the talking chiefs of Samoa, ability to manipulate argots might be one of the attributes of leadership in village India. The need for command of diverse styles increases as we go up the scale to the sub-regional and regional speech strata.

Some European scholars have utilized lexical data to trace the local effect of specific cultural movements. Thus, Frings (1948) has given us some studies on Roman influence in ancient Germany and on the itinerary of the Reformation in Germany in early modern times. Such studies, however, usually come as by-products of dialect surveys and are rarely specially planned. Further-more, linguistic indices employed have been based on loan words in vernaculars only and correlations applied only to social history. More detailed surveys covering the entire range of styles could find much wider application.

The effect of a new dialect or language, introduced into a speech community as a result of a change in the social system, can be traced by studies of bilingualism or of borrowings into the local speech. Widespread community bilingualism is equivalent to the creation of a new argot. The effect of the social change in question will be directly proportional to the number of speakers of this new argot, and the number and type of communication roles in which it is employed. It will be inversely proportional to the amount of linguistic interference in the speech of local users of the argot as measured against that of the innovating group. Thus, in most Indian urban communities English is the argot associated with the process of Westernization. Western influence in India is greatest in centers like Bombay, Calcutta, and Madras where we find the highest proportion of English bilinguals, many of whom carefully cultivate pronunciations modeled on Oxford English and use their English in formal as well as informal situations.

In the case of borrowing, the effect varies with the items borrowed. Lexical terms and certain syntactic patterns are more easily adopted than phonemic contrasts or morphemes and indicate less of a social change. The use to which these loans are put is also important. If the borrowed items become part of a new argot and are employed in limited situations only, the effect is less than if they enter into the vernacular itself. We may illustrate this by examining the spread of the Persian loan phonemes /z, f, x, k, g/ in the so-called Hindi language area of North India. These phonemes are integral parts of the vernacular only in certain urbanized Muslim homes. Elsewhere we find different degrees of adoption. In the Delhi and Lucknow urban circles the vernaculars include /z, f/ but /x, g, k/ are used only on formal occasions. In Bihar where Islamic penetration is less deep /k, g, x/ are not ordinarily found and /f, z/ are rare. The sub-regional and local dialect strata do not show any Persian loan phonemes, however the number of commonly used Persian lexical borrowings is greater in the West than in the East. Similar studies on the spread of modern urban Hindi in rural areas, for example, might form a basis for scaled indices for the measurement of social change and of the relative integration of rural areas in modern Indian national life.

Linguistic Measures of Argots and Vernaculars

The methods used in the study of argots should be quite different from those of the dialect survey of the linguistic geographer, which attempts to cover all variations in a single questionnaire and rarely contains safeguards against style switching. To begin with, distribution of argots does not follow the same pattern as that of vernaculars. Two social groups having the same argot may have different vernaculars. A high-caste villager may speak the same form of urban Hindi as his untouchable neighbor. Their vernaculars are likely to be quite distinct. Similarly, speakers of the same vernacular may use different argots depending on their training and occupation.

Linguistic characteristics also differ. Differences between vernaculars may appear on all levels of structure: phonetic, phonemic, morphological, syntactic, or lexical (Hill 1958). Between adjacent vernaculars, transitions are gradual. Phonetic differences often pattern, so that if in a dialect the front vowel [i] is slightly tenser than the equivalent front vowel [ɪ] in another dialect, similar variations are likely to exist for other front vowels such as [e]. Such differences are best discovered and most easily classified on the basis of detailed phonetic studies, using a highly refined system of transcription. Argots, on the other hand, tend to be symbolized by the presence or absence of distinct allophones, phonemic contrasts, morphemes, or lexical features. There is less of a gradual transition. Furthermore, a great deal of variation is permissible within the same argot. Hill (1958) mentions the fact that there are some Englishmen who say [bæš], [hæt], others say [baš], [hat] for "bash" and "hat"; both groups count as speakers of standard English. An argot is ordinarily learned after childhood often as a result of conscious effort, and its patterns are, so to speak, superimposed over those of the vernacular. To give a phonological example, a speaker of Hindi, residing in Delhi, will be phonetically similar to that of his Urdu-speaking neighbor. The two will differ to the extent that the Urdu speaker has learned to distinguish between /f, z, k̤, g̣, x/ and /ph, j, k, g, kh/ , whereas the Hindi speaker does not make all these distinctions but does distinguish between /ṇ/ and /n/ . When we compare our Urdu speaker from Delhi with another Urdu speaker from Bihar we find that, while they agree with respect to the above phonemic distinctions, the over-all phonetic aspects of the latter's speech will be closer to that of Hindi-speaking Biharis.

The total set of features which the linguist utilizes in identifying vernaculars, furthermore, includes both those which are known and recognized by natives as characteristic of that

vernacular as well as others that ordinarily are not noticed. Thus,
the pronunciated [bəyd] for "bird" is regularly identified as
characteristic of Brooklyn speech. Fewer laymen are aware of
the fact that there are some Americans who pronounce the words
"cot" and "caught" with the same vowel while other distinguish the
two. The dialectologist's techniques guard against the effect of
popular preconceptions about dialects. Items are elicited by
roundabout methods designed to keep the informant from being self-
conscious, so as to obtain natural, unguarded speech responses.
The resulting scientific classifications of dialects often come up
with groupings which have little relation to popular notions of
speech boundaries. Linguistic features characteristic of an argot
are generally recognized as such within the speech community.
As a matter of fact, they are the signals by which natives judge
and receive advance information about the nature of a communication
situation. Their social function is in every sense equivalent to
the sociologist's "symbols of social status. " It is the task of
linguistic studies first to establish the nature of these symbols
and then test for their presence or absence in certain well-defined
communication contexts. Detailed analyses of the total phonetic
system are less relevant. New methods will have to be devised for
work with argots, incorporating controls of the type used in social
science surveys and utilizing linguistic techniques derived from
dialectology as well as bilingual studies.

Conclusion

        The analysis of speech variation should form an integral
part of the study of South Asian civilization. Speech distribution
within a single speech community in India may be studied in terms
of vernaculars, or of argots. Differences in vernaculars are
attributable to breaks in over-all communication density, and may
reflect geographical or social distance. Differences in argot are
related to such concepts as level of integration, role, reference,
group, and the like, and may be utilized to study the interrelation
between local and supra-local networks. While vernaculars can
be studied by traditional methods of dialectology, new methods
will have to be developed for the study of argots.

NOTES

1. The first draft of this paper was presented at the 58th Annual Meeting of the American Anthropological Association, Mexico, D. F., 1959, under the title, "Speech Variation as an Index in the Study of South Asian Civilization."

I would like to thank Roman Jakobson, Susan M. Ervin, and Bernard Cohn for their helpful comments. Roman Jakobson suggests that the term "argot" as employed in this paper is somewhat awkward since it is most commonly used in the more restricted meaning of "secret language." Possibly "special parlance" would be a better term.

REFERENCES

Agraval, Ramesh P. 1959. A descriptive analysis of Bundeli dialect. Doctoral dissertation, Lucknow University.

Bach, Adolf. 1950. Deutsche Mundartforschung. Heidelberg, Carl Winter.

Bacon, Elizabeth. 1946. A preliminary attempt to determine the culture areas of Asia. Southwestern Journal of Anthropology 2:117-32.

Berreman, Gerald D. 1960. Cultural variability and drift in the Himalayan Hills. American Anthropologist 62:774-94.

Bloomfield, Leonard. 1933. Language. New York, Henry Holt.

Bright, William O. 1960. Linguistic change in some Indian caste dialects. In Linguistic diversity in South Asia, C. A. Ferguson and J. J. Gumperz, eds. Bloomington, Indiana, Research Center in Anthropology, Folklore and Linguistics.

Casagrande, Joseph B. 1959. Some observations on the study of intermediate societies. In Intermediate societies, social mobility
and communication. Seattle, Washington, American Ethnological Society.

Catford, J. C. 1958. Vowel systems of Scots dialects. Transactions
of the Philological Society 1957:107-17.

Chowdhury, Munier. 1960. The language problem in East Pakistan.
In Linguistic diversity in South Asia, C. A. Ferguson and
J. J. Gumperz, eds. Bloomington, Indiana, Research Center
in Anthropology, Folklore and Linguistics.

Cohen, Marcel. 1956. Pour une sociologie du langage. Paris, Paris
Editions, Albin Michel.

Cohn, Bernard S. 1957. India as a racial, linguistic and culture area.
In Introducing India in liberal education, Milton Singer, ed.
Chicago, The University of Chicago Press.

Cohn, Bernard S. and McKim Marriott. 1958. Networks and centers
in the integration of Indian civilization. Journal of Social
Research (Ranchi, Bihar) 1:1-9.

Diebold, A. Richard, Jr. 1961. Incipient bilingualism. Language 37:
97-112.

Dimock, Edward C. 1960. Literary and colloquial Bengali in modern
Bengali prose. In Linguistic diversity in South Asia, C. A.
Ferguson and J. J. Gumperz, eds. Bloomington, Indiana,
Research Center in Anthropology, Folklore and Linguistics.

Ferguson, Charles A. 1959. Diglossia. Word 15:325-40.

Ferguson, Charles A. and John J. Gumperz, Eds. 1960. Linguistic
diversity in South Asia. Bloomington, Indiana, Research
Center in Anthropology, Folklore and Linguistics.

Frings, Theodore. 1948. Grundlegung einer Geschichte der Deutschen Sprache. Halle (Saale), Max Niemeyer Verlag.

Gilliéron, J. and E. Edmont. 1903-1910. Atlas linguistique de la France. Paris.

Grierson, Sir George Abraham. 1916. Linguistic survey of India, Volume 9:1. Calcutta, Government of India.

Gumperz, John J. 1958a. Dialect differences and social stratification in a North Indian village. American Anthropologist 60:668-82. [In this volume, pp. 25-47.]
_____ 1958b. Phonological differences in three Hindi dialects. Language 34:212-24.

Gumperz, John J. and C. M. Naim. 1960. Formal and informal standards in the Hindi regional language area. In Linguistic diversity in South Asia, C. A. Ferguson and J. J. Gumperz, eds. Bloomington, Indiana, Research Center in Anthropology, Folklore and Linguistics. [In this volume, pp. 48-76.]

Hill, Trevor. 1958. Institutional linguistics. Orbis 7:441-55.

Hockett, Charles F. 1950. Age grading and linguistic continuity. Language 26:449-57.

Jaberg, Karl. 1936. Aspects géographique du langage. Paris, Droz.

Jaberg, Karl and Jacob Jud. 1928-40. Sprach und sachatlas Italiens und der Sudschweiz. Zofingen (Suisse), Ringmiret Co.

Kroeber, Alfred L. 1939. Cultural and natural areas of native North America. University of California Publications in American Archaeology and Ethnology 38:1-242.
_____ 1952. The Nature of Culture. Chicago, The University of Chicago Press.

Martinet, André. 1954. Dialect. Romance Philology 8:1-11.

McDavid, Raven. 1958. American English dialects. In The Structure of American English, W. Nelson Francis. New York, The Ronald Press Company.

McIntosh, Angus. 1952. Introduction to a survey of Scottish dialects. Edinburgh, Thomas Nelson and Sons.

Moser, Hugo. 1950. Deutsche Sprachgeschichte. Stuttgart, Curt E. Schwab.

Moulton, William G. 1960. The short vowel systems of Northern Switzerland. Word 16:155-82.

Pillai, M. Shanmugam. 1960. Tamil—literary and colloquial. In Linguistic diversity in South Asia, C. A. Ferguson and J. J. Gumperz, eds. Bloomington, Indiana, Research Center in Anthropology, Folklore and Linguistics.

Pickford, Glenna R. 1957. American linguistic geography: a sociological appraisal. Word 12:211-33.

Putnam, George N. and Edna M. O'Hern. 1955. The status significance of an isolated urban dialect. Language Supplement, Language Dissertation No. 53.

Rowe, William L. 1960. The marriage network and structural change in a North Indian Community. Southwestern Journal of Anthropology 16:299-311.

Smith, Jr., Henry L. 1952. Review of A word geography of the eastern United States, Hans Kurath. Studies in Linguistics 9:7-12.

Stankiewicz, Edward. 1956. The phonemic patterns of the Polish dialects: a study in structural dialectology. For Roman Jakobson. The Hague, Mouton. Pp. 518-30.

Steward, Julian H. 1951. Levels of socio-cultural integration: an
    operational concept. Southwestern Journal of Anthropology
    7:347-90.

Trager, George L. and Henry L. Smith, Jr. 1951. An outline of
    English structure. Norman, Oklahoma, The University of
    Oklahoma Press.

Troubetzkoy, N. S. 1949. Phonologie et géographie linguistique.
    Principes de Phonologie, Translated by J. Cantineau.
    Paris, Klincksieck. Pp. 343-50.

Wissler, Clark. 1938. The American Indian. 3rd ed. New York,
    Oxford University Press.

6 | Types of Linguistic Communities

Comparisons of linguistic and social behavior have been impeded by the fact that linguistic and anthropological studies are rarely based upon comparable sets of data. While the anthropologist's description refers to specific communities, the universe of linguistic analysis is a single language or dialect, a body of verbal signs abstracted from the totality of communicative behavior on the basis of certain structural or genetic similarities. To be sure, studies of individual languages vary greatly in range. They may deal with the speech of a small band of hunters and gatherers, a village dialect, or a literary language spoken by several hundred million speakers. But, on the whole, in selecting the data to be studied linguists give more weight to genetic relationships and structural homogeneity than to social environment. We think of English as a single whole, although a typical corpus may include texts stemming from rural England, urban United States, Australia or even former colonial areas of Asia or Africa.

The process of linguistic analysis, furthermore, is oriented towards the discovery of unitary, structurally homogenous wholes (Hymes 1961b:48). Stylistic variants, loans and the like are not excluded from grammars, but traditional interviewing techniques are not designed to measure their total range (Voegelin 1960:65) and the tendency is to relegate them to the category of free variation. The effect of such procedures is the selection of one single variety (Ferguson and Gumperz 1960:3) out of the complex of varieties which characterize everyday speech behavior. This one variety is then considered to be representative of the entire language or dialect.

Structural abstractions of this kind are quite adequate as long as interest is confined to language universals or typology and to comparative reconstruction. They have revolutionized our theories of grammar and in the field of language and culture they have disproved earlier naive notions which equated primitiveness of material culture with simplicity of language structure. But when we turn from a study of language as an institution to the analysis of speech behavior within particular societies, more detailed information is usually required. Thus views such as those of Linton who states that "there appears to be no correlation between the complexity of the language spoken by a people and the complexity of any other aspect of their behavior" (1936:81) are valid only with respect to the internal structure of any one single speech variety. They should not be interpreted to mean, as they sometimes are, that it is impossible to distinguish between the speech habits of simple tribal groups and complex urban societies. European linguists of the Prague school as well as some American anthropological linguists have shown that the existence of codified standard languages as distinct from every day casual speech is a "major linguistic correlate of an urban culture" (Garvin and Mathiot 1960:283).

The subject of intra-language variation, which had been neglected in the early days of descriptive linguistics is receiving renewed attention in recent years (Sebeok 1960). A number of scholars have called for a revision of the earlier "monolithic hypothesis of language structure." Instead they regard linguistic communication within a speech community in terms of an "interconnected system of subcodes" (Jakobson 1960:352). If we accept this we might hypothesize that linguistic complexity within a particular society is not a function of internal patterning within a single homogeneous system, but can be understood in terms of the relation among diverse systems of different extent. A similar view of social complexity is presented in some of the recent anthropological work on "intermediate societies" (Cohn and Marriott 1958:1, Casagrande 1959:1). In order to deal adequately with such linguistic and social systems, the focus of linguistic enquiry will have to shift from simple descriptive analysis to analysis followed by comparative or contrastive study.

Although comparative analysis may be synchronic or diachronic in nature, scholars interested in the relationship of language to social environment have until now confined themselves primarily to diachronic comparison. The predominant view is that of Sapir (1951:89), who tended to discount the effect of social environment and considered "drift" as the major factor in determining the structural peculiarities of a language. This view has also had considerable effect on synchronic studies, as can be seen from a paper by Triandis and Osgood dealing with the cross-cultural application of the semantic differential:

> Greek belongs to a subgroup of the Indo-European family of languages that is quite distinct from all other members of the family. Our present findings, then, support the assumption that the same general semantic structure will be found in all Indo-European languages. (Triandis and Osgood 1957:192)

Sapir's views on language change have never been completely accepted by all linguists and anthropologists. The work of Boas as well as that of European linguists concerned with Sprachbund phenomena has long since pointed to the limitations of the genetic approach (Hymes 1961a:23). In recent years Weinreich's studies on structural borrowing in Switzerland and in the Yiddish speaking areas of Eastern Europe have further emphasized the importance of social environment (1952:360, 1953). The areal approach to linguistic relationships was further developed by Emeneau (1956:3, 1961) in a number of carefully documented studies. Emeneau takes as his point of departure the South Asian culture area which he treats as a "single linguistic area." He points out the existence of numerous structural parallels among languages of Indo-Aryan, Dravidian and Munda stocks in Central India, as also between the Dravidian Brahui and the surrounding Indo-Aryan and Indo-Iranian language groups in the Northwest. Similar area-wide cross-language influences have been noticed in the California Indian language region, the very area from which Sapir draws his most striking examples of the lack of relationship between language and social environment. Catherine Callahan (1961) demonstrates the existence of a series of glottalized stops

in Lake Miwok which seem to be borrowed from the surrounding
Indian languages. William Shipley (1960) shows some striking
differences in the sentence structure of Northern and Southern
Maidu which also suggest the influence of environment.

The above studies in area linguistics, however, are
historically oriented and are of more interest to students of culture
history than to the social anthropologist. While the concept of
structural borrowing refers to the end result of a process of change,
it does not provide an insight into the dynamics of this process. Its
synchronic correlates, speech diversity and code-switching among
different dialects, styles or languages will probably hold more
interest for scholars oriented towards functional analysis. Such
studies must however begin with a specific community, not with
a linguistically defined entity (Gumperz 1951:94).

In his recent paper, The Ethnography of Speaking, Hymes
(1961b) reviews the literature on speech behavior and relates it
to the more traditional types of linguistic and anthropological
endeavor. He calls for a new approach to the "descriptive analysis
of speaking" and suggests that "the speech activity of a population
should be the primary object of attention." The present paper is
an effort in this direction.

Linguistic distribution within a social or geographical
space is usually described in terms of speech communities
(Bloomfield 1933:42). We find a number of instances of the use
of extra-linguistic criteria in defining such communities. Frings
and his group of German dialectologists have adopted techniques
from geography for the determination of cultural regions on the
basis of marketing and traffic patterns, distribution of items of
material culture and the like and have used these regions as the
focus for their study of speech distribution (Gumperz 1961a).
American linguists have dealt with small urban groups (Putnam
and O'Hern 1955), while Einar Haugen's monumental The Norwegian
Language in America is an example of an exhaustive study of an
immigrant group (1953). In all these studies, however, speech
communities are considered coterminous with a single language and
its dialects and styles. Bilinguals are said to "bridge speech

communities" (Hockett 1958). Some writers have gone so far as
to liken them to the sociologist's "marginal man" (Soffietti 1955).

There are no a priori grounds which force us to define
speech communities so that all members speak the same language.
Total bi- or multi- lingualism is the rule rather than the exception
in a wide variety of societies including the nineteenth century
Russian urban elite, the ruling groups of many modern Asian and
African nations, the American immigrant groups mentioned above
as well as many others. Weinreich as a matter of fact also speaks
of "bilingual speech communities" in describing the Yiddish
speakers of Eastern Europe (1953). Furthermore, from the point
of view of social function, the distinction between bilingualism
and bidialectalism is often not a significant one (Gumperz 1961a: 13;
Martinet 1954:1).

The present paper will therefore employ the term "linguistic
community" by analogy with Emeneau's term "linguistic area. "
We will define it as a social group which may be either monolingual
or multilingual, held together by frequency of social interaction
patterns and set off from the surrounding areas by weaknesses
in the lines of communication. Linguistic communities may consist
of small groups bound together by face-to-face contact or may
cover large regions, depending on the level of abstraction we wish
to achieve.

Social communication within a linguistic community may
be viewed in terms of functionally related roles, defined according
to Nadel (1957:31ff) as "modes of acting allotted to individuals
within a society. " Nadel's approach to the analysis of role is
couched in terms familiar to the linguist. He regards each role
as characterized by certain perceptual clues or "attributes"
consisting of "diacritics" implicit in role behavior such as dress,
etiquette, gestures, and presumably also speech behavior; and
by role names such as priest, father, or teacher which serve to
provide advance information regarding the nature of the role
behavior to be expected. A particular diacritic is considered as
peripheral if its presence or absence does not change the native's
perception of the role and relevant if it does change role perception.

Role behavior is further said to vary in accordance with the "interactional setting, " a term which seems to correspond to the
linguist's "context of situation" (Firth 1957:32) or "environment. "

    The totality of communication roles within a society may
be called its "communication matrix. " There are as yet no generally
agreed-upon procedures for isolating individual roles, although
correlations between language use or style and like behavior have
been noted in a number of recent studies (Fischer 1958:47, Chowdhury
1960:64, Ferguson 1959:2). For our purposes it will be sufficient
to isolate only those roles or role clusters which correlate with
significant speech differences. We assume then that each role has
as its linguistic diacritic a particular code or subcode which serves
as the norm for role behavior. We speak of the "code matrix" as
the set of codes and subcodes functionally related to the communication
matrix.

    The nature of the components of the code matrix varies
from community to community. In some all components are
dialects or styles of the same language. These we will refer to as
subcodes. In others the matrix also includes genetically distinct
languages, in which case we will use the term codes. The distinction
between code and subcode is largely a linguistic one, however; it
does not necessarily correspond to a difference in social function.
The peasant in Southern France uses his patois as the language of
the home and employs a regional variant of standard French towards
outsiders. In Brittany, Breton serves as the home language while
communication with outsiders is maintained through a second
variant of Standard French. Both Breton and the patois are used in
roughly equivalent contexts of situation and have similar social
function within the peasant community.

    The criterion for inclusion of a code in a study of a
linguistic community is that its exclusion will produce a gap in the
communication matrix. English is an important part of the
communication matrix of urban India while it could be omitted from
an ethnography of a remote tribal community. Similarly, Sanskrit
is relevant for the description of certain Hindu communities in
India but not for certain Muslim groups. The distinction between

uniformity and diversity of dialects or monolingualism and bilingualism thus becomes less important than the distinction between the
individual and the societal.

Subcodes of the same language within the code matrix also
show varying degrees of linguistic differences. Local dialects
may be either linguistically different or very similar to the other
superposed forms of speech. The same is true for styles. Ferguson
has recently pointed to some important linguistic differences between
the formal and informal media (1959:2) of certain urban populations.
We will use Weinreich's term, language distance (1952), to refer
to the totality of differences in phonology, grammar or lexicon
within the code matrix as measured by contrastive study.

Societies also vary in the way in which roles cluster within
the communication matrix. In rural India the role of the religious
preacher is closely associated with that of the social reformer,
while in American society, we would consider the two quite separate
(Gumperz 1961b). Another characteristic feature of some societies
is the distinction between behavior within the home and peer group
and behavior towards outsiders. In South Asia this distinction
in roles corresponds to sharp difference between local dialects and
superposed forms of speech. The sanctions against mixing the
two types of behavior have been long so strong that some Indians
have an almost insurmountable aversion to writing down informal
speech. Possibly such socially enforced distinctions in role
behavior are a major factor in the preservation of local dialects.
We will use the term role distinctness to refer to the degree to
which role behavior is kept separate.

An examination of linguistic communities in various parts
of the globe reveals a definite relationship between the overall
characteristics of the code matrix and certain features of social
structure. Connections of this type have often been noted (Greenberg 1956:109). Nineteenth century European dialectologists, for
instance, have demonstrated the relation between political and social
boundaries and present-day dialect isoglosses (Gumperz 1961a).
Other dialectologists have pointed to the contrast between relative
homogeneity of speech in recently settled areas such as the American

West and diversity in longer-settled areas on the East Coast. It is
assumed that this homogeneity is the result of processes of change
resulting from resettlement of populations of different origin under
conditions favoring fluidity of roles and statuses. This conclusion
is also supported by our own experience with foreign language
settlements in the United States where the language tends to be
preserved as long as the settlers remain a distinct social group,
as is the case in some rural settlements, but will disappear when
the settlers are merged into urban society.

We have already referred to the work of the Prague school
linguists and of Garvin on the relationship between urban societies
and standard languages (1960:283). Garvin and Mathiot define
a standard language as a "codified form of a language accepted by
and serving as a model to a larger speech community." They list
a number of criteria as characteristic of a standard language.
Two of these, codification and language loyalty are of special
interest. Codification relates to the fact that rules of pronunciation
and grammar are explicitly stated (e.g. in the form of standard
grammars and dictionaries), while language loyalty, a concept
introduced by Weinreich (1953:106), is the attitude which lends
prestige to a language and leads people to defend its "purity"
against "corruption" in pronunciation or "foreign" loans.

The above and similar references to the relation between
speech distribution and social environment are all limited to
specific cases. More generalized formulations should become
possible through the application of concepts such as code matrix,
role distinctness, language distance and language loyalty to
linguistic communities of different degrees of social complexity.
Such classifications might show rough parallels between speech
distribution and social groups of the type now classified by social
scientists as bands, larger tribal groups and modern urbanized
communities. Any formulations of this kind will of necessity
be extremely tentative, especially since social scientists themselves
do not seem to agree on the theoretical basis for distinguishing
between simple and complex societies (Schneider 1961) and since
reliable cross-cultural information on speech behavior is almost

non-existent. They are offered here only in the hope that they may
stimulate further research.

We begin with the least complex communities, consisting
of small bands of hunters and gatherers such as we find among
American Indians of the Great Basin. Social contacts in these
groups are limited to face-to-face communication, there is a
minimum of social stratification, and contacts with outsiders are
relatively infrequent. Speech is not completely uniform, however;
perceptible differences may be observed between what has been
called casual every-day speech and non-casual styles used in
singing, recitation, myth-telling and similar ritually defined
situations. There are some cases in such societies, where ritual
formulas contain words, sentences or songs in a language which is
unintelligible to the natives themselves. In general, however,
the language distance between casual and non-casual speech is
relatively small and control of the non-casual style does not seem
to be confined to a particular group (Hymes 1958:253; Yegerlehner
1953:264; Voegelin 1960:57 ff).

Diversity may be somewhat greater in the case of larger,
economically more advanced tribal communities which, although
not integrated into larger societies, maintian some trade relations
with the outside. There, to the extent that ritual activities requiring
the use of non-casual language become specialized, these styles
may become associated with particular groups. Trade with other
tribes speaking other languages requires bilingualism but speaking
in these languages tends to be confined to certain roles only. In
many societies, trade relations are limited and superficial and
surrounded by ritual intended to keep the trader from trespassing
on tribal society. As trading activities expand in scope and
specialized groups of traders arise, one or the other tribal
language may spread over wide areas as a trade language, as in
the case of Hausa in Africa. The forms of language used in trade
situations tends to be quite distinct from that used within the
tribal group. They differ from standard languages in that they
usually lack codification and tend to have no special prestige
outside the trading situation. Socalled pidgin or mixed languages
are not as a rule found in purely tribal societies but are the result

of contact between an economically developed society and a tribal group or groups.

Tribal societies may have outside relations other than trade through intermarriage or religious ritual. In such situations, there is evidence to show that bi- and multi-lingualism is much more common than most linguistic and ethnographic studies would lead one to believe. Such bilingualism, however, is rarely of the societal type. Within the community only the tribal language is spoken. In certain California Indian tribes (the Yurok, Karok and Hupa) living in the same general area and maintaining regular contact, this is carried to such an extreme that each tribe has a different name for the same physical landmark. Evidently the tribal language is the symbol of communal identity, although it does not show the formal characteristics of a standard language. We may say that for such tribes, language loyalty applies to the tribal language, although the communication matrix may also include certain trade languages.

Community bilingualism, speech stratification, or major stylistic variance seems to become possible only as the economic base expands to allow economic stratification. One common type of variation found in societies which, although relatively advanced, still preserve some tribal characteristics, is that between "high" and "low" language styles (Garvin and Riesenberg 1952:201; Uhlenbeck 1950). One characteristic of such societies is the existence of a ruling group representing conquerors from the outside who maintain considerable social distance from the rest of the population. High and low styles tend to vary in lexicon, morphophonemics, and allomorphy but not in phonology. They also utilize different borrowing sources: high Javenese borrows from Indo-Aryan languages while high Balinese, it is said, borrows from Javanese. Regardless of the difference between high and low forms, both seem to be regarded as part of the same language by local populations.

Diversity tends to reach a maximum in the more typical intermediate societies characterized by the existence of peasant,

herder or even tribal strata or population in various degrees of
integration in the socially dominant groups. Social systems in
these societies exhibit a high degree of social stratification and
occupational specialization. Social behavior is characterized by
role distinctness, so that individuals act differently in different
contexts. These distinctions are emphasized by elaborate ritual
and behavioral conventions (i. e. etiquette) as well as by differences
in dress, food habits, and the like. An extreme example of this
is the Indian caste society, which gives the impression of a
multitude of distinct populations living side by side and communicating
only with respect to a limited portion of their total activities. Other
less complex intermediate societies tend to differ in degree of
complexity, not in kind. The code matrix in such societies may
include several distinct languages and in addition, the language
distance between subcodes varies from purely lexical and phonetic
variances to important structural divergences. One interesting
phenomenon is the occurrence of deliberate speech disguise of the
type found in modern "Pig Latin." This type of disguise while
rendering the subcodes mutually unintelligible is describable in
terms of relatively simple transformation rules (Halle and
Chomsky 1961).

In discussing speech distribution in these societies we will
distinguish between the vernacular form of the language learned at
home, and argots or special parlances, learned after childhood and
used only in certain limited situations (Gumperz 1961a:12).
Geographic diversity of speech forms is greatest in the case of the
vernaculars used among the rural populations. This diversity
may take the form of variant dialects or of genetically distinct
local languages. In both cases the social functions are similar;
they serve as in-group languages and co-exist with superposed
codes used for communication with strangers. In medieval Europe,
for example, we find islands of Celtic speech in the Alpine regions
interspersed among Romance and Germanic dialect continua.
Slavic languages alternate with Germanic dialects in the East
while Basque occurs with Romance in southwestern Europe. Similarly
in India the North Dravidian tribal languages and Munda languages
such as Korku are found deep in the Indo-Aryan territory.

Argots or special parlances are of several types. The
first, which we may call subregional or regional dialects, serve
for communication in the market place and as media of inter-group
communication. They resemble the trade languages of tribal areas
in that they show little codification and carry no great prestige. The
language distance between these codes and local forms of speech
may be small if both are dialects of the same language. If local
populations speak a genetically distinct language, those local
residents whose business requires contact with the outside tend to
be bilingual.

The second set of argots is that employed by certain social
and occupational groups in the pursuit of their special activities.
We may include here the special parlances spoken by commercial
groups, thieves' argots, and literary and recitation styles of
popular story tellers. The social function seems to be that of
maintaining group exclusiveness. They tend to be guarded and
preserved from outsiders in somewhat the same way that craft
guilds guard their craft skills. Codes in this set may on occasion
be written; and to the extent that proper pronunciation and grammar
serve as a means of group identification, they may be said to show
some codification, but their prestige as a rule is limited.

The third category includes the sacred and administrative
codes which are distributed over wider and geographically and
socially more diverse regions than the previous set. Thus, in
medieval Europe, Latin was used as both administrative and sacred
language in Germanic, Romance, and Slavic speech areas. Sanskrit
and Persian in medieval India had similar functions. These codes
serve as the language of special administrative and priestly classes
but they are not necessarily spoken by the actual rulers. They
share some of the characteristics of occupational codes in that
they function to maintain group exclusiveness; they are characterized
by extreme codification, symbolized by the necessity for a large
investment of time in the study of grammar and rhetoric and, of
course, by the existence of schools for this, with their complements
of scholars. When administrative and sacred codes differ, the
sacred codes are accorded the greatest amount of prestige.
Intermediate societies, then, in contrast to tribal societies, tend

to show language loyalty to codes which may be quite distinct
from the vernacular.

Extreme diversity and language distance between the
administrative and sacred codes and other codes in the code matrix
is maintainable only as long as government remains in the hands of
a small ruling group (Havranek 1936:151). As a greater proportion of
the population is drawn into the national life and becomes mobilized,
the old administrative code may be replaced by one drawn from the
regional strata. The new administrative subcodes characteristic
of this type of society are as a rule not quite identical with the
spoken idiom of the urban mobilized groups; considerable language
distance may be maintained in a number of instances (Ferguson 1959).
In general, however, the tendency is for the code matrix to
become less and less diverse as local populations are integrated
into the dominant groups or "mobilized" as Deutsch (1953) has
called it and as role distinctness decreases.

Language distances within the code matrix are lowest in
some highly urbanized communities such as we find in parts of
modern Europe and in the United States. In these communities,
the distinction between standard and local dialects has almost
disappeared. It is reflected only in the form of regional standards
such as we have in the American Midwest, Southwest, or West.
Some social speech distinctions persist. In addition there are a
number of distinct formal and informal subcodes, as well as
technical and scientific parlances. In contrast to what we find
in intermediate societies, however, language distances among
these forms tend to be confined to the syntactical and lexical levels.
We rarely find two or three different sets of inflectional allomorphs
or function words such as characterize stylistic differences in
some of the Asian languages. A large portion of the differences
that do occur are justified by special requirements for technical
terminology. It almost seems that shallow linguistic contrast in
styles is a direct correlate of the fluidity of roles symbolized by
the distinction between caste and class. Language loyalty in these
societies is bestowed on the standard, which now closely reflects
the majority speech.

NOTE

I am grateful to Catherine Callahan, Paul Friedrich, Dell Hymes and William Shipley for their helpful comments.

BIBLIOGRAPHY

Bloomfield, Leonard. 1933. Language. New York: Henry Holt.

Callahan, Catherine. 1961. Phonemic Borrowing in Lake Miwok. Typescript.

Casagrande, Joseph B. 1959. Some Observations on the Study of Intermediate Societies. In Intermediate Societies, Social Mobility and Social Communication, Proceedings of the 1959 Annual Spring Meeting of the American Ethnological Society, pp. 1-10.

Chomsky, Noam and Morris Halle. 1968. The Sound Pattern in English. New York: Harper and Row.

Chowdhury, Munier. 1960. The Language Problem in East Pakistan. In C. A. Ferguson and John J. Gumperz, eds. Linguistic Diversity in South Asia, pp. 64-78.

Cohn, Bernard S. and McKim Marriott. 1958. Networks and Centers in the Integration of Indian Civilization. Journal of Social Research (Ranchi Bihar) 1.1-9.

Deutsch, Karl W. 1953. Nationalism and Social Communication. Cambridge, Mass.: The M.I.T. Press.

Emeneau, M. B. 1956. India as a Linguistic Area. Language 32.3-16.
_____ 1962. Brahui and Dravidian Comparative Grammar. University of California Publications in Linguistics, Volume 27. Berkeley: University of California Press.

Ferguson, Charles A. 1959. Diglossia. Word 15.325-40.
_____ and John J. Gumperz, eds. 1960. Linguistic
    Diversity in South Asia. Bloomington, Indiana: Research
    Center in Anthropology, Folklore and Linguistics.

Firth, J. R. 1957. A Synopsis of Linguistic Theory, 1930-1955.
    In Studies in Linguistic Analysis, Special Volume of the
    Philological Society, pp. 1-32.

Fischer, John L. 1958. Social Influences on the Choice of a Linguis-
    tic Variant. Word 14. 47-61.

Garvin, Paul and Madeleine Mathiot. 1960. The Urbanization of the
    Guarani Language - A Problem in Language and Culture.
    In Men in Cultures, A. F. C. Wallace, ed. Philadelphia:
    University of Pennsylvania Press.
_____ and S. H. Riesenberg. 1952. Respect Behavior on
    Ponape: An Ethnolinguistic Study. American Anthropologist.
    54:201-20.

Greenberg, Joseph H. 1956. The Measurement of Linguistic Diver-
    sity. Language 32:109-15.

Gumperz, John J. 1961a. Speech Variation and the Study of Indian
    Civilization. American Anthropologist 63. 976-88.
_____ 1961b. Religion and Social Communication in Village
    North India. Typescript of talk presented to Seminar on
    Hinduism, August 1961, University of California, Berkeley.
    [In this volume, pp. 225-38.]
_____ and C. M. Naim. 1960. Formal and Informal
    Standards in the Hindi Regional Language Area. In
    Linguistic Diversity in South Asia, C. A. Ferguson and
    J. J. Gumperz, eds. pp. 92-118.

Haugen, Einar. 1953. The Norwegian Language in America. A study
    in Bilingual Behavior. Philadelphia: University of Pennsyl-
    vania Press.

Havranek, B. 1936. Zum Problem Norm in der heutigen Sprachwissenschaft und Sprachkultur, International Congress of Linguists,
4th, Actes . . ., Copenhagen, 151-57.

Hockett, Charles F. 1958. A Course in Modern Linguistics. New York
Macmillan.

Hymes, D. H. 1958. Linguistic Features Peculiar to Chinookan Myths.
International Journal of American Linguistics 24:253-57.
_____ 1961a. Alfred Louis Kroeber. Language 37:1-28.
_____ 1961b. The Ethnography of Speaking. In Anthropology
and Human Behavior, T. Gladwin and W. C. Sturtevant, eds.
Washington, D.C.: Anthropological Society of Washington.

Jakobson, Roman. 1960. Linguistics and Poetics. In Style in Language
Thomas A. Sebeok, ed. pp. 350-77.

Linton, Ralph. 1936. The Study of Man. New York: Appleton-
Century.

Martinet, André. 1954. Dialect. Romance Philology 8.1-11.

Nadel, S. F. 1957. The Theory of Social Structure. Glencoe,
Illinois: The Free Press.

Putman, George N. and Edna M. Hern. 1955. The Status Significance
of an Isolated Urban Dialect. Language, Supplement 31.

Sapir, Edward. 1951. Language and Environment. In Selected
Writings of Edward Sapir, David Mandelbaum, ed. pp. 89-103
Berkeley: University of California Press.

Schneider, David M. 1961. Comment on Studies of Complex Societies.
Current Anthropology 2.215.

Sebeok, Thomas A. ed. 1960. Style in Language. Cambridge,
Massachusetts: The M.I.T. Press.

Shipley, William. 1961. Maidu and Nisenan. A Binary Survey. International Journal of American Linguistics 27.46-51.

Soffietti, James P. 1955. Bilingualism and Biculturalism. Journal of Educational Psychology 46. 222-27.

Triandis, H. C. and C. E. Osgood. 1958. A Comparative Factorial Analysis of Semantic Structures in Monolingual Greek and American College Students. Journal of Abnormal and Social Psychology 57. 187-96.

Uhlenbeck, E. M. 1950. De Tegenstelling Krama: Ngoko, Haar Positie in het Javaanse Taalsysteem. Djakarta. 28 pp.

Voegelin, C. F. 1960. Casual and Non-Casual Utterances within Unified Structure. In Style in Language, T. A. Sebeok, ed. pp. 57-68.

Weinreich, Uriel. 1952. ŠABESDIKERLOSN in Yiddish: A Problem of Linguistic Affinity. Word 8. 360-77.
_____ 1953. Languages in Contact. Publications of the Linguistic Circle of New York, Number 1. New York: Linguistic Circle of New York.

Yegerlehner, John. 1958. Structure of Arizona Tewa Words, Spoken and Sung. IJAL 24. 264-67.

7 | The Speech Community

Although not all communication is linguistic, language is by far the most powerful and versatile medium of communication; all known human groups possess language. Unlike other sign systems, the verbal system can, through the minute refinement of its grammatical and semantic structure, be made to refer to a wide variety of objects and concepts. At the same time, verbal interaction is a social process in which utterances are selected in accordance with socially recognized norms and expectations. It follows that linguistic phenomena are analyzable both within the context of language itself and within the broader context of social behavior. In the formal analysis of language the object of attention is a particular body of linguistic data abstracted from the settings in which it occurs and studied primarily from the point of view of its referential function. In analyzing linguistic phenomena within a socially defined universe, however, the study is of language usage as it reflects more general behavior norms. This universe is the speech community: any human aggregate characterized by regular and frequent interaction by means of a shared body of verbal signs and set off from similar aggregates by significant differences in language usage.

Most groups of any permanence, be they small bands bounded by face-to-face contact, modern nations divisible into smaller subregions, or even occupational associations or neighborhood gangs, may be treated as speech communities, provided they show linguistic peculiarities that warrant special study. The verbal behavior of such groups always constitutes a system. It must be based on finite sets of grammatical rules that underlie the production of well-formed sentences, or else messages will not be intelligible. The description

of such rules is a precondition for the study of all types of linguistic
phenomena. But it is only the starting point in the sociolinguistic
analysis of language behavior.

Grammatical rules define the bounds of the linguistically
acceptable. For example, they enable us to identify "How do you
do?" "How are you?" and "Hi" as proper American English
sentences and to reject others like "How do you?" and "How you
are?" Yet speech is not constrained by grammatical rules alone.
An individual's choice from among permissible alternates in a
particular speech event may reveal his family background and his
social intent, may identify him as a Southerner, a Northerner, an
urbanite, a rustic, a member of the educated or uneducated classes,
and may even indicate whether he wishes to appear friendly or
distant, familiar or deferential, superior or inferior.

Just as intelligibility presupposes underlying grammatical
rules, the communication of social information presupposes the
existence of regular relationships between language usage and social
structure. Before we can judge a speaker's social intent, we must
know something about the norms defining the appropriateness of
linguistically acceptable alternates for particular types of speakers;
these norms vary among subgroups and among social settings.
Wherever the relationships between language choice and rules of
social appropriateness can be formalized, they allow us to group
relevant linguistic forms into distinct dialects, styles, and occupational or other special parlances. The sociolinguistic study of
speech communities deals with the linguistic similarities and
differences among these speech varieties.

In linguistically homogeneous societies the verbal markers
of social distinctions tend to be confined to structurally marginal
features of phonology, syntax, and lexicon. Elsewhere they may
include both standard literary languages, and grammatically divergent local dialects. In many multilingual societies the choice of
one language over another has the same signification as the
selection among lexical alternates in linguistically homogeneous
societies. In such cases, two or more grammars may be required

to cover the entire scope of linguistically acceptable expressions
that serve to convey social meanings.

Regardless of the linguistic differences among them, the
speech varieties employed within a speech community form a
system because they are related to a shared set of social norms.
Hence, they can be classified according to their usage, their origins,
and the relationship between speech and social action that they
reflect. They become indices of social patterns of interaction in the
speech community.

Historical orientation in early studies

Systematic linguistic field work began in the middle of
the nineteenth century. Prior to 1940 the best-known studies were
concerned with dialects, special parlances, national languages, and
linguistic acculturation and diffusion.

Dialectology. Among the first students of speech communities were the dialectologists, who charted the distribution of
colloquial speech forms in societies dominated by German, French,
English, Polish, and other major standard literary tongues. Mapping
relevant features of pronunciation, grammar, and lexicon in the
form of isoglosses, they traced in detail the range and spread of
historically documented changes in language habits. Isoglosses
were grouped into bundles of two or more and then mapped; from
the geographical shape of such isogloss bundles, it was possible to
distinguish the focal areas, centers from which innovations radiate
into the surrounding regions; relic zones, districts where forms
previously known only from old texts were still current; and
transition zones, areas of internal diversity marked by the coexistence
of linguistic forms identified with competing centers of innovation.

Analysis along these lines clearly established the importance
of social factors in language change. The distribution of rural
speech patterns was found to be directly related to such factors as
political boundaries during the preceding centuries, traditional

market networks, the spread of important religious movements, etc. In this fashion dialectology became an important source of evidence for social history.

    Special parlances, classical languages. Other scholars dealt with the languages of occupationally specialized minority groups, craft jargons, secret argots, and the like. In some cases, such as the Romany of the gypsies and the Yiddish of Jews, these parlances derive from foreign importations which survive as linguistic islands surrounded by other tongues. Their speakers tend to be bilinguals, using their own idiom for in-group communication and the majority language for interaction with outsiders.

    Linguistic distinctness may also result from seemingly intentional processes of distortion. One very common form of secret language, found in a variety of tribal and complex societies, achieves unintelligibility by a process of verbal play with majority speech, in which phonetic or grammatical elements are systematically reordered. The pig Latin of English-speaking schoolchildren, in which initial consonants are transferred to the end of the word and followed by "-ay," is a relatively simple example of this process. Thieves' argots, the slang of youth gangs, and the jargon of traveling performers and other occupational groups obtain similar results by assigning special meanings to common nouns, verbs, and adjectives.

    Despite their similarities, the classical administrative and liturgical languages—such as the Latin of medieval Europe, the Sanskrit of south Asia, and the Arabic of the Near East—are not ordinarily grouped with special parlances because of the prestige of the cultural traditions associated with them. They are quite distinct from and often unrelated to popular speech, and the elaborate ritual and etiquette that surround their use can be learned only through many years of special training. Instruction is available only through private tutors and is limited to a privileged few who command the necessary social status or financial resources. As a result, knowledge of these languages in the traditional societies where they are used is limited to relatively small elites, who

tend to maintain control of their linguistic skills in somewhat the
same way that craft guilds strive for exclusive control of their
craft skills.

The standard literary languages of modern nation-states,
on the other hand, tend to be representative of majority speech.
As a rule they originated in rising urban centers, as a result of
the free interaction of speakers of a variety of local dialects, became
identified with new urban elites, and in time replaced older administrative languages. Codification of spelling and grammar by means
of dictionaries and dissemination of this information through public
school systems are characteristic of standard-language societies.
Use of mass media and the prestige of their speakers tend to carry
idioms far from their sources; such idioms eventually replace many
pre-existing local dialects and special parlances.

Linguistic acculturation, language shift. Wherever two or
more speech communities maintain prolonged contact within a broad
field of communication, there are crosscurrents of diffusion. The
result is the formation of a Sprachbund, comprising a group of
varieties which coexist in social space as dialects, distinct neighboring
languages, or special parlances. Persistent borrowing over long
periods creates within such groups similarities in linguistic structure,
which tend to obscure pre-existing genetic distinctions; a commonly
cited example is the south Asian subcontinent, where speakers of
Indo-Aryan, Dravidian, and Munda languages all show significant
overlap in their linguistic habits.

It appears that single nouns, verbs, and adjectives are
most readily diffused, often in response to a variety of technological
innovations and cultural or religious trends. Pronunciation and
word order are also frequently affected. The level of phonological
and grammatical pattern (i.e., the structural core of a language),
however, is more resistant to change, and loan words tend to be
adapted to the patterns of the recipient language. But linguistic
barriers to diffusion are never absolute, and in situations of
extensive bilingualism—two or more languages being regularly

used in the course of the daily routine—even the grammatical cores
may be affected.

Cross-cultural influence reaches a maximum in the cases
of pidgins and creoles, idioms combining elements of several
distinct languages. These hybrids typically arise in colonial societies
or in large trading centers where laborers torn out of their native
language environments are forced to work in close cooperation with
speakers of different tongues. Cross-cultural influence may also
give rise to language shift, the abandonment of one native tongue in
favor of another. This phenomenon most frequently occurs when
two groups merge, as in tribal absorption, or when minority groups
take on the culture of the surrounding majority.

Although the bulk of the research on speech communities
that was conducted prior to 1940 is historically oriented, students of
speech communities differ markedly from their colleagues who
concentrate upon textual analysis. The latter tend to treat languages
as independent wholes that branch off from uniform protolanguages
in accordance with regular sound laws. The former, on the other
hand, regard themselves primarily as students of behavior,
interested in linguistic phenomena for their broader sociohistorical
significance. By relating dialect boundaries to settlement history,
to political and administrative boundaries, and to culture areas and
by charting the itineraries of loanwords in relation to technical
innovations or cultural movements, they established the primacy of
social factors in language change, disproving earlier theories of
environmental or biological determinism.

The study of language usage in social communities, furthermore, revealed little of the uniformity ordinarily ascribed to protolanguages and their descendants; many exceptions to the regularity
of sound laws were found wherever speakers of genetically related
languages were in regular contact. This led students of speech
communities to challenge the "family-tree theory," associated with
the neogrammarians of nineteenth-century Europe, who were
concerned primarily with the genetic reconstruction of language
history. Instead, they favored a theory of diffusion which postulates

the spread of linguistic change in intersecting "waves" that emanate
from different centers of innovation with an intensity proportionate
to the prestige of their human carriers.

Thus, while geneticists regarded modern language distribution
as the result of the segmentation of older entities into newer and
smaller subgroups, diffusionists viewed the speech community as a
dynamic field of action where phonetic change, borrowing, language
mixture, and language shift all occur because of social forces, and
where genetic origin is secondary to these forces. In recent years
linguists have begun to see the two theories as complementary. The
assumption of uniformity among protolanguages is regarded as an
abstraction necessary to explain existing regularities of sound
change and is considered extremely useful for the elucidation of
long-term prehistoric relationships, especially since conflicting
short-term diffusion currents tend to cancel each other. Speech-
community studies, on the other hand, appear better adapted to the
explanation of relatively recent changes.

Language behavior and social communication

The shift of emphasis from historical to synchronic
problems during the last three decades has brought about some
fundamental changes in our theories of language, resulting in the
creation of a body of entirely new analytical techniques. Viewed in
the light of these fresh insights, the earlier speech-community
studies are subject to serious criticism on grounds of both linguistic
and sociological methodology. For some time, therefore, linguists
oriented toward formal analysis showed very little interest. More
recent structural studies, however, show that this criticism does
not affect the basic concept of the speech community as a field of
action where the distribution of linguistic variants is a reflection
of social facts. The relationship between such variants when they
are classified in terms of usage rather than of their purely
linguistic characteristics can be examined along two dimensions:
the dialectal and the superposed.

Dialectal relationships are those in which differences set off the vernaculars of local groups (for example, the language of home and family) from those of other groups within the same, broader culture. Since this classification refers to usage rather than to inherent linguistic traits, relationships between minority languages and majority speech (e.g., between Welsh and English in Britain or French and English in Canada) and between distinct languages found in zones of intensive intertribal contact (e.g., in modern Africa) can also be considered dialectal, because they show characteristics similar to the relationship existing between dialects of the same language.

Whereas dialect variation relates to distinctions in geographical origin and social background, superposed variation refers to distinctions between different types of activies carried on within the same group. The special parlances described above form a linguistic extreme, but similar distinctions in usage are found in all speech communities. The language of formal speech making, religious ritual, or technical discussion, for example, is never the same as that employed in informal talk among friends, because each is a style fulfilling particular communicative needs. To some extent the linguistic markers of such activities are directly related to their different technical requirements. Scientific discussion, for instance, requires precisely defined terms and strict limitation on their usage. But in other cases, as in greetings, forms of address, or choosing between "isn't" and "ain't," the primary determinant is the social relationship between speakers rather than communicative necessity. Language choice in these cases is limited by social barriers; the existence of such barriers lends significance to the sociolinguistic study of superposed variation.

This distinction between dialectal and superposed varieties obviates the usual linguistic distinction between geographically and socially distributed varieties, since the evidence indicates that actual residence patterns are less important as determinants of distribution than social interaction patterns and usage. Thus, there seems to be little need to draw conceptual distinctions upon this basis.

Descriptions of dialectal and superposed variation relate primarily to social groups. Not all individuals within a speech community have equal control of the entire set of superposed variants current there. Control of communicative resources varies sharply with the individual's position within the social system. The more narrowly confined his sphere of activities, the more homogeneous the social environment within which he interacts, and the less his need for verbal facility. Thus, housewives, farmers, and laborers, who rarely meet outsiders, often make do with only a narrow range of speech styles, while actors, public speakers, and businessmen command the greatest range of styles. The fact that such individual distinctions are found in multilingual as well as in linguistically homogeneous societies suggests that the common assertion which identifies bilingualism with poor scores in intelligence testing is in urgent need of reexamination, based, as it is, primarily on work with underprivileged groups. Recent work, in fact, indicates that the failure of some self-contained groups to inculcate facility in verbal manipulation is a major factor in failures in their children's performances in public school systems.

Attitudes to language choice. Social norms of language choice vary from situation to situation and from community to community. Regularities in attitudes to particular speech varieties, however, recur in a number of societies and deserve special comment here. Thieves' argots, gang jargons, and the like serve typically as group boundary maintaining mechanisms, whose linguistic characteristics are the result of informal group consensus and are subject to continual change in response to changing attitudes. Individuals are accepted as members of the group to the extent that their usage conforms to the practices of the day. Similar attitudes of exclusiveness prevail in the case of many tribal languages spoken in areas of culture contact where other superposed idioms serve as media of public communication. The tribal language here is somewhat akin to a secret ritual, in that it is private knowledge to be kept from outsiders, an attitude which often makes it difficult for casual investigators to collect reliable information about language distribution in such areas.

Because of the elaborate linguistic etiquette and stylistic conventions that surround them, classical, liturgical, and administrative languages function somewhat like secret languages. Mastery of the conventions may be more important in gaining social success than substantive knowledge of the information dispensed through these languages. But unlike the varieties mentioned above, norms of appropriateness are explicit in classical languages; this permits them to remain unchanged over many generations.

In contrast, the attitude to pidgins, trade languages, and similar intergroup media of communication tends to be one of toleration. Here little attention is paid to linguistic markers of social appropriateness. It is the function of such languages to facilitate contact between groups without constituting their respective social cohesiveness; and, as a result, communication in these languages tends to be severely restricted to specific topics or types of interaction. They do not, as a rule, serve as vehicles for personal friendships.

We speak of language loyalty when a literary variety acquires prestige as a symbol of a particular nationality group or social movement. Language loyalty tends to unite diverse local groups and social classes, whose members may continue to speak their own vernaculars within the family circle. The literary idiom serves for reading and for public interaction and embodies the cultural tradition of a nation or a sector thereof. Individuals choose to employ it as a symbol of their allegiance to a broader set of political ideals than that embodied in the family or kin group.

Language loyalty may become a political issue in a modernizing society when hitherto socially isolated minority groups become mobilized. Their demands for closer participation in political affairs are often accompanied by demands for language reform or for the rewriting of the older, official code in their own literary idiom. Such demands often represent political and socio-economic threats to the established elite, which may control the distribution of administrative positions through examination systems based upon the official code. The replacement of an older official

code by another literary idiom in modernizing societies may thus
represent the displacement of an established elite by a rising
group.

    The situation becomes still more complex when socio-
economic competition between several minority groups gives rise to
several competing new literary standards, as in many parts of
Asia and Africa, where language conflicts have led to civil disturbance
and political instability. Although demands for language reform
are usually verbalized in terms of communicative needs, it is
interesting to observe that such demands do not necessarily reflect
important linguistic differences between the idioms in question.
Hindi and Urdu, the competing literary standards of north India, or
Serbian and Croatian, in Yugoslavia, are grammatically almost
identical. They differ in their writing systems, in their lexicons,
and in minor aspects of syntax. Nevertheless, their proponents
treat them as separate languages. The conflict in language loyalty
may even affect mutual intelligibility, as when speakers' claims
that they do not understand each other reflect primarily social
attitudes rather than linguistic fact. In other cases serious linguistic
differences may be disregarded when minority speakers pay language
loyalty to a standard markedly different from their own vernacular.
In many parts of Alsace-Lorraine, for example, speakers of
German dialects seem to disregard linguistic fact and pay language
loyalty to French rather than to German.

    Varietal distribution. Superposed and dialectal varieties
rarely coincide in their geographical extent. We find the greatest
amount of linguistic diversity at the level of local, tribal, peasant,
or lower-class urban populations. Tribal areas typically constitute
a patchwork of distinct languages, while local speech distribution
in many modern nations takes the form of a dialect chain in which
the speech of each locality is similar to that of adjoining settlements
and in which speech differences increase in proportion to geographical
distance. Variety at the local level is bridged by the considerably
broader spread of superposed varieties, serving as media of supra-
local communication. The Latin of medieval Europe and the Arabic
of the Near East form extreme examples of supralocal spread.

Uniformity at the superposed level in their case, however, is achieved at the expense of large gaps in internal communication channels. Standard languages tend to be somewhat more restricted in geographical spread than classical languages, because of their relationship to local dialects. In contrast to a society in which classical languages are used as superposed varieties, however, a standard-language society possesses better developed channels of internal communication, partly because of its greater linguistic homogeneity and partly because of the internal language loyalty that it evokes.

In fact, wherever standard languages are well-established they act as the ultimate referent that determines the association of a given local dialect with one language or another. This may result in the anomalous situation in which two linguistically similar dialects spoken on different sides of a political boundary are regarded as belonging to different languages, not because of any inherent linguistic differences but because their speakers pay language loyalty to different standards. Language boundaries in such cases are defined partly by social and partly by linguistic criteria.

Verbal repertoires. The totality of dialectal and superposed variants regularly employed within a community make up the verbal repertoire of that community. Whereas the bounds of a language, as this term is ordinarily understood, may or may not coincide with that of a social group, verbal repertoires are always specific to particular populations. As an analytical concept the verbal repertoire allows us to establish direct relationships between its constituents and the socioeconomic complexity of the community.

We measure this relationship in terms of two concepts: linguistic range and degree of compartmentalization. Linguistic range refers to internal language distance between constituent varieties, that is, the total amount of purely linguistic differentiation that exists in a community, thus distinguishing among multilingual, multidialectal, and homogeneous communities. Compartmentalization refers to the sharpness with which varieties are set off from each other, either along the superposed or the dialectal dimension. We speak of compartmentalized repertoires, therefore, when several languages are spoken without their mixing, when dialects are set off from each other by sharp isogloss bundles, or when special parlances are sharply distinct from other forms of speech. We speak of fluid repertoires, on the other hand, when transitions between adjoining vernaculars are gradual or when one speech style merges into another in such a way that it is difficult to draw clear borderlines.

Initially, the linguistic range of a repertoire is a function of the languages and special parlances employed before contact. But given a certain period of contact, linguistic range becomes dependent upon the amount of internal interaction. The greater the frequency of internal interaction, the greater the tendency for innovations arising in one part of the speech community to diffuse theoughout it. Thus, where the flow of communication is dominated by a single all-important center—for example, as Paris dominates central France—linguistic range is relatively small. Political fragmentation, on the other hand, is associated with diversity of languages or of dialects, as in southern Germany, long dominated by many small, semi-independent principalities.

Over-all frequency in interaction is not, however, the only determinant of uniformity. In highly stratified societies speakers of minority languages or dialects typically live side by side, trading, exchanging services, and often maintaining regular social contact as employer and employee or master and servant. Yet despite this contact, they tend to preserve their own languages, suggesting the existence of social norms that set limits to freedom of intercommunication. Compartmentalization reflects such social norms. The exact nature of these sociolinguistic barriers is not yet clearly understood, although some recent literature suggests new avenues for investigation.

We find, for example, that separate languages maintain themselves most readily in closed tribal systems, in which kinship dominates all activities. Linguistically distinct special parlances, on the other hand, appear most fully developed in highly stratified societies, where the division of labor is maintained by rigidly defined barriers of ascribed status. When social change causes the breakdown of traditional social structures and the formation of new ties, as in urbanization and colonialization, linguistic barriers between varieties also break down. Rapidly changing societies typically show either gradual transition between speech styles or, if the community is bilingual, a range of intermediate varieties bridging the transitions between extremes.

BIBLIOGRAPHY

Barth, Frederik. 1964. Ethnic Processes on the Pathan-Baluch Boundary. Pages 13-20 in Indo-Iranica: Melanges présentés a Georg Morgenstierne, a l'occasion de son soixante-dixieme anniversaire. Wiesbaden (Germany): Harrassowitz.

Bernstein, Basil. (1958) 1961. Social Class and Linguistic Development: A Theory of Social Learning. Pages 288-314 in A. H. Halsey et al. (editors), Education, Economy, and Society. New York: Free Press → First published in Volume 9 of the British Journal of Sociology.

Bloomfield. Leonard. (1933) 1951. Language. Rev. ed. New York: Henry Holt.

Brown, Roger W. 1965. Social Psychology. New York: Free Press.

Gumperz, John J.; and Hymes, Dell H. (editors). 1964. The Ethnography of Communication. American Anthropologist New Series 66, no. 6, part 2.

Halliday, Michael A. K.; McIntosh, Angus; and Strevens, Peter. (1964) 1965. The Linguistic Sciences and Language Teaching. Bloomington: Indiana Univ. Press.

Haugen, Einar. 1956. Bilingualism in the Americas: A Bibliography and Research Guide. Alabama University: American Dialect Society.

Haugen, Einar. 1966. Language Conflict and Language Planning. Cambridge, Mass.: Harvard Univ. Press.

Hertzler, Joyce O. 1965. A Sociology of Language. New York: Random House.

Hymes, Dell H. (editor). 1964. Language in Culture and Society: A Reader in Linguistics and Anthropology. New York: Harper.

Jespersen, Otto. (1925) 1964. Mankind, Nation and the Individual, From a Linguistic Point of View. Bloomington: Indiana Univ. Press. → First published as Menneskehed, najon og individ i sproget.

Kurath, Hans (editor). 1939-1943. Linguistic Atlas of New England. 3 vols. and a handbook. Providence, R. I.: Brown Univ. Press.

Labov, William. 1966. The Social Stratification of English in New York City. Washington, D.C.: Center for Applied Linguistics.

Passin, Herbert. 1963. Writer and Journalist in the Transitional Society. Pages 82-123 in Conference on Communication and Political Development, Dobbs Ferry, N.Y., 1961, Communications and Political Development. Edited by Lucian W. Pye. Princeton Univ. Press → Contains a discussion of the relationship of national languages to political development.

Weinreich, Uriel. 1953. Languages in Contact: Findings and Problems. New York: Linguistic Circle of New York.

8 | Language, Communication, and Control in North India

In Collaboration with J. Das Gupta

Since linguists have only recently turned from grammatical analysis to consider the role of language in society, the study of modernization has been left largely to social scientists who can hardly be expected to deal with linguistic questions. Yet, language problems are known to plague developing societies. In post-independence India, for example, national language, the linguistic states issue, problems of script and minority group claims for linguistic autonomy have long played a dominant part in public life. So far, however, such problems tend to be treated primarily as cultural or political issues. Few, if any attempts have been made to examine their relation to mass communication, social mobility, social control and other aspects of socioeconomic development. [1]

Karl Deutsch's early writings suggest that language and literacy are important measures of socioeconomic change, along with other indices such as the rise of political consciousness, the development of marketing systems, etc. [2] But his suggestions have not been followed up systematically. Studies in communication, even when they refer to language, tend to focus on values, attitudes and ideologies — i.e., the content of what is transmitted, without attempting any systematic analysis of the structure of the verbal channels by which messages are propagated. [3]

The present paper explores this latter problem by examining the linguistic policies and practices of twentieth century language societies in the North Indian state of Uttar Pradesh. We will attempt to demonstrate the close interdependence between communication

and political processes by showing how the policies and activities
of these interest groups both affect internal communication channels
and are in turn affected by them.

By making use of the concepts of mobilization and technical
specialization, two distinct processes involved in modernization,
we are able to treat specific phenomena being studied as indices
of a more general process of change. Social mobilization has been
described by Deutsch as the process by which hitherto isolated
sectors of the population are drawn into fuller participation in public
life, through the opening of channels of communication capable of
transmitting information from centers of political control, economic
power and innovation to outlying areas. [4] The relatively more intensive communication among individuals of such a mobilized population
implies the creation of mass media circulating widely, increased
literacy, and a general educational system to sustain both.

The concomitants of technical specialization, on the other
hand, have been discussed by Keller. [5] She argues that technology
and knowledge in industrialized society have become so diversified
and complicated that no single individual can hope to make all
relevant decisions. Hence the emergence of strategic elites,
groups of experts, whose power depends only on their specialized
skill. These strategic elites differ from traditional upper class
ruling groups in that they are recruited on the basis of their
performance in their speciality, rather than upon any criterion of
family or social background. Although Keller does not state this
directly, it seems evident that implicit in the concept of strategic
elites is the existence of a mobilized population, where social
barriers limiting the individual's participation in public affairs are
minimized. However, the particular requirements of many of the
technical specialities supporting strategic elites tend to limit
members' contacts to others with similar skills; once membership
in an elite group is obtained, members are relatively cut off from
other technical elites and from the general public.

The two processes, mobilization and technical specialization,
are thus complementary. Modernization serves at once to broaden

popular participation in public life and to increase its technological
and communicative complexity. In both modernized and traditional
societies, the individual ability to understand all the details of his
environment is limited, but whereas in the latter the barriers are
largely social, in the former they are (at least, in principle)
technical — i.e., directly connected with the task performed.

Our discussion is based on the premise that social organization is more directly reflected in the language distance — the
grammatical and lexical distinctions among the languages, dialects,
and speech styles — of the community linguistic repertoire[6] than in
the structure of a single language. This approach leads us to
predict that whenever interaction among speakers is restricted by
social or ecological boundaries, preexisting language differences
are reinforced. With the breakdown of such barriers through
modernization, or other social change, language differences would
be expected to decrease.

The Czech linguist Havranek calls attention to important
implications of this approach to verbal communication systems. [7]
He observes that because of the widespread use of classical literary
languages like Greek and Latin in ancient and medieval times,
writings produced in one region could be read and appreciated
throughout the contemporary civilized world. Such linguistic
uniformity was possible, he argues, only because literary skills
were the preserve of a small exclusive literary elite, which had
little or no direct contact with vernacular speaking local populations.
Communicability over large areas was thus achieved at the expense
of serious gaps in internal communication. The rise of national
consciousness and the broadening of political and economic
participation during the last several centuries has generated pressures
tending to remove such intra-societal language barriers.

Following this argument to its logical conclusion, one
might suppose that the ideal language situation is one where, to use
Ferguson's terms, a single accepted norm of pronunciation, grammar
and vocabulary is used for all levels of speaking and writing. [8] Such

a system would be well suited for the transmission of objective information. Members would have access to literary resources and could otherwise participate in the full range of available occupations and activities with a minimum of vocabulary learning, and without having to master pronunciation and grammatical rules not acquired as part of their home background.

But such a system would be limited in other ways. Wherever language variation is regularly associated with speakers' home background or certain role performances, its very occurrence encodes important social information. A native's ability to diagnose pronunciation differences and choice of word and sentence structure gives him information about his interlocutors' social identities, their attitudes and the probable content of their message. In small, homogeneous, closed groups where actors know each other intimately, and where the range of possible discussion topics is limited, this information is largely redundant. Such communities in fact tend to show a minimum of speech diversity. In complex and industrial societies, however, speakers deal with individuals of widely varying cultural background, whose attitudes and values differ from their own. They frequently know little about their interlocutors. Here clues derived from speech performances serve an important function in evaluating what is said, in singling out some items as more important than others, and in generally facilitating the processing of information.

Aside from differences in social background, the communications of technical specialists such as lawyers, physicians, and scientists, are a further source of language variants. Members of these groups communicate more intensively with each other than with outsiders in the area of their specialty and so tend to generate their own terminological conventions. Knowledge of these conventions becomes part of the skills required for admission to the group. For members themselves, technical parlance serves as a shorthand way of alluding to a whole body of shared knowledge. It eliminates the need for unnecessary elaboration and explanation, speeds up communication within the group, and facilitates development of the specialty. On the other hand, however, the greater the number of technical terms, the greater the communication difficulties for the lay public.

While linguistic diversity thus serves necessary functions in large speech communities, this diversity need not take the form of languages grammatically distinct from local idioms such as Greek and Latin in ancient and medieval Europe. Command over the grammatical intricacies of an otherwise foreign language is obviously unrelated to the performance of most technical and literary tasks, when special styles of one's own language will suffice. Wherever such command is a requirement for recruitment to elite positions, or even more important, wherever it is made a precondition for access to communication media, barriers to mobilization can be quite as restrictive as purely ascriptive barriers of kin and family background. The development of modern standard languages can thus be viewed as a direct consequence of the increasing pressures for democratization and greater popular participation in public life in recent times.

Although the standard languages of modernized nation states are never identical with the spoken idiom, they tend to be similar enough for easy switching from formal or technical speech styles to informal language. The technological requirements of mass communication, and especially those of mass distribution, require that spelling, morphology, and syntax be uniform. There must be generally accepted rules of codification defining what is acceptable grammar and writing, and these must be set down in readily available dictionaries and grammars.

But communicative efficiency requires only that diversity be controlled; it need not be eliminated. Since codification rules apply only to formal modes of communication, they need not apply to all styles of the standard language. Minor differences in accent do not affect communicability; on the contrary, they serve as carriers of social information.

Technical terminologies and the special communicative conventions of strategic elites, on the other hand, pose serious communication problems. For example, very few laymen in the United States can expect to understand the Journal of the American Chemical Society or the full meaning of the official text of a new law, although both follow the codification rules of standard English. But in the U.S., as in other modernized societies, there exists secondary communication media such as Scientific American, Popular Mechanics, Time, etc. These media make a specialty of translating technical terminologies into a language intelligible to the layman. The styles they employ represent a linguistic bridge between strategic elites and the rest of the mobilized population. Internal diversity is functionally related to the requirements of technical tasks and is controlled by codification so that everyone has direct access to as much information as he can utilize without having to rely on others.

Although the Indian situation is in many ways more complex, the general trend toward a decrease in dysfunctional diversity, accompanied by an increase in functional diversity, follows the same pattern as in western societies. Initially, internal diversity was even greater than in ancient Europe. Long before the trends of westernization began, most regions in India exhibited concurrent use of three literary languages, each having its own distinct function. Sanskrit was used mainly for Hindu religious and high literary purposes; Persian as the dominant medium of administration and the regional languages such as Marathi, Bengali and also the precursors of Modern Hindi, Khari Boli and Braj Bhasa served as additional literary media. All these literary languages furthermore were grammatically distinct from the many often mutually unintelligible local dialects used in informal interaction. A third group of spoken trade or bazaar languages was used for rather limited transactional purposes among the various local communities in market relations and festival situations. To complicate the picture even further many commercial or artisan castes maintained their own special parlances often marked by special secret script which served to protect their activities from outsiders.

Since they were regularly employed in what on other grounds must be considered a single social system, all these language varieties formed a single communication system. But where modernized communication systems are fluid, marked largely by gradual transitions in phonology and lexicon, the traditional Indian system was segmented into a limited set of discrete subdomains, each set off from the others by sharp grammatical and sometimes even script distinctions, as well as by lexical and phonological features. The barriers of ethnic origin, caste and occupation which characterized Indian society were thus reflected by compartmentalization of verbal interaction into distinct communicative spheres.

The implications of such a communication system for social mobility and participation have already been mentioned. Deep barriers of language served to cut off the ordinary resident from much of the information which he needed to conduct his daily affairs. Since land records, money lenders' accounts, administrative regulations and even the religious texts which he needed for his ceremonials were often kept in different languages, he had to rely on the personal mediation of others for access. The system thus favored the formation of a large number of mediating groups whose literary skills were their main stock in trade.

Individuals wishing to enter linguistically marked occupations found their tasks made more difficult by the fact that they had to learn not only the relevant technical skills and the appropriate terminologies but also a whole new set of grammatical rules and the stylistic norms associated with them. In the absence of a public education system, this training could be acquired only through personal apprenticeship; education was a privilege, depending on personal relationships with teachers and on the parent's social standing in the community, not a right. The lack of explicit and generally available codification rules furthermore left the teachers themselves as the sole guardians of what constituted closed communities, whose literary skills were their main assets. Self interest led them to make every attempt to preserve these assets

for their own kind. Since each group served as guardian and judge
of the authenticity of its own style, it could by manipulation of
standards of correctness erect almost unsurmountable access barriers
to the technical skills it controlled.

The introduction of English as the official language in the
early nineteenth century led to the disappearance of Persian and
reduced the social importance of Sanskrit. But for a long time the
pattern of internal linguistic barriers remained as before. Historical
records from the early days of English occupation in fact give evidence
of certain dominant caste groups' attempts to capitalize on their control
of English in much the same way that their ancestors had controlled
previous literary languages. [9]

English education, however, was public, open to all who
had the financial means. This, combined with the fact that the growing governmental bureaucracy opened up more and more opportunities
for those with literary skills, soon led to the development of new
groups of literati who were outside of the system of traditional
occupational ties. [10] Under the influence of these new groups, new
vernacular prose styles modeled on English were developed.
Gradually, as these were adopted as the official media in the lower
rungs of administration, they began to gain more general acceptance
and to displace previous literary languages and special craft idioms.
In what is now known as the Hindi area there were two such developing vernaculars, Hindi and Urdu. In the initial stages of their
development, they differed primarily in script. The grammatical
and lexical base was largely the same. It derived from Hindustani
which had been current as a bazaar language throughout Northern
India since Mughul times.

The extension of the communication system, liberalization
of the access barriers, along with the improved educational facilities,
materially increased the size of the mobilized population, providing
a base for the spread of nationalism with its demand for further
linguistic reforms. With the gradual entry of the masses to the
extended political and social scene there arose a general agreement

among nationalists that English would eventually have to go. [11] The language of the foreign conqueror could hardly serve as a symbol for the new Indian nation.

Hindustani and its derivatives, Hindi-Urdu, were, to be sure, widely used but they lacked the literary prestige and respectibility of English. It was felt therefore that these new idioms needed to be changed so as to more closely reflect the genius of the nation— i.e., the native literary traditions—and to become the intellectual equal of English.

This goal lent itself to a number of different interpretations, in accordance with the special interests of its advocates. The leaders of the predominantly westernized Muslim elite came largely from Western Uttar Pradesh where Persian influence had been strongest. This led them to introduce a large number of Persian borrowings into what they considered acceptable Urdu. A rival group of Hindi intellectuals, on the other hand, was based in Eastern Uttar Pradesh and Bihar where Sanskrit learning had remained strongly rooted. [12] Their language reforms leaned heavily on Sanskrit. Each of these groups identified language with their community, invoking and glorifying the history of their respective religious and cultural backgrounds, and in this way each tended to drift away from the other. As the Hindu-Muslim conflict grew, literary Hindi and Urdu began to grow more and more distinct, not only from each other but also from the spoken everyday idiom of the urban middle classes. Rising social mobilization and political consciousness were thus accompanied by a widening rift between these two groups and within each group, between the elite and the yet unmobilized masses.

It was Gandhi, the initiator of the first all-India based political mass movement, who first realized the dangers to mobilization which were inherent in the political particularism of the new Hindu and Muslim elites. He accused both the 'Hindi Pandits of Prayag' and the 'Urdu Maulvis of Aligarh' of exaggerating the mutual differences between Hindi and Urdu, pointing out that much of what they rejected as mixed forms was in fact commonly employed throughout North India. He felt that a common language for India should build on popular usage and convention and not on literary injunctions of the Pandits and their political defenders. Gandhi's emphasis on basing linguistic reform on the common elements of popular speech was intended to emphasize three points: unity of the national movement, social and political mobilization of the masses, and the linking of the masses to the successively higher levels of social and political authority. [13]

The intended, as well as the unintended, consequences of the struggle waged over the question of language reform can be better appreciated if one looks into the groups processes involved in language politics in India during the late nineteenth and twentieth centuries. The first organized association devoted to the cause of propagation of Hindi was established in Banaras as the Nagari Pracharani Sabha (1893). It began as a literary association but was soon converted into a political promoter of the cause of Hindi. [14] In 1910, a more exclusively politically oriented association, the Hindi Sahitya Sammelan (HSS), was established at Allahabad by the Hindi oriented leaders of the Indian National Congress. [15] During the earlier years of its existence Gandhi and the Gandhian leaders of Indian National Congress partially succeeded in getting this organization to work for popularizing the idea of a commonly comprehensible national written language as a means of breaking through the barriers of communication between the elite and the masses and bridging the linguistic gulf separating the various regions of India.

Linguistic consensus among the nationalists was short lived. With the broadening of the base of the national movement, and with the widening mobilization of the masses in the late nineteen twenties, the Hindu-Muslim conflict began to intensify again. Within the Congress Party a new group of political leaders rose who revived the concern for the purity of Hindi. They resisted what they called Gandhi's efforts to conciliate the Muslim demands for Urdu. In their search for symbols of identity, these leaders increasingly identified Hindi with Hindu and Sanskrit culture and returned to the policy of magnifying and sometimes manufacturing divergences between Hindi and Urdu. Frequently, Urdu was branded as an alien

language imported by former invaders. In 1935, control over the
Hindi Sahitya Sammelan passed into the hands of this latter group of
leaders and ultimately Gandhi, Nehru and other proponents of 'broader
Hindi' or Hindustani had to resign from the Sammelan.

     In 1942, Gandhi and his followers founded the Hindustani
Prachar Sabha in order to promote the Hindustani form of Hindi. But
this new organization did not succeed in influencing the course of the
Hindi movement in North India. It should be noted, however, that
the Gandhian efforts were eminently successful in South India. Already
in 1918 Gandhi had founded the Dakshina Bharat Hindi Prachar Sabha
in Madras for propagating Hindi in South India. This organization
had always worked in close cooperation with the Hindi Sahitya
Sammelan. After the split in the Sammelan, it remained aligned
more with the Hindustani Prachar Sabha than with the Sammelan.[16]
These organizations continued with their efforts to implement
Gandhi's policy for a common Indian language. Their Hindi was as
close as possible to the urban colloquial style current in Western
Uttar Pradesh, Delhi or in the Eastern Punjab (i.e., the area where
Hindi originated and where it is commonly spoken by the middle
classes, both Muslim and Hindu, and a high proportion of the lower
classes), drawing for its technical terms on whatever seemed most
popularly accepted, whether Persian, Sanskrit or English. It could
be written in either the Urdu or Nagari script, and both were taught
in their schools. In line with the Gandhian policy of basic education
they emphasized rural literacy programs as an integral part of
village development through many centers. In addition, a number
of highly influential centers for the propagation of Hindi in non-
Hindi speaking areas of the South were created.

     Whereas Hindi is the most commonly accepted spoken
language in Western U. P., the traditional centers of literary
learning are largely located in Eastern U. P. Here, the spoken
medium of home and friendship groups are such local dialects as
Avadhi and Bhojpuri, which are grammatically quite different from
Hindi. Hindi is learned as a second language by the Hindu middle
classes. Urban Muslim middle classes speak local dialects and
learn literary Urdu.[17] Because of the attitude to Hindi as a

language of scholarship, the utilitarian policies and lack of literary sophistication found little support here, and instead urban literati tended to align themselves with the HSS.

The HSS spread its organizational roots throughout most of North India, but unlike the Gandhians, its educational efforts were directed primarily toward those who were already somewhat literate in Hindi. It succeeded in gathering around it the most important Hindi scholars, literary critics, and philologists, as well as some of the most active and productive writers in the Hindi language, many of whom came from Eastern U. P. A new school of Hindi writing developed, including such famous critics as Ram Chandra Shukla and such prose writers as Hazari Prasad Dwivedi and poets such as Maithili Sharan Gupta, who through their writings succeeded in giving literary respectability to the new Hindi. [18] While the works of these writers never achieved the popular success and the wide popular distribution of modern Bengali or Marathi authors, they nevertheless were highly successful in rallying around them the younger Hindi literary elite. There was, in many cases, no formal connection between this group of writers and the HSS, but it was frequently highly Sanskritized style of these writers which the HSS employed and attempted to promulgate.

One of the most significant organizational achievements of the HSS was the establishment of a network of examination centers for secondary and college diplomas and degrees. Before independence, these Hindi training and examination centers, as well as the Gandhian basic education centers, competed directly with government sponsored educational institutions. After independence, these competing systems were reorganized and directly aided by the U. P. and the national state government. [19]

These educational centers have been unique sources of support for the HSS organization. Financially, they provide substantial funds through training and examination fees. Structurally the HSS acquired a regular, routinized bureaucracy supervising its educational and literary activities in North India and outside. Even before independence few voluntary associations in India working with a political purpose could match the resources of the HSS. [20]

The importance of the HSS educational activities and its vast scale of operation are, however, significant on another level. Thousands of teacher-publicists or 'pracharaks' working through the vast network of educational centers have proved to be effective instruments for codifying the literary Hindi that is learned by the students. This control mechanism is important because it has tended to standardize Hindi in accordance with the HSS leaders' norm of Sanskritized Hindi. The concerted efforts of the examination centers at the base and the Hindi literary elite at the top have tended to remake Hindi in the image of the Eastern U. P. literary language at the expense of many colloquial forms generally accepted in the West.

The fact that most Hindi literary scholars are imbued with attitudes towards literary language similar to those of the HSS has had a profound effect on the Indian government's language planning efforts. Under the official government policy, Hindi is eventually to become the national language[21] of India. While English continues to play an important part, more and more the official business both at the state and national level is being transacted in Hindi. In implementing its task of developing Hindi, almost every ministry at the state and national level has set up official committees charged with the task of creating legal and technical terminologies suitable for the new functions the language is filling.

The Board of Scientific Terminology was constituted in 1950. It was assigned the task of preparing 350,000 new terms in Hindi, of which by 1963, 290,000 were already in. [22] For fields other than science, another committee has the responsibility of coining new terms. Various standard manuals are being prepared for different subjects. Glossaries, dictionaries, and encyclopedias are being prepared either directly by official committees or by private organizations with official patronage. [23] In 1956, the work of creating an encyclopedia in Hindi was entrusted to the Nagari

Pracharani Sabha, a voluntary association for the promotion of
Hindi. In ten years it has produced six volumes.

The stated official policy in regard to newly introduced terms
is that they be commonly intelligible. But since Gandhians have paid
little attention to the technical aspects of language planning, government language committee staffs have had to be drawn primarily
from the ranks of Hindi scholarship, with the result that these
terminilogies, as well as the official writings in Hindi, are in effect
quite close to the literary style advocated by the HSS.

Once pressed into service, the Hindi scholars were quick
to bring their basic conviction to bear on the task of language planning.
One respected Hindi expert has articulated some of these convictions
in clear terms. [24] He begins with the premise that the development
of Hindi is dependent on the creation of a vocabulary that is consistent
with the genius[25] of the Indian languages. According to him this is
a way of rescuing India from the denationalizing effects of alien
languages. [26] All these imply that the development of Hindi is
dependent on a conscious policy of Sanskritization. This would be a
way of purifying Hindi by purging it of the influence of English
and Urdu.

In this sense, the Hindi scholars have interpreted the task
of language development as being synonymous with increasing
classicalization. [27] But classicalization implies that the literary
language diverges sharply from the common speeches bringing in its
trail an increasing separation between the media of elite communication and mass comprehension. Evidently, the Hindi scholars are
less concerned with standardizing the language for popular use than
for retaining its purity from the contamination of the outside
influences. Hence, the policy of elitist sanctity has been of greater
salience to their conception of language planning than the policy of
extension of mass communication.

This conception of language planning has to a certain extent
been facilitated by the ambiguity in the constitutional provision

concerning the style of official Hindi which while paying homage to the "genius" of Hindi, requires at the same time the reflection of "composite culture" in official Hindi. [28] It is not clear whether "composite culture" refers to a reconciliation of culture conflict based on religion or on resolving the dichotomy between elite and mass culture or both of them taken together. A leading coalition of factions within the Congress and some other parties maintained that official Hindi should be of sufficient common comprehension and, therefore, should be based on composite culture. On the other hand, the Hindi interest associations and generally the Hindi literary elite emphasized more on the question of the genius of Hindi which they identified with classical Sanskritic language and tradition. However, by virtue of political influence and actual influence on language planning, the Hindi scholars and associations have successfully impressed their views on official Hindi as well as the general new Hindi style.

Here are some examples of the new literary style. Items one and two are taken from signboards intended for the public. Item three is from the text of the Indian Constitution as given in the Government of India, Ministry of Law, Manual of Election Law. [29] In each case, line a gives the official text, line b the English translation and line c an approximate equivalent in the colloquial educated style.

Item 1

    a. dhuumrpaan varjint hai
    b. smoking prohibited
    c. sigret piinaa manaa hai

Item 2

    a. binaa aagyãã pravee š nišeedh
    b. entrance prohibited without permission
    c. binaa aagyãã andar jaanaa manaa hai

Item 3

    a. raastrapati kaa nirvacin eek aisee nirvaacik gan kee
        sadasy kareẽegee jisjmeẽe
    b. the president's election will be done by electors chosen
        to include
    c. raastrapati kaa canaaoo eek aisee cunee huwee sadasy
        kareẽegee jisjmeẽe

    a. (k) sansad-kee doonõõ sadnõõ-kee nirvaacit sadasy
        tathaa
    b. (a) the elected members of both houses of parliament
        and
    c. (k) sansad kii doonõõ sabhaaoo kee cunee huwee sadasy
        aur

    a. (kh) raajyõõ kii vidhaan sabhaaõõ-kee nirvaacit sadasy
        hõõgee
    b. (b) the elected members of the lower houses of state
        legislatures will be
    c. (kh) raajyõõ kii vidhaan sabhaaõõ-kee cunee huwee

On the surface the official language seems to differ from
the colloquial style largely in vocabulary. Colloquial terms like
manaa, 'prohibited', are replaced by varjit or niseedh, nirvaacin replaces
cunaaoo, 'election', etc. Such innovations are common in most
complex societies and can in part be justified for technical reasons.
Many new official terms (all borrowed from Sanskrit) such as
sadasy 'member', raastrapati 'president', udyoog 'industry', etc.
are in fact becoming more and more commonly accepted in every
day Hindi speech. But the substitution of tathaa for the colloquial
aur serves no such technical function. This is one of a series of
literary-colloquial alternates which affect a large proportion of the
commonly used Hindi conjunctions, post-positions (post-positions
correspond in Hindi to prepositions in English), number terms and
other grammatically important function words. Other examples are:
yadi for agar 'if', kintu for magar 'but', atah for isliyee 'therefore',
saabit for saath 'with', pratharm for pahlaa 'first', etc. Such
grammatical variation is more commonly found in traditional
literary languages than in modern standard languages.

Furthermore, a number of new grammatical features are
being introduced into the literary language, along with the lexical
borrowings. Varjit 'prohibited' is derived from the norm varjan by
addition of the participal suffix -it. This suffix also occurs in other
Sanskrit borrowings such as prakaasit 'published', staapit 'established',
etc. Along with the suffix -ik in nirvaacik or audyoogik 'industrial'
(from udyoog 'industry'), it is one of a group of new derivative
suffixes which are beginning to be more and more frequent. They
differ from the other derivational rules in that they affect only words
borrowed from Sanskrit and that they may require certain vowel
alternations such as the change of initial u- to au- in audyoogik which
were common Sanskrit but are not found in the modern vernacular.
In syntax, furthermore, the literary style tends towards new norm
constructions such as pravees 'entrance', where colloquial Hindi
would simply use a verbal derivative such as andar jaanaa (literally)
'going inside. '

Other important innovations are beginning to affect the
sound system. The final consonant clusters -mr, -jy, -sy in
dhuumr, raajy, sadasy, the final short vowels -i and -u in raastrapati
and kintu do not occur in colloquial speech. Words like raajy were
used in their colloquial raaj in early Hindi writings. The -y seems to
have been added around the turn of the last century as part of the
general trend toward Sanskritization.

It seems evident that the new grammatical differences between
colloquial and literary Hindi resulting from recent language reform
materially add to the ordinary speaker's task of learning literary
Hindi. Many of the new rules are irregular in that they affect only
certain parts of the vocabulary. Others affect deeply ingrained
pronunciation patterns. Considerable exposure time is required
before such rules can be mastered. Many native speakers of Hindi,
including some educated persons, feel uneasy about their control of
literary Hindi. On the other hand, those who have been exposed
to the present form of literary Hindi as part of their family background
have considerable advantage in the educational system. New barriers
to mobilization are being created providing an opportunity for elite
particularism to assert itself.

The work of the language planners has aroused considerable
public dissatisfaction. Newspapers periodically carry articles
which are highly critical of the new Hindi. At one point even Nehru
exclaimed in Parliament that the Hindi broadcasts of his own speeches
were incomprehensible to him.[30] But since linguistic scholarship
in Hindi continues to be under the influence of the Hindi elite,
and of those sympathetic to its aims, any effort to stem the present
trends involves more than simply a policy decision. Present
language training programs will have to be reexamined in light of
the need for mobilization and socioeconomic development.

However, even in the absence of government efforts for
change, the present language elite as represented by the HSS leaders
and their allies, though dominant in the Hindi area and to some
extent within the Congress Party language policy makers, cannot
take their dominance for granted. Historically, their power has
depended upon the fact that their interests were identical with those
of the political groups in power. The pattern of dominance achieved
so far however must be maintained against substantial opposition
both within and outside the ruling party. Because of the relatively
fluid nature of the faction system represented by the structure of
the Congress Party, the Hindi elite must constantly guard its
political resources. Only in this way can it maintain its strategic
position in language planning on a national scale.

The structure of politics in which modern elites operate
in India compels them to seek the aid of other groups. Hindi elites
cannot achieve their aims without the support from the wider
uneducated Hindi-speaking masses including those who themselves
would have difficulty in using Sanskritized literary styles. In
addition the Hindi elite must build coalitions against the supporters
of English and in doing so it must recruit support of non-Hindi
associations.

As the struggle over language continues attitudes towards
language purity are increasingly affected by the necessity for
political compromise. In their efforts to gain mass circulation and
general acceptance by new Hindi speakers, recently created literary
journals as well as a significant number of younger prose writers are

beginning to reject overly Sanskritized literary styles. Thus the logic of mass politics under democracy may once more lead to a decrease in the dysfunctional grammatical differences between colloquial and literary Hindi and create more tolerance for deviant accents. To the extent that the Hindi elite is ready to push the case of Hindi political dominance its efforts should have the unintended consequences of reducing internal communication barriers and facilitating social mobilization and linguistic modernization.

NOTES

Work on this paper was in part supported by grants from the National Science Foundation and from the Institute of International Studies, University of California, Berkeley. We are grateful to Miss Patricia Calkins and Dr. Om Talwar for comments and assistance.

1. For some exceptions to this see Frank A. Rice (ed.), Study of the Role of Second Languages, Washington, D. C. : Center for Applied Linguistics, 1962; John J. Gumperz, "Linguistic and Social Interaction in Two Communities" in J. J. Gumperz and Dell Hymes, The Ethnography of Communication, American Anthropologist, 1964. [In this volume, pp. 186-211.]

2. See Karl W. Deutsch, Nationalism and Social Communication. Cambridge, Mass. : M.I.T. Press, 1966.

3. For instance, see Lucian W. Pye (ed.), Communication and Political Development, Princeton, N. J. : Princeton University Press, 1963, or Richard R. Fagen, Politics and Communication, Boston: Little, Brown, 1966.

4. See Karl W. Deutsch, "Social Mobilization and Political Development," American Political Science Review, vol. 55, no. 3, September 1961, p. 494.

5. See Suzanne Keller, Beyond the Ruling Class, Strategic Elites in Modern Society, New York: Knopf, 1963.

6. John J. Gumperz, op. cit.

7. B. Havranek, "Zum Problem Norm in der Heutigen Sprachwissenschaft und Sprachkultur," International Congress of Linguistics, 4th Actes... Copenhagen, 1936, pp. 151-157.

8. Charles A. Ferguson in Frank A. Rice (ed.), Study of the Role of Second Languages, Washington, D.C.: Center for Applied Linguistics, 1962, p. 4.

9. R. E. Frykenberg, "Traditional Processes of Power in South India: An Historical Analysis of Local Influence," Indian Economic and Social History Review, vol. 1, 1963, pp. 122-142.

10. Ellen McDonald, "Social Mobilization and Vernacular Publishing in 19th Century Maharashtra," mimeo, 1967, 28 pp.

11. For a representative collection of views of the nationalist leaders see Z. A. Ahmad, ed., National Language for India, Allehabad: Kitabistan, 1941. See especially P. D. Tandon's advocacy of Hindi: "I believe that political freedom cannot come out of cultural slavery to the English language and things English. I have therefore always stood strongly... for the exclusion of English from our national... work. India's real self must assert itself through her own languages and particularly through Hindi..." P. 93. (Emphasis added)

12. For accounts of the Hindu and Muslim efforts to emphasize the difference between Hindi and Urdu, see Aziz Ahmad, Studies in Islamic Culture in the Indian Environment, London: Oxford University Press, 1964, especially pp. 239-262, and Ram Gopal, Linguistic Affairs of India, Bombay: Asia Publishing House, 1966, especially chapters 4 and 8.

13. For Gandhi's views see M. K. Gandhi, Thoughts on National Language, Ahmedabad: Navajivan, 1956.

14. For an account of the origin of this organization, see Hirak Jayanti Granth, Benaras: Nagari Pracharani Sabha, Sambat 2011, p. 3 (in Hindi).

15. On the development of the H.S.S., see Kantilal Joshi in Rajat Jayanti Granth. Wardha: Rashtrabhasha Prachar Samiti, 1962, pp. 581 ff. (in Hindi).

16. Gandhi also founded in 1936 the Rashtradhasha Prachar Samiti, Wardha for promoting Hindi in the non-Hindi areas not covered by the scope of the Madras Sabha. For accounts of these organizations see Kantilal Joshi's chapter, ibid., pp. 592 ff.

17. See John J. Gumperz, "Language Problems in the Rural Development of North India" in The Journal of Asian Studies, vol. 16, no. 2, February 1957, pp. 251-259. [In this volume, pp. 12-24.]

18. For a brief discussion of the impact of these writers on the new Hindi, see R. A. Dwivedi, A Critical Survey of Hindi Literature. Delhi: Motilal Banarsi Dass, 1966, especially pp. 164-216.

19. In 1962 the H.S.S. and in 1964 the D.B.H. P.S. were recognized by the state as Institutions of National Importance.

20. The financial and other resources of the major Hindi associations are indicated in their annual reports.

21. This means primarily official language of the Union but Hindi is also being made a general link language for non-official purposes. See Report of the Education Commission, 1964-66, Education and National Development, New Delhi: Ministry of Education, Government of India, 1966, pp. 13-16.

22. The Board was later replaced by the Standing Commission for Scientific and Technical Terminology.

23. For samples of the official efforts see for example A Consolidated Glossary of Technical Terms, (English-Hindi), Delhi: Central Hindi Directorate, Ministry of Education, Government of India, 1962, and on translation problems, plans and programs, The Art of Translation, New Delhi: Ministry of Scientific Research

and Cultural Affairs, 1962. On the problem of translating legal works
see M. C. Sharma, Rendering of Laws in Hindi — Its Problems,
New Delhi: Ministry of Law, Government of India, 1964. The
private efforts have been conspicuously led by Dr. Raghuvira. His
ideas on language planning are summarized in his India's National
Language, New Delhi: International Academy of Indian Culture,
1965 (in English and Hindi).

24. The reference here is to Dr. Raghuvira. See ibid.

25. His attempt to develop Hindi "in consonance with the
genius of Indian languages" is discussed in ibid, p. 221.

26. As he points out, "Our languages will again go into the
lap of mother Sanskrit, when she was free. We shall have again
our own words." Ibid, p. 207.

27. For a valuable discussion of standarization with special
reference to major Indian languages see P. S. Ray, Language
Standardization: The Hague, Mouton, 1963, especially p. 125 ff.

28. For instance Art. 351 states: "It shall be the duty of
the Union to promote the spread of Hindi language, to develop it
so that it may serve as a medium of expression for all the elements
of the composite culture of India and to secure its enrichment by
assimilating without interference with its genius, the forms, style
and expressions used in Hindustani and in other languages of India
specified in the Eighth Schedule and by drawing, wherever necessary
or desirable, for its vocabulary, primarily on Sanskrit and secondarily
on other languages."

29. Ministry of Law, Government of India, Manual of
Election Law, Revised Second Edition; Delhi: Manager of Publications
Government of India, 1961.

30. See National Herald, April 5, 1958, and G. C. Awasthy,
Broadcasting in India, Bombay: Allied Publishers, 1965, p. 132.

Part II. Language Usage and Social Interaction

9 | Linguistic and Social Interaction in Two Communities

The Universe of Sociolinguistic Analysis

Sociolinguistics has been described as the study of verbal behavior in terms of the social characteristics of speakers, their cultural background, and the ecological properties of the environment in which they interact (Hymes 1962; Ervin-Tripp 1964). In this paper we will explore some of the formal aspects of this relationship. We will examine the language usage of specific groups and attempt to relate it to linguistically distinct dialects and styles on the one hand and variables employed in the study of social interaction on the other.

The raw material for our study is the distribution of linguistic forms in everyday speech. As is usual in descriptive analysis, these forms are first described in terms of their own internal patterning at the various strata (phonemic, morphemic, etc.) of linguistic structure (Lamb 1964; Gleason 1964). Ultimately, however, the results of this analysis will have to be related to social categories. This condition imposes some important restrictions on the way in which data are gathered. Since social interaction always takes place within particular groups, linguistic source data will have to be made commensurable with such groups. We therefore choose as our universe of analysis a speech community: any human aggregate characterized by regular and frequent interaction over a significant span of time and set off from other such aggregates by differences in the frequency of interaction. Within this socially defined universe forms are selected for study

primarily in terms of who uses them and when, regardless of purely
grammatical similarities and differences. If two grammatically
distinct alternatives are employed within the same population,
both will have to be included. On the other hand, in those cases
where socially significant differences in behavior are signaled by
grammatically minor lexical or phonemic correlates, the latter
cannot be omitted from consideration.

Verbal Repertoires

        Procedures such as these enable us to isolate the verbal
repertoire, the totality of linguistic forms regularly employed in
the course of socially significant interation. Since spoken communication of all kinds is describable by a finite set of rules which underlie the formation of all possible sentences, verbal repertoires
must have structure. The structure of verbal repertoires, however, differs from ordinary descriptive grammars. It includes
a much greater number of alternates, reflecting contextual and
social differences in speech. Linguistic interaction, as Bernstein
(1964) has pointed out, can be most fruitfully viewed as a process
of decision making, in which speakers select from a range of
possible expressions. The verbal repertoire then contains all
the accepted ways of formulating messages. It provides the
weapons of everyday communication. Speakers choose among this
arsenal in accordance with the meanings they wish to convey.

Grammatical and Social Restraints on Language Choice

        Ultimately it is the individual who makes the decision,
but his freedom to select is always subject both to grammatical
and social restraints. Grammatical restraints relate to the
intelligibility of sentences; social restraints relate to their
acceptability. In expressing his opinion about the weather, Smith
might say, "It looks as if it isn't going to rain today," or "It
looks like it ain't gonna rain today." Both messages have similar
referents and, in comparison to ungrammatical sentences like
"Its look it like gonna ain't rain today," are equally likely to

be understood. Since linguistic analysis deals with grammatical
restraints on language choice, alternations such as the above are
not considered part of the linguistic structure. If they are listed
at all they are relegated to the realm of free variation. What then
can be the reason for their persistence and what is their function in
the overall communication process ?

   If the choice among them were completely a matter of
individual freedom, the connotations of his message would be
idiosyncratic to the speaker and this would result in misunderstanding. The power of selection is therefore limited by commonly
agreed-on conventions which serve to categorize speech forms as
informal, technical, vulgar, literary, humorous, etc. To be
sure, such conventions are subject to considerably greater variations
than grammatical restraints, but wherever they are well established,
the style of a message also gives advance information about its
content. When we hear, "Mr. President, Ladies and Gentlemen, "
we suspect that we are in for something like a formal address or
a political speech. We can turn on the radio and recognize a news
broadcast without actually understanding the words that are being
spoken. In listening to someone talking on the telephone, we can
make a good guess as to whether he is talking to a friend or
taking care of routine business. The more we know about a particular society, the more efficiently we can communicate in it. Speech
styles provide advance information about the nature of messages and
speed up communication in somewhat the same way that titles
and tables of contents help in reading a book. The social etiquette
of language choice is learned along with grammatical rules and
once internalized it becomes a part of our linguistic equipment.
Conversely, stylistic choice becomes a problem when we are
away from our accustomed social surroundings. Expressions
which are customary in our own group might quite easily offend
our interlocutor and jeopardize our mutual relationship by mis-
labeling messages.

   When regarded from this point of view, social restraints
on language choice are an important component of the relationship
between signs and their meanings. Every message must conform
to the grammatical restraints of the verbal repertoire but it is

always interpreted in accordance with social restraints. As
Bernstein (1964) says, "Between language and speech there is social
structure." This connection must be statable in terms of regular
rules allocating particular sets of forms to particular kinds of
interaction. These rules should allow us to predict which of the
several possible alternative realizations of messages is most likely
to be employed in any instance.

Social Relationships and Social Occasions

Our discussion of social interaction will employ the term
social relationship to refer to regular patterns or types of interaction. Every society has a finite number of such relationships.
They are abstracted from everyday behavior in somewhat the
same way that linguistic forms are derived from language texts.
Some common examples are: The father-son relationship, sales-
man-customer relationship, husband-wife relationship, etc. All
such types of interaction are carried on by individuals, but in
analyzing social relationships we think of participants not as persons
but as occupants of statuses defined in terms of rights and obligations. An individual occupies a number of such statuses. He
may be a father, an employer, a passenger on a public conveyance,
a member of a club, etc. Each is associated with fairly well-
defined norms of behavior. Any one social relationship focuses on
one of these while others remain suspended.

As Goffman (1963) has shown, social acts always form
part of broader social settings——more or less closely defined
behavioral routines which are regarded as separate in a society.
Our usual round of activities is segmented into a number of such
routines: we eat breakfast, travel to the office, participate in
meetings, go out on dates, etc. Social occasions limit the
participants and more importantly limit the kinds of social relationships that may be brought into play. They are in turn divisible
into subroutines, encounters, or speech events (Goffman 1964;
Hymes 1961). On our way to work we may first turn to our
neighbor and then strike up a conversation with a stranger. During
a meeting we may step aside with one or two participants to talk

about a side issue. While generally related to broader social settings, encounters more narrowly restrict the selection of social relationships and thus bear a somewhat closer relation to modes of acting and speaking.

Let us now examine some common variants such as "dine— eat," "house—mansion," "talk—lecture," or even "going —goin'." All such sets refer to broadly similar classes of objects and activities. They share some attributes, but differ in other more specific features. Dining and eating both indicate consumption of food, but the former tends to imply more elaborate menus and more rigidly defined etiquette than the latter. Similarly mansions are more spacious and better furnished than houses. Beyond this, however, the difference in referents also carries some important implications about the social positions of the actors concerned. Not everyone can "dine." Certainly not two laborers during a dinner break, no matter how well prepared the food they consume and how good their table manners. To use dine in their case might be appropriate in jest, but not in normal conversation.

Alternation of this type may thus be viewed from two perspectives. In the realm of semantics it selects among subclasses of referents. In the sphere of social interaction it reflects the positions actors wish to assume relative to each other, i.e., the quality of their relationship. Whenever a set of linguistic forms is interchangeable within the same frame without significant change in meaning, it is this second aspect which becomes most important. In the course of any one encounter mutual relationships are constantly defined and redefined in accordance with the speaker's ultimate aim. But each encounter sets bounds to this type of variation. Social restraints on language choice express the norms defining such bounds. If he violates these, an actor risks misunderstanding.

Co-occurrence Restrictions

Aside from their purely social aspects, restraints on language choice have one other important set of characteristics.

This concerns the linguistic relationship among the constituents of
a statement. An alternant once chosen sets limits to what can
follow within the same utterance. In the example of alternation
given above, the form "ain't" must be followed by "gonna"; similarly,
"as if" in the first example requires a following "isn't going to. "

Speech events differ in the rigidity with which such co-
occurrence restrictions apply. In some cases (e.g. , public
ceremonies, religious ritual, etc.) modes of speaking are narrowly
prescribed; in others (e.g. , conversations among personal friends,
party chitchat, etc.) there may be scope for a wide range of
alternate sequences. Regardless of particular instances, however,
discourse of all types always shows some form of co-occurrence
restrictions. From the point of view of linguistic structure, it is
important to note that co-occurrence restrictions apply, not to
any particular segment within an utterance, but always to the
utterance as a whole. The informal ending "-in" in items such
as "going" could hardly appear with learned verbs like "purchase. "
Substitution of a learned alternant for a colloquial word also
requires elimination of colloquial pronunciations. Co-occurrence
rules effect all linguistic strata (Joos 1960). They simultaneously
condition the morphological and phonological realizations of
messages. This property enables us to segment verbal repertoires
into distinct speech varieties. A verbal repertoire then is not
simply composed of linguistic forms. It is always a set of varieties,
each with its own internal grammatical structure.

A survey of the literature on bilingualism and dialectal
variation from the point of view of language choice shows that
linguistic interaction in all communities involves alternation among
distinct varieties. But this is not to say that the same or similar
connotational meanings are realized through grammatically
equivalent choices in all cases. In an American community, the
substitution of "goin'" for "going" may signal a switch from
formality to informality (Fischer 1958); in France, on the other
hand, like ends may be accomplished by selecting tu rather than
vous (Brown and Gilman 1960). In Java, the rules of linguistic

etiquette may require alternate use of High Javanese, Low Javanese, and local dialect forms (Geertz 1961). Whenever several languages or dialects appear regularly as weapons of language choice, they form a behavioral whole, regardless of grammatical distinctness, and must be considered constituent varieties of the same verbal repertoire.

Compartmentalized and Fluid Repertoires

The concept of the verbal repertoire allows us to deal with speech communities of all types. Monolingual and multilingual repertoires can be analyzed within the same general framework. They differ in internal grammatical diversity and more importantly in the co-occurrence rules. In multilingual repertoires, co-occurrence rules tend to be more rigid. Verbal behavior seems to be neatly divided among a series of compartments: choice of an initial form commits the speaker to a particular line of approach. The monolingual repertoires, on the other hand, show a greater degree of flexibility. Different types of verbal behavior seem to shade off into one another.

Allocation of speech varieties to social relationships, co-occurrence rules, and internal language distance provide the structural criteria for the analysis of speech behavior. As indices, these are independent of particular languages and cultures. They form a general framework for the study of speech communities of all types in terms which are commensurable with the anthropologist's social structure.

Social Organization in Khalapur[2]

The data for our analysis are drawn from Khalapur, an agricultural village about 80 miles north of Delhi, India, in the Gangetic doab (the plain between the Ganges and Jumna rivers), and Hemnesberget (Hemnes), a small commercial settlement in the Rana fjord of Northern Norway just south of the Arctic circle.

The Gangetic <u>doab</u> is one of the most fertile and densely
settled regions of northwestern India. Since the turn of the century,
it has developed into a major sugar producing region. With its
population of about 3,000, Khalapur is somewhat larger than most
neighboring villages, but its economy and social organization are
typically rural. The main Delhi railroad and a major highway
pass within three miles of Kalapur; and two industrial sugar mills
six miles away employing several hundred persons consume most
of the village cane crop. Until recently, the village remained quite
separate from the interurban communication network. There are
many signs that this isolation is beginning to break down. Community
development is showing its effect and a recently established Inter-
college (Junior College) provides instruction up to the college
sophomore level to students from many surrounding localities.
Paved roads have recently been constructed, and a regular <u>tonga</u>
service (horse-drawn taxi) now connects with the railroad.

Khalapur inhabitants are divided by profound differences
in ritual status, wealth, political power, occupation, and education,
affecting every aspect of daily interaction. In the ritual sphere,
31 distinct castes or extended kin groups are recognized. Ninety
per cent of these are Hindu, and ten per cent are Muslim. Each is
set off from its neighbors by differences in marriage patterns and
ritual practices. Castes may be ranked along the usual ritual
prestige scale with Brahmans, Rajputs (Warrior-landholders),
and merchants at the top, and untouchable Chamars (landless
laborers) and Sweepers at the bottom.

Distribution of wealth and political power shows only
partial agreement with this ranking. Rajputs are the dominant
caste. They constitute more than 40% of the population and own
90% of the land. All other, including Brahmans, are dependent
on them for their subsistence. But Rajputs are in turn sectioned
off by residence patterns into seven neighborhoods. Political
and economic control in each neighborhood is held by a few wealthy
families. As a result of their wealth, political power, and education,
these families have become an aristocracy set off from their poorer
Rajput neighbors, whose holdings are small compared to theirs.

These latter are often tenants and may be economically no better
off than the bulk of the lower caste population. Wealthy families
often maintain friendlier relations with powerful merchants or
artisans and with other landholding castes from neighboring villages
than with their poorer caste brothers.

The new intercollege and the resulting increase in educational
opportunities have added another dimension to the ritual and socio-
economic distinctions. Education is now within the reach of all
groups. The majority of students still come from the Rajputs and
upper castes, but now both the poor and the wealthy have access
to schooling. Many lower caste persons have obtained government
or commercial employment and have become the equals of the
influential Rajput families in education and general sophistication.

Although the recent changes in technology and education have
begun to loosen the rigidity of intergroup separation, social
stratification is still an integral part of the village value system and
is symbolized in a variety of ways in dress, posture, and everyday demeanor. Untouchable women are readily recognizable by
their lahnga (skirts) and their silver jewelry. Educated men tend
to wear Western type shirts and pajamas or khaki trousers, while
the ordinary farmer wears the traditional kurta and dhoti, which
may be made of mill cloth or of material grown and woven within
the village. Others oriented towards Congress Party politics are
beginning to replace their locally made cloth with the homespun
material produced in the Gandhi centers and sold through the local
Congress organization stores.

Whenever two or more people sit together on the cots
which serve for most seating, rigid seating rules are observed.
If all are members of one caste, the oldest person sits at the head
of the cot (which has a special name); others sit next in order of
prestige ranking. If a Brahman is present he will be offered
the head seat. Lower caste persons and sometimes also poor
Rajputs will sit on the floor and untouchables at a slight distance
from the group. Wealthy merchants or artisans or other distinguished visitors however may find a seat on a special cot. Similar

patterns apply also to seating at a feast where the upper castes tend
to sit together in an order determined partly by ritual status and
partly by wealth whereas the poorer lower castes sit aside in their
own separate place. Only caste brothers may smoke from the
same hookah (water-pipe) and they do so in order of rank. Special
pipes may be kept for respected guests from other castes.

   In speaking, each caste is designated by a special caste
title and each person by a term of reference which usually reflects
his caste affiliation or his occupation. Relatively strict rules of
deference seem to apply to interaction with everyone except one's
closest friends and one's family members. Since the term "friend"
may be synonymous with "relative," the two groups tend to overlap.
So great is the guardedness which governs interaction that even an
age mate from an adjoining neighborhood is accorded respect
behavior and is addressed by his title rather than by his family
name.

Khalapur Verbal Repertoire[3]

Local Speech and Standard Language

   Intra-village communication in Khalapur is carried on
primarily in the local dialect (Grierson 1916). The official standard
language, however, is Hindi and villagers list themselves as
speakers of Hindi for census purposes. The standard is learned
either in elementary school, through residence in cities or through
outside contacts. Educated persons, village leaders, businessmen,
and all those who deal regularly with urbanites speak it. In village
interaction Hindi symbolizes the new status relationships created
by the increasing involvement of villagers in state politics, modern
commerce, village development, and state education. Norms call
for the use of Hindi in contacts with representatives of the post-
independence elite, as well as in the classroom and on the lecture
platform. Those individuals who do not speak Hindi modify their
speech with appropriate loan words when the social occasion
demands. Purely local relationships, on the other hand, always

require the dialect and everyone, including highly educated villagers, uses it to symbolize participation in these relationships.

The dialect and standard Hindi define the linguistic bounds of the verbal repertoire. A portion of the grammatical characteristics of this repertoire are common to all speech varieties. There is, for example, a common core of phonemes which are realized by the same pronunciations regardless of which style is spoken. Similarly the basic grammatical categories of noun and verb inflection are shared. But we also find a significant number of differences and these constitute the inventory of structural variants from which speakers select in accordance with situational and co-occurrence restraints. Some examples of these are given below.

On the level of phonology, the dialect shows a special set of contrasts between retroflex and nonretroflex /n/ and /ṇ/ and /l/ and /ḷ/ and between retroflex flap /ṛ/ and retroflex stop /ḍ/ , as well as a special set of diphthongs consisting of vowels followed by a short up glide: /ūi/ /āi/ /ōi/ . The Hindi distinction between alveolar /s/ and palatal /š/ is lacking. Another dialect feature is the frequency of medial double consonants in words such as dialect (K) loṭṭa 'jug' vs. Hindi (H) loṭa. Word pairs resulting from this difference in phonemic distribution are frequently mentioned in popular stereotypes of dialect speech. Morphological differences are most frequent in the phonological realization of shared morphemic categories, i.e., in inflectional endings. The dialect lacks a feminine plural suffix, e.g., (K) bhæ̃s 'female buffaloes,' (H) bhæ̃sẽ. The plural oblique case suffix is (K) o and (H) õ, e.g., (K) bhæ̃so-ka 'of the female buffaloes' (H) bhæ̃sõ-ka. Dialect verbs have the infinitive suffix -n and the past participle ending -ya in place of Hindi ending -na and past participle -a, e.g., (K) bolaṇ,'to speak' (H) bolna, (K) bolya 'spoke' (H) bola. There are syntactical differences in the use of inflected subjunctive forms, e.g. (K) bolæ 'he speaks' when Hindi calls for a complex construction of present participle plus auxiliary, e.g., (H) bolta hæ 'he speaks.' Striking differences occur in the system of function words, i.e., grammatically important pronouns, adverbs of place and manner, conjunctions, post-positions (corresponding to prepositions in English), e. g.:

Dialect	Hindi	English
o	wo or wah	he
wa	wo or wah	she
mhara	həmara	our
-lo	-tak	until
-tæ	-se	from
ib	əb	now
inghæ	yəhā	here
tə læ	nīce	below
kyukkə r	kæ sa	how
kətek	kitna	how much

Additional Speech Varieties

The Khalapur repertoire is subdivided into several additional speech varieties with somewhat more limited occurrence. In a previous study, several minority subdialects were described which reflect the social isolation of the three local untouchable groups (Gumperz 1958). These groups are segregated residentially wear special clothing and ornaments, and are in many ways culturally distinct. Here we will deal with superposed variants (i. e., variants occurring within a single population) in the speech of the majority of Rajputs and touchable castes. Members of these groups distinguish between two forms of the vernacular: moṭī bolī and saf bolī. The former is used primarily within the family circle, with children and with close relatives as well as with animals and untouchable servants. It symbolizes the informality that attends these relationships. Saf bolī, on the other hand, reflects the guardedness of the relationships outside the immediate friendship group and the respect towards elders. Moṭī bolī contains the greatest number of purely local features. Among its phonetic

characteristics are: a special high allophone [ɨ] of the phoneme
/ə/ occurring before /i/ in the next syllable; a pronounced pitch
glide on the vowel preceding the medial voiced aspirate in words
such as pidha 'steel'; a very pronounced up glide in the phonetic
realization of diphthongs /ūi/ /ai/ /oi/ . Morphologically this
style shows greater frequency of deviant function words of the
type listed in the dialect column above. In saf boli , on the other
hand, the above phonetic features are closer to standard Hindi
and dialect function words such as kətek and kyukkə ŗ tend to be
replaced by their Hindi equivalents.

Yet another speech variety characterizes interaction of
villagers with merchants in the local bazaar, wandering performers,
and priests——the traditional hinge groups of rural India. This
regional speech variety is grammatically intermediate between the
local vernacular and Hindi. In pronunciation it shows no dipththongs
of the type /ui/ but retains the retroflex/ nonretroflex nasal and
lateral distinction. In grammar the Hindi-like present tense
construction is employed and Hindi function words prevail. There
are furthermore three varieties of what is ordinarily called Hindi.
Before independence Urdu served as a medium of instruction and
some of the elder village residents still employ Urdu forms
(Gumperz 1960) in interaction with strangers. Such usages have
a distinctly old-fashioned flavor. Village Hindi itself has a conversational and an oratorical style. The latter is characterized by
a large number of Sanskrit loan words which affect both the
lexicon and the system of functors (e. g. conversational aur
'and,' oratorical tətha 'and'), and by initial and final consonant
clusters in words such as krišna 'name of the God,' gram
'village' (conversational gãw). In phonology this style shows many
special initial and final consonant clusters. The oratorical style,
as its name implies, serves as the norm for public lectures and
for some classroom lectures. It is used on such social occasions
even though the audience often does not understand the Sanskrit
expressions. Intelligibility is achieved by interspersing such
lectures with explanatory passages in conversational Hindi or in
the regional dialect.

Social Organization in Hemnesberget[4]

Hemnesberget (or Hemnes), is a commercial settlement
of about 1,300 inhabitants in the Rana Fjord of Northern Norway.
Until the 19th century, the Rana area, located in one of the most
sparsely settled regions in Europe, was directly controlled by a
small aristocracy of merchants, landowners, and government
officials who controlled the land and monopolized the trading
rights. Vast differences in wealth and education separated them
from the majority of the population, who were their tenants,
fishermen, and estate laborers. In the late 19th century, trade
monopolies were abolished and land turned over to settlers. The
region is now one of small farmers, who earn their livelihood
through dairying, lumbering, fishing, and boatbuilding.

Government-sponsored economic development during the
last three decades has turned the Rana area into an important iron
and steel producing center. The area of Mo-i-Rana at the head
of the fjord has grown from about 1,000 inhabitants in the 1920s to
almost 20,000 in 1960, largely through immigration from southern
Norway and Trondheim. The city reflects this growth in its several
department stores, hotels, restaurants, and cinemas. A railroad
from Trondheim to Mo-i-Rana and on to Bodø was recently
completed, and the road system is steadily improving. But
Hemnes remains relatively unaffected by these developments.
Although regular once-a-day boat service to Mo and two daily
buses to the nearby railroad station are available, and a few
people commute to Mo by private auto or motorcycle, for the bulk
of local residents, life centers in and around Hemnes. They form
their friendships primarily with other local inhabitants. Our
interviews showed that events in Mo-i-Rana or even in neighboring
small towns are only of marginal interest to them.

With the disappearance of the earlier aristocratic upper
classes, the bulk of the inhabitants now stem from similar social
backgrounds. The social system shows a fluidity of class structure
quite similar to that described by Barnes for Southern Norway

(1954). Extremes of poverty and wealth are absent. Occupationally the residents fall into four groups: artisans and workers, small shopkeepers and farmers, large merchants, and officials. These differences in occupation carry with them some real distinctions in authority. Yet for all but a few individuals who tend to identify with the older aristocratic classes, the local value system tends to minimize such distinctions, the usual way of expressing this sentiment being, "we are all equal here in Hemnes."

Hemnesberget Verbal Repertoire

The internal social homogeneity of Hemnes is reflected in the somewhat lessened compartmentalization of the verbal repertoire. Inhabitants speak both a local dialect, Ranamål (R), and a standard. The former is the native tongue and the chief medium of intra-village communication. But whereas the Khalapur vernacular is divided into several linguistically distinct subdialects and superposed speech varieties, the Hemnes variety shows only minor distinctions relating to residence patterns and generational discrepancies rather than rigid social cleavages.

The Hemnes standard is Bokmål (B) (or Riksmål as it used to be called), one of the two officially recognized literary languages in Norway (Haugen 1959). Bokmål is universally accepted throughout Northern Norway, while the other literary language, Nynorsk (formerly Landsmål), is more current in central and western coastal districts. Children learn the standard in school and in church and through regular exposure to radio broadcasts. Since education is universal and Hemnes residents are highly literate, Bokmål can be said to be somewhat more firmly established in Hemnes than Hindi in Khalapur.

In spite of their familiarity with Bokmål, villagers take considerable pride in the dialect as a vehicle for spoken discourse. Unlike its Khalapur equivalent, Ranamål is not simply an in-group tongue, regarded as out of place in urban contexts and not worthy

of serious scholarly attention. Hemnes residents consider their
local speech suitable for oral interaction both in their home surroundings and outside. Although they may often employ Bokmål in their
dealings in the city they insist on their right to use the dialect, to
show, as they put it "that we are not ashamed of our origin." Local
norms thus confine Bokmal to a very limited number of social
relationships, relating to literature, church, and some types of
interaction with nonlocals.

Grammatical Differences

        Some of the more important grammatical distinctions
between Bokmål (B) and Ranamål (R) are listed below. The dialect
has a series of alveolar palatalized consonants /tj dj nj lj/ which
contrast with their nonpalatalized counterparts. Some differences
in the distribution of vowel phonemes are frequent correspondences
between (B) /i/ and (R) /e/ and (B) /e/ and (R) /æ/ , e.g.,
men/ mæn 'but' and til/ tel 'to, towards.' As in Khalapur, broader
grammatical categories are shared and distinctions occur primarily
in the phonological realizations of particular allomorphs. Thus
the plural suffix with nouns like hæ st 'horse' is (B) -er and (R) -a.
The present tense for the verb 'to come' is (R) çæm and (B)
komer. Other important differences affect commonly employed
function words:

Bokmål	Ranamål	English
dere	dɔk	you (plural)
han	hanj	he
vem	kem	who
wa	ke	what
vordan	ke...lesn	how
til	tel	towards
fra	ifrɔ	from
mellom	imelja	in between

Linguistic Characteristics of Khalapur and Hemnes Repertoires

Comparison of our two verbal repertoires with respect to the internal linguistic distinctions among constituent varieties brings out some interesting points of similarity. Ultimately verbal repertoires are socially defined concepts, but it would seem from our study and from other work along similar lines (Gumperz 1964) that they also have certain linguistic characteristics which set them off from verbal repertoires in other societies. These characteristics stem from the fact that internal differences tend to be localized in specific strata of structure. We have already suggested that there is considerable overlap in our two verbal repertoires. In terms of the stratificational model of language structure proposed by Lamb (1964), this overlap tends to be greatest in the sememic (semantic categories) and lexemic (grammatical categories) strata and in phonetics. Major form classes and inflectional categories as well as word order rules seem almost identical within our two repertoires. In the realm of phonology, the totality of distinct segments can be divided into two sets: a common core, i.e., a set of obligatory distinctions which everyone in the community makes, and a set of optional distinctions. The phonetic realizations of alternants in constituent varieties vary only with respect to the optional distinctions and not with respect to the obligatory distinctions. Thus in (K) kətek and (H) kitna, 'how much,' the allophones of /k/ and /t/ are the same in each case and (K) /ə/ is phonetically the same as (H) /ə/ in həmara 'our.' In Hemnes also, (B) til and (R) tel 'to' share the same relizations of initial /t/, and the /e/ of tel is the same as the /e/ in (B) vem 'who.' Similar instances of phonetic overlap were also noted by Ferguson (1959).

Aside from optional distinctions in phonology, linguistic differences among constituent varieties seem to be concentrated largely in what Lamb (1964) calls the morphemic stratum (the phonological realizations of lexemic categories). It would seem that wherever alternation among linguistic variants by the same populations creates grammatical overlap, this overlap provides the structural basis for the isolation of verbal repertoires.

Speech Variation and Social Relationships in Khalapur and Hemnes

The fact that verbal repertoires in both communities are compartmentalized has some important social implications. From the point of view of local populations it means that many of the activities that individuals might be called on to engage in require considerable linguistic as well as technical skill. To talk to a government official, or to deal with a local merchant, a Khalapur villager must control distinct rules of linguistic etiquette. He must be able to manipulate not one, but several grammatical systems. In all societies there are certain specialized activities which require special vocabularies. Scientific and legal discourse as well as communication among artisans would be difficult without carefully defined technical vocabularies. Furthermore, oral and written communications require different types of syntax. But phonemic and morphophonemic differences of the type found in our study are hardly related to the nature of the activities they symbolize. They constitute cultural restraints imposed upon interaction above and beyond what can be justified on purely technical grounds and are thus ritual in the sense in which this word is used by Leach (1954:10).

Ritual barriers to interaction affect different spheres of activity in our two communities. In Hemnes they apply only to a limited number of scholarly, literary, administrative, and religious relationships, while the bulk of intra-village communication reflects the lack of rigidly defined stratification within the community. In Khalapur, on the other hand, ritual barriers affect every aspect of community life. They are part of the elaborate rules of etiquette which are also evident in dress, seating, and smoking, and seem to mirror the guardedness which attends the bulk of interpersonal relations. In contrast to Hemnes, Khalapur village life is not a single whole, but rather a broad grouping of sets of distinct relationships signaled by differences in linguistic and other modes of behavior. The details of this grouping are in themselves of interest, since they provide interesting insights into social structure. Thus servants as well as junior kin may be addressed in moṭī bolī. The two statuses seem to share some common characteristics.

Similarly religious, political, and educational activities all require the oratorical style and are thus regarded as related. The difference between Hindi and the regional dialect suggests a status distinction between two types of non-locals: traditional merchants and itinerants and modern businessmen and government officials. More detailed analysis of this type should furnish fruitful insights into native status definitions.

Linguistic Interaction in Khalapur and Hemnes

Our discussion of verbal repertoires so far has dealt only with normative aspects of language choice. We have described the constituent speech varieties in terms of the social relationships they normally symbolize. Behavior in actual encounters, however, is not always predictable on the basis of these associations alone. Just as individual words may be used in meanings which are different from their primary referents, so also speech styles need not always signal the exact social relationships with which they are associated. Thus speakers may employ the word 'fox' either in its primary meaning to designate an animal or to refer to a human being to whom they wish to assign some of the connotations of 'foxiness.' Similarly some aspects of formal lecture style can be introduced into informal discussions to convey some of the connotations of formality for the sake of emphasis.

This use of superposed variation constitutes a different dimension of linguistic behavior. We account for it by distinguishing two types of interaction: transactional and personal. Transactional interaction centers about limited socially defined goals, i.e., a religious service, a petition, a job interview, etc. Participants in such interaction in a sense suspend their individuality in order to act out the rights and obligations of relevant statuses. Hence their linguistic and other modes of behavior must be predictable from the social definition of these statuses.

In personal interaction, on the other hand, participants act as individuals, rather than for the sake of specific social tasks.

This behavior predominates in periods of relaxation among friends, and within peer groups. It is also common in scholarly discussions where the subject is more important than the social characteristics of participants. It gives scope to all facets of experiences, and individuals may resort to changes in speech style in order to under-score particular meanings. Personal switching is associated with differences in emphasis and in topic, and thus contrasts with transactional switching, which correlates with such alterations in the formal characteristics of encounters as changes in participants or in their relative statuses.

The linguistic effect of personal switching is a loosening of co-occurrence restrictions. Forms which would not appear together in transactional encounters may now co-occur. Some social restraints on language choice of course always remain. Strictures on obscenity and other types of taboos are rarely violated no matter how free the dialogue. Baby talk is not appropriate in most discussion among adults.

It is important to note that personal switching achieves its effect in nontransactional encounters because there exists a regular association between choice of linguistic form and social relationships in transactional encounters. It is this latter association which gives rise to relevant differences in connotation. Stylistic alter-nation which remains confined to transactional encounters need not necessarily lead to linguistic change, since the differences between variants are reinforced by nonlinguistic correlates. When switch-ing occurs in personal encounters, on the other hand, situational reinforcement is lacking and hence there is a greater likelihood of change. Both types of linguistic alternation therefore must be taken into account in sociolinguistic study.

The balance of personal and interactional switching varies both from community to community and from subgroup to subgroup within the same population. An individual's expertise in manipulat-ing speech varieties is a function of his position within the social system. In Khalapur, poorer Rajputs and members of the lower castes who spend their days in physical labor and interact primarily within the immediate kin group tend to use moṭī bolī. They sound ill at ease when required to switch to saf bolī and have a tendency to revert to moṭī bolī when they become agitated. Their knowledge of the regional speech and of standard Hindi furthermore is limited to a few stereotyped phrases which they tend to intersperse with moṭī bolī forms. Wealthier Rajputs, merchants and artisans, those who held clerical positions, and especially political leaders, show the greatest skill in switching. Intergroup differences in linguistic expertise are somewhat smaller in Hemnes but there are nevertheless many farmers and local artisans who show less skill in spoken Norwegian than those who are called upon to use it regularly.

In Khalapur only moṭī bolī and saf bolī alternate in personal switching. Hindi and regional speech occur exclusively in trans- actional interaction. Our field observations furthermore show personal switching primarily in gatherings of politically more active Rajputs who are not necessarily close kin. Here saf bolī is the usual form of speech while moṭī bolī is used in joking and in quarreling. Although there seems to be some correlation between linguistic expertise and personal switching in Khalapur, the connection is probabilistic rather than causal, since not all speakers who are highly adept at stylistic manipulation engage in the latter.

Personal switching was the object of a special study in Hemnesberget, reported in greater detail elsewhere (Gumperz 1964; Blom 1964). Linguistic data were collected through tape recorded informal discussions with groups of two types: members of purely local "closed" friendship networks (Barnes 1954) and members of "open" networks. The former included individuals whose significant social relationships were confined to Hemnes. The latter were made up of university students, a clerk in a local office, and others who maintained relationships both with Hemnes residents and with the urban elite.

All groups were exposed to topical stimulae ranging from local issues such as fishing, personal relationships in Hemnes, etc., to superlocal issues such as city life, government investment, national politics, etc. It was found that local groups tended not to switch from the dialect to standard Norwegian except in transactional encounters (i. e. , when talking to the anthropologist observers). Internal discussion within the group was carried on entirely in the dialect regardless of topic. Open network groups on the other hand engaged both in transactional and in personal switching. They tended to use a high proportion of standard Norwegian forms both when talking to the observers and in their own internal discussion dealing with supralocal topics.

In our field interviews we were unable to determine any differences in attitude toward language use among these groups. Members of both groups adhered to the prevalent norms which call for dialect forms in all types of oral interaction. In fact, when tapes of open network groups discussions were played back to one participant, she expressed surprise and stated she had not realized that she had been using Bokmål forms.

Our data seem to indicate that intergroup distinctions in linguistic behavior are attributable to the different ways in which participants of open and closed network groups in Hemnes society define their mutual relationships. All members of open network groups share in a much broader range of experiences than those who belong to closed networks. They regard each other as students, literati, or part of the politically conscious national elite as well as friends and fellow Hemnes residents. Hence they feel compelled to symbolize these additional relationships through stylistic shifts when the discussion demands it.

In assessing the effect of personal switching for linguistic change we take into account both the specific varieties which are affected as well as the position of the group within the local social system. In the case of Khalapur we might predict that moṭī bolī is on its way out since the behavior of upper class Rajputs who use it in personal switching is being increasingly imitated by others. The prevalence of personal switching among open network groups in Hemnes however is not necessarily an indication that the local dialect is about to be replaced by standard Norwegian. Open network groups such as we studied are relatively marginal in the community as a whole. Their members will probably find employment elsewhere and pass out of the community. Any radical shift in the verbal repertoire such as changeover from a compartmentalized to a fluid structure (which the loss of the local dialect would imply) should, if our analysis is correct, also require a restructuring of social relationships within the majority group.

Conclusion

Our comparison of verbal behavior in Khalapur and Hemnes is intended to be suggestive rather than definitive. Nevertheless we hope that the information we present demonstrates the fruitfulness of the verbal repertoire as a sociolinguistic concept. We have stated that a verbal repertoire is definable both in linguistic and social terms. As a linguistic entity it bridges the gap between grammatical systems and human groups. The common view that language stands apart from social phenomena, which is held by anthropologists of many persuasions (Sapir 1921:228; Radcliffe-Brown 1957:143; Nadel 1951:89), would seem to be valid only if we confine our analysis to single homogeneous systems abstracted from the totality of communicative behavior. If, however, we follow the procedure suggested in this paper and consider the linguistic resources of human groups to be divisible into a series of analytically distinct speech varieties, showing various degrees of grammatical overlap and allocated to different social relationships, then the connection between linguistic and social facts is readily established. It is the language distance between these varieties rather than the internal phonological or morphological structure of specific varieties which most readily reflects the social environment. Since language distances can be studied through contrastive linguistic analysis independently of extralinguistic phenomena, their measurement provides a valuable index for the study of society.

Social restraints on language choice, on the other hand, are also a part of social structure. They are thus susceptible to analysis in terms of generalized relational variables which apply to interaction in all human groups. The study of particular sets of grammatical systems and cultural norms in terms of these variables enables us to treat linguistic behavior as a form of social behavior, and linguistic change as a special case of social change.

NOTES

1. The study of verbal behavior in Hemnesberget was sponsored by the Institute of Sociology, University of Oslo, Norway, and was carried out in cooperation with Jan-Petter Blom. Thanks are due to the latter, to Sverre Holm, Professor of Sociology, University of Oslo, and to Dr. Hallfrid Christiansen for assistance in the project. The author's stay in Norway was made possible by a grant from the National Science Foundation.

2. For more detailed ethnographic data on Khalapur, see Hitchcock and Minturn 1963.

3. A detailed analysis of Khalapur phonology is given in Gumperz 1958b. Our phonetic transcription here differs slightly from the above. The vowels ə, i., and u are short; vowels ī, ū, e, o, æ, ɔ, and a are long. For discussion of the various subvarieties of Hindi in the Hindi language area, see Gumperz 1960.

4. Ethnographic data cited is based largely on the work of Jan-Petter Blom (1964), although the author takes full responsibility for the interpretation presented here. In local usage the term Hemnes refers to both the town and the entire region, while Hemnesberget is the name of the town proper. In the present paper the two terms are sometimes used interchangeably.

REFERENCES

Bernstein, Basil. 1964. Elaborated and restricted codes: their social origins and some consequences. [American Anthropologist 66:6 (Part 2). 55-69.]

Blom, Jan-Petter. 1964. Friendship networks in Hemnes. Typescript.

Brown, R. W. and A. Gilman. 1960. The pronouns of power and solidarity. In Style in Language. Thomas Sebeok, ed. Cambridge, Massachusetts: The M.I.T. Press.

Ervin-Tripp, Susan. 1964. An analysis of the interaction of language, topic, and listener. American Anthropologist 66:6/2:86-102.

Ferguson, Charles A. 1959. Diglossia. Word 15:325-340.

Fischer, John L. 1958. Social influences in the choice of a linguistic variant. Word 14:47-56.

Geertz, Clifford. 1963. The Javanese family. Glencoe, Free Press.

Gleason, H. S. 1964. The organization of language: a stratificational view. Georgetown University Monograph Series on Languages and Linguistics, No. 17, pp. 75-95. Washington, D. C.: Georgetown University Press.

Goffman, Erving. 1963. Behavior in public places. Glencoe, Free Press.

Gumperz, John J. 1958a. Dialect differences and social stratification in a North Indian village. American Anthropologist 60:668-681. [In this volume, pp. 25-47.]

_____ 1958b. Phonological differences in three Hindi dialects. Language 34:212-224.

_____ 1960. Formal and informal standards in the Hindi regional language area (with C. M. Naim). In Linguistic diversity in South Asia. C. A. Ferguson and J. J. Gumperz, eds. Indiana University Research Center, Bloomington, Indiana. [In this volume, pp. 48-76.]

Gumperz, John J. 1966. On the ethnology of linguistic change. Sociolinguistics, ed. by W. Bright (The Hague: Mouton and Co., 1966), pp. 27-49.

Hitchcock, John T. and Leigh Minturn. 1963. The Rajputs of Khala-pur. In Six cultures: Studies in child rearing. Beatrice B. Whiting, ed. New York, John Wiley.

Hymes, Dell. 1962. The ethnography of speaking. In Anthropology and human behavior. T. Gladwin and W. D. Sturtevant, eds. Washington, D. C., Anthropological Society of Washington, pp. 15-53.

Joos, Martin. 1960. The isolation of styles. Report of the 10th Annual Round Table Meeting on Linguistics and Language Studies. R. S. Harrell, ed. Georgetown University.

Lamb, Sidney M. 1964. The sememic approach to structural seman-tics. American Anthropologist 66, No. 3, Part 2, pp. 57-78.

Leach, E. R. 1954. Political systems of highland Burma. Cambridge, Mass., Harvard University Press.

Nadel, S. F. 1951. The foundations of social anthropology. Glencoe, Free Press.

Radcliffe-Brown, A. R. 1957. A natural science of society. Glencoe, Free Press.

Sapir, Edward. 1921. Language. New York, Harcourt, Brace.

10 Linguistic Repertoires, Grammars, and Second Language Instruction

In his Postulates for a Science of Language, Leonard Bloomfield defines a language as the totality of utterances that can be made in a speech community (1926). His statement emphasizes the view that the sounds and grammatical patterns we study are always abstracted from social activity. They form part of a complex of communicative symbols, produced by members of particular societies interacting in specific social settings in accordance with culturally defined norms of behavior. Few linguists would disagree with this formulation. In asserting that speaking is a form of social interaction, Bloomfield is merely following long established tradition. But so far, such assertions constitute little more than professions of faith. The important contribution of modern linguistic scholars lies in their analysis of verbal signs in terms of their purely linguistic environment. Bloomfield and his followers were able to achieve the explicitness and reliability of statement for which they are justly famous largely because of their insistence that segmentation and classification of verbal forms be based on observable sound. Source data for linguistic analysis were, to be sure, collected from native informants, but once recorded, items were grouped purely on the basis of their formal similarities and differences. Meaning and context were left aside for later consideration.

The last decade has seen a radical break with the basic position of post-Bloomfieldian linguistics. The modern view of grammars as theories of a language rather than as classifications of pre-existing elements has also brought about important changes in the nature of linguistic descriptions. No matter what our opinion regarding these new developments, it is evident that these grammars cover a considerably broader range of phenomena than the earlier formal statements. Along with phonology and morphophonemics, syntax and semantics have once more become an integral part of linguistic descriptions. But the expansion in scope of linguistic description is also accompanied by new efforts to reassert the independence of formal linguistic analysis. A recent article on semantic theory by Katz and Fodor (1963) makes a major contribution toward the incorporation of semantics into grammar, but in this article the authors also go to great lengths to argue that information about what they call sociophysical settings should be excluded from linguistic descriptions. The semantic theory they envisage is, among other things, capable of dealing with cases of homonymy in sentences such as "The bill is large," where the noun subject may refer either to a bird's beak, a document demanding payment, or to a currency note. On the other hand, the difference in meaning between the objects of the sentences "This store sells horseshoes" and "This store sells alligator shoes" is declared to be outside the scope of linguistics, since knowledge of the difference is a matter of personal experience, and thus not subject to formalization. Despite the increase in the scope of linguistic descriptions, therefore, the new theory continues to make sharp distinctions between grammars and the social context in which utterances are used. Linguists and social scientists operate with similar source data, but the products of the linguists' analysis remain independent entities whose relationship to social facts we are unable to specify in any clear terms.

In work on grammatical theory or internal reconstruction of protolanguages there is, of course, little need to go beyond the ordinary grammatical statement. But claims for the applicability of formal linguistics are usually much broader.

Since the 1940's, for example, the importance of descriptive analysis in the construction of foreign language texts has been emphasized. This emphasis has been justified to a large extent. Contrastive analysis of grammatical systems serves as the basis for drill materials which have been strikingly effective in teaching the ability to produce grammatical sentences in a new language.

But it is also fair to say that we have not been completely successful in providing students with the linguistic ability they need to communicate effectively in speech communities where these languages are spoken. Problems of this type are especially severe in Asia, where the learners encounter a radically different cultural environment.

Consider the case of an American who, after completing the conventional language course and having attained reasonable fluency in spoken Hindi, arrives in New Delhi, the capital of India. In his background reading he has most probably learned that Hindi is not the only language spoken there, that many of the educated classes speak English, and that in addition Urdu, Punjabi, and a variety of other local dialects are used. Since he has grown up in a monolingual community, however, he has little idea of what this multilingual situation implies for day-to-day communication. He therefore tends to be unprepared for the problems he finds.

A typical difficulty, which is the subject of frequent complaints by returning students, concerns the lack of opportunity to use and practice the Hindi that had so laboriously been learned. Wherever the Westerner goes, in hotels, in shops, at parties, in public offices, Indians address him in English. Their English may be barely intelligible but, nevertheless, he is given little opportunity to switch to Hindi. On occasion, when with a group of Indians, he may find his companions talking among themselves in highly abbreviated, idiomatic Hindi, or even in what seems like a mixture of English and Hindi. Nevertheless, they address him only in English, almost as if they were capitalizing on the language barrier in order to exclude him from the intimacy of their in-group relations.

When, in spite of all this, the Westerner does insist on speaking Hindi, he is frequently misunderstood. Some interlocutors will object to the conversational forms he has learned on the grounds that they are Hindustani, sometimes called khaanaa khaaoo, "eat your food," forms. These were used by the English in their relations with Indian servants, but are not regarded as suitable for free India. On the other hand, the Westerner's attempts to employ

expressions such as <u>maaf kiijiyee</u>, "excuse me," as mere politeness
formulas are inappropriate, as Indians use such expressions only
to beg forgiveness for a real wrong. Similarly, polite forms of
address when used with porters, waiters and similar service
personnel, produce awkwardness rather than appreciation.

When questioned about the appropriateness of particular
forms, native speakers commonly give conflicting responses.
Interminable arguments may arise over the proper form of the
subject pronoun and the direct object in sentences such as "he knows
it," in which Hindi has several alternates:

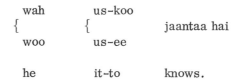

	wah	us-koo	
	{	{	jaantaa hai
	woo	us-ee	
	he	it-to	knows.

Since native speakers contradict each other, the Westerner hardly
knows where to turn.

In sum, learning appropriate Hindi usage in a modern
Indian city is a difficult and frustrating task——almost as difficult
as learning the grammar in the first place. Since our textbooks
provide no guidance for this task, the result is that an unusually
large proportion of Westerners in India tend after a while to drop
their efforts at mastering the vernacular and revert to using English
on all occasions. It seems necessary, therefore, at least for the
purposes of applied linguistics, to reopen the question of the
relationship between linguistic and social facts. More specifically,
the question arises: given a grammatical analysis of the languages
involved, what additional information can the sociolinguist provide
in order to enable the language teacher to give his students the
skills they need to communicate effectively in a new society?

This discussion suggests a somewhat different approach
to the problem than that taken by Katz and Fodor. They, along

with most linguists, tend to be concerned primarily with the cognitive functions of language. They look at language almost exclusively in terms of the way in which objects and concepts are encoded through verbal signs. In language instruction, however, our concern is also with behavior, as it affects language usage. The question, then, is not how to specify the relation between words and sociophysical settings in more detail, but rather, given several alternate ways of formulating a message, which of these is most appropriate according to the social norms of the particular occasion. Contrastive analysis furnishes the relevant grammatical patterns; what we need is information on the social factors which govern the employment of grammatically acceptable alternates.

Modern social anthropologists have formulated a set of concepts for the study of social interaction which seem general enough to apply to linguistic as well as to non-linguistic behavior, and which may be useful for the present discussion. In this framework the actions of individuals within particular settings may be analyzed in terms of their status, i.e., the positions they occupy within the social system, as defined by the rights and duties which the culture assigns to such positions. A person may act as a father, as a friend, as a judge, a customer, etc. In each case his behavior is determined by different norms. The term 'social relationship' may be used to describe interaction between two or more statuses. Every society has a finite number of such relationships, and each carries certain social norms. Some common examples are the father-son, customer-salesman, husband-wife relationships, etc. The daily round of activities in a society can be regarded as segmented into a series of distinct social occasions (Goffman, 1963)——more or less closely defined behavioral routines which are kept separate by members of a society. For example, we eat breakfast, travel to the office, participate in meetings, go out on dates, etc. In each such social occasion only a limited number of social relationships may occur. Thus, behavioral norms applying to any particular speech event should be predictable from knowledge of the social occasion and of the social relationships involved. What follows is an attempt to apply some of these concepts to problems of language usage.

Basic to the present approach is the assumption, also
suggested in the work of scholars such as Brown and Gilman (1960)
and Fischer (1958), that language usage reflects the quality of social
relationships in particular social occasions. In dealing with linguistic
phenomena in this way, we are thus operating in a new "ethnographic"
dimension (Hymes, 1964) where linguistic alternates are grouped not
in terms of their purely linguistic similarity, but in terms of the
norms which govern their usage. We therefore introduce the concept
of linguistic or verbal repertoire (Gumperz, 1964 and 1965), defined
as the totality of linguistic forms regularly employed within the
community in the course of socially significant interaction. Repertoires
in turn can be regarded as consisting of speech varieties, each
associated with particular kinds of social relationships. In monolingual speech communities, such as we find in the highly industrialized societies of the West, repertoires tend to be co-extensive with
the linguists' grammars. The difference is that many of the speech
varieties which must be recognized on social grounds are so similar
linguistically that they have not been noted in ordinary grammars.
In linguistically diverse speech communities like the one we find
in Delhi, on the other hand, constituent varieties may require
separate though related grammars. Switching among languages in
communities of the latter type has the social function similar to
stylistic switching in monolingual communities (Rubin, 1961). The
linguistic repertoire, therefore, is a general concept which allows
us to compare any two communities in terms of the way in which
internal speech distribution reflects social structure, regardless of
any pre-established criteria of linguistic homogeneity or hetero-
geneity.

To make formal statements of the relationship between
social norms and language choice would, in view of our present
limited knowledge, be a formidable task. It would require ethnographies much more detailed than we now have available. For the
purpose of language instruction, however, the anthropologists'
experience, based on several years of participant observation of
interaction in typically Indian small town and village contexts, can
at least provide a useful approximation. The Hindi teaching materials
prepared at the University of California (Gumperz and Rumery, 1962)

attempt to utilize this experience to make at least a beginning in the direction of introducing realism of social context into a language course.

A brief survey of common encounter types found in Indian and American societies reveals some important differences. Dating, parties governed by complete informality of relations, casual gatherings in doctors' offices or other public locations such as have been described by Hall in his popular The Silent Language (1959) are, for example, unknown in India. On the other hand, some common Indian practices have no Western counterpart. Consider, for example, the puja, or meditation period, which many Indians observe daily and which involves a half hour or more of silence. A Western visitor arriving during such a period will be completely ignored. If he is familiar with the local custom, he will leave without speaking and return later, or he will sit unobtrusively until the meditation period is over. Lack of acquaintance with such behavior, on the other hand, may cause awkwardness or misunderstanding. In other instances, what on the surface seem like similar encounters carry radically different behavioral norms in the two societies. It is, for example, usually inappropriate in India to discuss an interlocutor's wife and family in a casual encounter.

A crucial characteristic of Indian society in this respect is the importance placed on the interlocutors' formal status in most types of interaction. In the bulk of encounters outside the family and close friendship circles individuals are treated as occupying statuses, rather than as individuals. This fact is, as a rule, symbolized by verbal clues. Different greetings and different modes of address are used for Hindus, Muslims, officials, friends, respected elders, etc. A switch from Hindi to Urdu to English may have similar status-marking functions.

The need for such status markers is dropped only in personal interaction among friends. In view of the severe social barriers to interpersonal friendships, however, such friendship relations are considerably more difficult to achieve in Indian society than in Western societies. In a sense, therefore, we can say that the

Indian's persistent attempts to use English in interaction with
Westerners serves as a boundary maintenance device marking the
social differences involved. This can be overcome only after long
periods of close contact.

It might be objected that since selection of linguistic form
is ultimately a matter of individual choice, individuals might easily
be induced to change their attitudes. Ethnographic experience
suggests that this is easier said than done. Behavioral norms such
as those referred to here are, as a rule, deeply ingrained since
childhood. They form part of unconscious linguistic behavior
(Levi-Strauss, 1964) in much the same way that purely linguistic
habits do. They are violated only at the risk of considerable social
disapproval, and such violation usually results in extreme conflict
on the part of individuals involved. The recent 'foul speech'
controversy at the University of California in Berkeley, involving
the public use of four-letter words, is a case in point. On the
surface, all the individuals involved did was to exercise their
freedom of choice. But in doing so they violated one of our most
firmly held social norms governing conduct at public meetings,
exposing themselves thereby to the ire of all concerned. Reactions
to the foreigner's stylistically inappropriate speech in India is,
of course, never so extreme, but nevertheless it may cause
considerable discomfort.

An important task in constructing a socially realistic
conversational sequence is, then, to isolate those encounter types
in which a newly arrived Westerner might have occasion to use
his Hindi. Since much of the Westerner's life is spent in Western-
type, specially constructed, insulated residential colonies and
modern shopping districts which confine him to contact with the
Western-trained elite and keep him from intimate contact with
typically Indian society, this proves to be not as simple as it may
seem. Here the Westerner is restricted to meeting Indians who
are bilingual in English and who, for the reasons explained above,
tend to have little understanding of his efforts to practice Hindi.
When contact with the few monolinguals who penetrate these
enclaves becomes necessary, a host of bilingual intermediaries

are ever ready to interpret and thus preserve him from direct contact
with them.

Special efforts will therefore have to be made to find monolingual Indian settings where these difficulties may be overcome.
The Westerner will have to seek out native bazaars or small
provincial towns and learn to insist on dealing with monolinguals,
avoiding English-speaking intermediaries. Only after considerable
length of stay in the country and after acquiring a knowledge of the
situational proprieties of language usage, when he has established
close friendship ties with Indians, can the Westerner expect to
converse freely in Hindi with his interlocutors.

After setting up a list of likely conversational situations
and identifying each with respect to their cultural labels, these
situations and the statuses of participants can then be graded in
terms of their social complexity and in terms of the amoung of
knowledge of the culture that they require. The Indian bazaar
behavior provides a convenient starting point for such an arrangement. In a country as diverse as India, the bazaar provides a
neutral meeting place, where distinctions of caste and ethnic background remain suspended in social interaction. All actors become
vendors or customers, regardless of their social background.
Bazaar language thus shows relatively simple lexicon and sentence
structures and avoids complex patterns of greetings and social
introductions and politeness formulas.

Beginning with bazaar situations, it is possible to establish
a range of complexity ranging from interaction with uneducated
service personnel such as shoemakers and washermen, dealings
with drivers of horse- or bicycle-drawn public conveyances,
tourist guides in out-of-the-way places, conversations with fellow
passengers on trains, to informal friendship relations with social
equals and discussions on literary and political topics, towards
the end of the scale.

As a next step in the preparation of the text, each encounter
was enacted on the scene with a Westerner and actual Indian shopkeepers,

service personnel, etc. , as actors, and recorded by means of
sequence photography. A set of color slides was then selected to
represent conversation content somewhat in the way in which comic
strip artists represent action. Texts to fit each slide set were
then written by linguist-native speakers associated with the project.
The conversations served as the basis for pronunciation and grammar
drills such as those found in ordinary spoken language texts.

The Berkeley Hindi materials have now been in use for
about two years at a number of institutions throughout the country.
On the whole, native speakers tend to agree that the texts are
appropriate to the social occasions illustrated. Students returning
from India have commented on the 'realism' of the course. But
the contextual approach also has a number of advantages for the
purely linguistic content of the course.

Linguists, for example, have long objected to the educator's
preference for word frequency counts, claiming that they are
time-consuming and do not necessarily produce significant results.
The procedure followed here makes word frequency counts unnecessary.
If the encounter type if accurately defined, then the vocabulary which
is appropriate to it by definition also has the proper frequency
distribution.

More importantly, the association of stylistic variants
with visual and social clues provides the student with a natural
introduction to the social factors which underlie the style switching
which is so important in India. English loans and even entire
Indian English slang phrases will appear natural in student
conversations. Urdu pronunciations and lexicon will correlate
with Muslim dress and gestures, etc. It is even possible to switch
styles within the same encounter and change from what Indians
call 'chaste' Hindi to Westernized Hindi to Urdu within the same
conversation, provided such changes are justified by the status
relationship of participants within the encounter. Thus a speaker
may use the Urdu tashriif rakhiyee in asking a Muslim to sit down,
and then turn to someone with the Hindi equivalent, padhaariyee,
for the same message.

      The initial assumption regarding the dependence of linguistic form on social setting receives partial confirmation from the fact that in our text grammatical grading of conversational material emerges as a natural consequence of contextual grading. For example, among the important grammatical distinctions between Hindi and English are case-gender-number agreement of nouns and verbs and the verbal tense-mood system. Agreement is more basic to the system since it affects both nouns and verbs. It would be ideal therefore if problems of verb morphology could be left aside while agreement is practiced. The bazaar situations allow us to do just that with natural Hindi conversations, since the only verb forms that appear are the morphologically simple request forms.

      In other cases our approach provides criteria for choosing among what would otherwise seem freely alternating modes of expression. Thus sentences like the <u>woo us-koo jaantaa hai</u> 'he knows it,' cited above, alternate with <u>pataa hai</u> (literally, 'knowledge exists'). The former occurs frequently in texts elicited by the usual linguist-informant interview method. With its subject-object-verb structure it is a relatively close translation equivalent of English and hence it might seem natural on grounds of ease of learning to emphasize it in drill materials. The latter expression shows a noun plus auxiliary type predication, somewhat more difficult for Americans to learn. It is, however, very common in informal Hindi, and furthermore has close parallels in local dialects and other South Asian languages. In general, wherever alternate Hindi expressions are possible, contextual eliciting tends to select those alternates with more direct translation equivalents in other Indian languages, whereas linguist-informant eliciting technique yields a higher proportion of English-like constructions.

      Our examination of social interaction has revealed some important differences between behavioral norms in the American and North Indian speech communities. Further work in South Indian, Dravidian-speaking speech communities seems to indicate that behavioral norms there are quite similar to those in North India. Thus Tamil-speaking informants, when shown slide sequences taken in North India, seem to have no difficulty in producing natural conversations to fit these sequences. Indications are, therefore, that while the contextual approach requires considerable additional work, once an analysis is made it may at least in part be transferable to other speech communities within that culture area, resulting in a considerable gain in generality.

REFERENCES

Bloomgield, Leonard. 1926. "A set of postulates for the science of language," Language 2:153-156.

Brown, Roger W. and H. Gilman. 1960. "The pronouns of power and solidarity," Style in Language, Thomas A. Sebeok, ed. New York, Wiley, pp. 253-256.

Fischer, John L. 1958. "Social influences on the choice of a linguistic variant," Word 14:47-56.

Goffman, Irving. 1963. Behavior in public places. Glencoe: Free Press.

Gumperz, John J. 1964. "Linguistic and social interaction in two communities," American Anthropologist 66: no. 6, 137-153. [In this volume, pp. 151-176.]

_____ 1968. "Some desiderata in South Asian areal linguistics," Studies in Indian linguistics: M. B. Emeneau Felicitation Volume, Bh. Krishnamurti, ed. Poona, India, Linguistic Society of India and Deccan College, pp. 118-123.

Gumperz, John J. and June Rumery. 1962. Conversational Hindi-Urdu. Berkeley, Institute of International Studies, University of California.

Hall, Edward T. 1959. The Silent Language. Garden City, New York, Doubleday and Co.

Hymes, Dell. 1964. "Toward ethnographies of communication,"
American Anthropologist, 66, no. 6, 1-34.

Katz, Jerrold J. and Jerry A. Fodor. 1963. "The structure of a
semantic theory," Language 39:170-210.

Lévi-Strauss, Claude. 1964. "Structural analysis in linguistics and
anthropology," in Language in Culture and Society, A Reader
in Linguistics and Anthropology, Dell Hymes, ed. New York,
Harper and Row.

Rubin, Joan. 1961. "Bilingualism in Paraguay," Anthropological
Linguistics 4:52-58.

11 | Religion and Social Communication in Village North India

      Although India presents a scene of great local cultural diversity, in the study of religion the subcontinent may be viewed as a single large field of social action. Within this field new movements are constantly arising, whose practices and ideas interact with others and penetrate from one section of the subcontinent to the other, filtering across deep political and social barriers. Thus in ancient times Brahminical Hinduism spread south from the Northwest, and Hinduism and Jainism, originating in the Northeast, followed closely upon its path. In medieval times the various bhakti movements which arose in South India spread northward, but have continued to play an important part in the life of all regions. Similarly reform Hinduism, born under the impact of contact with the West, affects areas far from its points of origin.

      Action and interaction on this large scale are hardly possible without a highly developed system of mass communication. In fact, communication is a major function of many Indian religious institutions. Side by side with the local priest and the scholastic, who confine their activities to officiating at religious rites and to commentaries on traditional texts, we find the religious communicators; the sanyasi , the guru, the theatrical performer, and the musician. These often wander from region to region, penetrating into remote areas far from public transportation. In assuming their religious role, they are freed from many restrictions of the caste system, they interact freely with many individuals with whom they otherwise would not come into contact, and their message is assured a more sympathetic hearing than that of ordinary strangers.

Anthropologists studying the media employed in the communication of religious values have recently pointed out the importance of religious performances (Singer, 1957:141; McCormack 1959:119; Damle 1959). The present paper deals with such performances in a single village and attempts to analyze their social function in respect to other aspects of the local communication network. Observations made here are based on an eighteen-month study of rural Hindi dialects carried out in cooperation with a team of American and Indian anthropologists in and around the village of Khalapur.

Khalapur is located in the Gangetic valley, about eighty miles north of Delhi, not far from the main communication arteries leading to the Punjab in the West. With its population of about five thousand, it is somewhat larger than the surrounding villages, but its economy and social organization are typically rural. Inhabitants fall into thirty-one endogamous caste or jati groups, ninety per cent Hindu and ten per cent Muslim. Rajputs constitute the dominant caste and make up forty-eight per cent of the total population. Untouchable Chamars are next with twelve per cent, and after them come Brahmans with five per cent. The remaining thirty-five per cent of the population is divided into twenty-eight caste groups (Hitchcock 1956, 1959).

From the point of view of communication, we may visualize Khalapur as part of a complex grid, of the type proposed by Cohn and Marriott (1958), consisting of a series of major and minor religious, commercial, and administrative centers, each with its own hinterland. Innovations arising in one center spread both to other centers and into the hinterland. On the village level, we find a further process of diffusion, which seems to be determined largely by networks of social relationships such as the marriage networks recently described by Rowe (1960:299).

The town of Deoband, six miles away, is the most important of the many centers affecting the life of Khalapur. Formerly the seat of a local Muslim feudal ruler, it now serves as the tahsil (sub-district) headquarters. Among its attractions are a well-known mosque and several Hindu shrines, a sugar mill, and the bazaar which is the closest and most convenient of several surrounding marketing facilities. Muzzafarnagar, sixteen miles south of Deoband and twelve miles from Khalapur, the headquarters of the neighboring district with its large bazaar and extensive whole-sale grain market, offers a somewhat greater selection of goods and services. Saharanpur, the district headquarters for Khalapur, thirty miles to the north of Deoband, is primarily of administrative and religious importance. Both Muzzafarnagar and Saharanpur are easily accessible from Deoband via the main Delhi-Saharanpur railroad or by bus via the paved highway following the same route. Hardwar, in the Himalayan foothills at a distance of five hours by bus or train, is the chief religious center of the area. Here the ashes of the dead are consigned to the Ganges. Hardwar has a great variety of well-known shrines, and many of the most important Hindu sects maintain their headquarters there.

In addition, a number of religious fairs are regularly held in the countryside, and some shrines located as far away as Rajasthan are well known to Khalapur villagers. Marriage relation-ships for the upper castes extend as far as Ambala and Patiala, about one hundred miles to the west, to Moradabad, one hundred miles to the east, and to Delhi, to the south; the lower castes tend to marry within a circle of about thirty miles.

Most information filtering into the village from these various sources reaches the average villager via oral channels either through travellers returning from abroad or through visitors. Although Khalapur has never been very isolated as Indian villages go, contacts with the outside have increased manyfold within the last fifteen years. The railroad and the interurban road system have been in operation ever since the turn of the century, but the village itself was cut off from this urban grid. It is surrounded on three sides by a stream and a swampy tract fordable only in the dry season. Roads leading to the main Deoband-Muzzafarnagar arteries were unimproved and almost impassable to vehicular traffic. Construction of an all-weather bridge and a paved road during the last ten years has eliminated most obstacles to regular travel. Villagers may now travel to Saharanpur and back within a single day. Horse tongas have begun to ply between the village and the Deoband railroad station. Most upper castes and many artisan castes have family members who visit Deoband several times a week on foot or by bicycle. For the lower castes such trips are only slightly rarer. Longer trips outside the Deoband, Saharanpur, Muzzafarnagar area, made either for religious pilgrimage purposes, to visit relatives, or in connection with marriage parties, also seem to have increased in number.

While villagers have begun to travel more, their opportunities for informal contact with strangers are less extensive than one might suppose. Trade negotiations are accompanied by a great deal of suspicion on both sides, a fact which limits the nature of the social relationship. Individuals who visit a city frequently have a regular circle of contacts there. In each bazaar in fact, there are shops frequented by members of one caste group, where individuals may congregate and smoke a hukka (waterpipe) without fear of pollution. Longer trips in connection with marriage parties often lead through large cities such as Merut or Delhi and often there is as much as eight hours delay between trains. On the occasion of such delays, villagers rarely venture outside the railroad station into the strange city. They show little desire to sightsee in places where they have no personal relations. If for any reason it is necessary to stay overnight in a strange location, the preferred spot is a dharmshala, a place for religious pilgrims, or if that is not available, the railroad platform. All these restrictions on outside contact limit the ways in which innovations may reach the village.

The recent improvements in communication have also materially increased the number of non-resident visitors to the village. A great variety of peddlers arrive daily and sell their wares from house to house among the well-to-do. This is a recent phenomenon since most villagers still recall the day when any stranger would find himself harrassed by groups of children, and strange peddlers from abroad had reason to feel unsafe in the village lanes. The number of outside visitors to the village is further increased by the new inter-college (junior college) established in the early 1950's, which attracts students from many surrounding villages, where they mingle with the local boys. In addition since the establishment of the village development project in 1953, a village level worker has been permanently stationed in the village and block development officers frequently arrive for special visits. Other officials come in connection with collection of taxes, cooperative society business, or tubewell or canal irrigation.

Within the village itself, the spread of innovations is greatly hampered by caste- and kinship-determined restrictions on free social interaction. Although in Khalapur, as in most small village communities, the division of labor is such that most members of all castes come into regular contact, interaction among different groups is limited to certain neutral spheres. A low-caste person will not ordinarily engage in free and equal discussion with those of greatly superior status. One frequently finds a lower-caste individual sitting or standing at a slight distance from a higher group engaged in discussion, listening to what is said, but not participating. Although news of current events may spread with relative ease, intergroup contact is not sufficiently intense to eliminate differences in attitude on such matters as home life, social and religious values, village politics, etc., which thus tends to restrict conversational subject matter. We find some evidence in support of this in a study of social dialects, which shows that the speech of untouchable Sweepers diverges significantly from that of the majority. These Sweepers spend a great deal of their day in the homes of their upper-caste masters, talk to them regularly, but do not adopt their speech patterns (Gumperz, 1958).

Observations on social interaction in the village show that free discussion and interchange of opinion are most likely to occur in small groups which we might call social nuclei. These are made up of men of one or more joint agricultural families, i.e., those who jointly own and operate their farm or business or share in the income from wage labor. They congregate either in the family chopal (men's house) or in cattle compounds or workshops, which are often hidden from public view. Group members are usually but not always of the same caste. It is possible for one person to be part of more than one nucleus. As a matter of fact, intercaste friendships are fairly frequent among touchable classes with roughly similar position in the hierarchy, so that a Rajput may have Brahman, merchant, or goldsmith friends; a carpenter may be in close contact with a group including merchants and goldsmiths; other carpenters may in turn be friendly with potters; and so on down the hierarchy. Among the Rajputs, many of the wealthier joint farm families divide their work in such a way as to allow some members enough time for cultivating other social groups.

Most informal social life in the village takes place within individual social nuclei. We find no functioning public assembly hall or square, accessible to all, where members of different groups may mingle. Village lanes are empty during leisure hours, and it is rare to find anyone just strolling or visiting from house to house. The community center, built with government funds, serves as a school during the day and is usually empty in the evening. Occasionally the local youth group uses the hall for an evening of devotional songs. Membership in this group is limited to a few upper-caste social nuclei and is by no means representative of the community as a whole.

Direct contacts of outsiders with villagers also tend to be channeled through individual nuclei. Casual visitors usually see only their own friends and relatives. Government officials, including development officers whose task it is to promote social change, invariably stop at a selected family chopal. If they require information about the village, this is obtained by enquiries from members of their host's social nucleus. If direct contact with other villagers is necessary, these villagers are called to see the officer at the host's chopal. Whatever information the officer has to convey reaches the public through the host group. The village level worker similarly must work through the dominant caste. The fact that he has no public offices but is forced to seek quarters in a village home further limits his freedom of movement.

In the absence of any central mechanism which would provide simultaneous access to a variety of groups, the flow of innovations within the village is dependent primarily on intergroup

contact. The study of dialect distribution, for example, shows a
direct correlation between speech differences and the number of
intercaste friendships. Those untouchable groups which are the
most divergent linguistically also show the lowest number of intergroup friendships. Similar conditions might be expected to hold in
the field of social values.

A number of the newer media of mass communication have
recently been added to the already mentioned outside contacts, but
these have done little so far to disturb the described pattern of
dependence on person-to-person oral channels. Newspapers are
not sold in the shops; they reach the villager primarily through
individual subscriptions. Periodical literature and pamphlets
intended for general distribution through the panchayat ordinarily
circulate no further than the village headman's social nucleus. Moreover, the number of individuals capable of reading these papers is
much smaller than would appear from the literary statistics, since
the style employed in the news stories is quite different from either
the village dialect or the conversational style of standard Hindi.
Those few individuals who do read may often be found reading aloud
to their own friends and commenting on the content of the news in
the local dialect, thus reverting to oral communication.

The local youth group receives a number of posters dealing
with village development. Some of these can be found adorning the
chopal of the youth group leader; others are placed in his private
room within the women's quarters, and are accessible to none
except close family members. There is no public place in which
to display posters. A lending library made available to the youth
group is also stored in a private home and suffers from the same
limitations of accessibility.

There are at least five radios in the village. Two of them
are publicly owned. The one belonging to the village council fell
into disrepair two months after it was purchased and no effort
was made to have it repaired, in spite of the fact that repairmen

are easily available in the neighboring bazaar town. Another one,
which is owned by the local junior college, is occasionally used by
small groups of students. The three private radios serve only a
few of the social nuclei. They are used with such discretion that
anthropologists working in the village were not aware of their
existence for several months. This contrasts sharply with Muslim
or Christian villages in the Near East where radios are set up in
most public places and the voice of Radio Cairo is heard by all.

To summarize, therefore, if we leave aside the nature of
a particular item, the spread of innovations in the village is
determined by: (1) the nature of the message source and, if the
source is human, its position in the social hierarchy; (2) the nucleus
or nuclei through which it is channeled into the village and their
relative status in the hierarchy; (3) the number of intergroup friendship ties of the mediating nuclei. It is obvious that high-caste
families whose representatives travel frequently and who receive
the greatest number of outside visitors have the best access to
information from the outside. In the absence of a functioning
system of mass communication, low-caste groups who, for economic
reasons, tend to be confined to the village are the most isolated.

Religious performances avoid many of the limitations
which the village social structure imposes on other media of
communication. They may take place during the spring or fall
seasons of religious festivals or in connection with weddings or sometimes whenever a troupe happens to pass through the village. In
view of the almost total absence of any form of public entertainment,
they form a welcome break in the daily routine and tend to draw
large audiences.

Performances observed in the village are of two types.
The first are religious lectures, based on traditional texts either
read or spoken by a single performer. The narrative alternates
with song. Often they are presented in dialogue form and acted out
with vivid gestures. The lecturer is sometimes accompanied by
a group of musicians, or he may provide his own accompaniment

with his own instrument. Performers usually are members of a
particular religious sect or order.

The second type, dramatic troupes, consist of several
people acting out mythological themes usually on a platform stage.
Dialogue is again interspersed with song, and music is provided
by a group of musicians. Performances follow the general pattern
outlined by Hein for the Ram Lila spectacle (1959).

Drama troupes or religious lecturers frequently visit the
village on invitation of a particular family. But the actual performances are held in a public place, an open square or a field, and
members of all castes including untouchables may attend. One
performance was observed in the untouchable Chamar section of
the village and much of the audience consisted of upper-caste
individuals. This section of the village is not ordinarily frequented
by touchables except when on business.

The troupe receives food, lodging, and occasionally presents
of clothing and money from the inviting family. Most of the cash
income derives from voluntary audience contributions. Individuals
pass their money over to the actors in public during the performance.
Their names and the amount contributed are then announced.

Of special interest is the caste composition of the various
performing groups. In the case of religious lecturers, caste
varies with the nature of the sect. Some sects draw their members
exclusively from a Brahmin caste; in others, members of a single
non-Brahmin caste predominate; while others, like the Arya
Samaj troupe mentioned below, are of mixed composition. Dramatic
troupes, as a rule, are composed of persons whose families are
engaged in agriculture and who travel about for part of the year.
Some come from neighboring villages, others are drawn from
villages which may be several hundred miles distant from one
another. One of the troupes observed was entirely Brahmin;
another included only Dooms (a traditional Muslim caste of musicians
and beggars). Several other troupes had intercaste composition.

One combined Rajputs and Brahmins, another Rajputs, Brahmins, as well as Dooms, who occupy a place close to that of untouchable in the caste hierarchy. Regardless of caste, performers tend to be well treated on their travels and are accorded a measure of respect which recalls that given to the sanyasi, who is casteless by definition. When the performers take up their roles, the audience tends to forget their secular states and accepts their message as if it were spoken by the characters they represent.

The communicative advantages of religious performances are thus twofold. They differ from other types of social interaction in that they take place in a public location and are capable of simultaneously reaching a large number of diverse social nuclei. By virtue of their religious character, they are able to overcome many of the usual limitations of caste and social status. These features make them effective mass communication media.

An examination of the structure of traditional performances shows that they lend themselves to the transmission of a variety of messages, not always related to the overt religious theme. Let us take an example from music to illustrate the mechanics of this process. The basis of Indian music is the rag or melody type, consisting of a fixed sequence of notes within a certain interval. A piece of music or composition consists of variations on one or another of the rags in the traditional repertory. The result is closer to what in Western music we might call variations on a theme than to free composition. In classical Indian music, the number of available rags and the permitted range of variations are so large that a great degree of melodic variety is possible. The village system, however, is much more limited. Melodies as a rule are few and well known and rarely present a new esthetic experience. Rags are usually associated with certain themes: the holi rag or the biaahii rag sung at weddings is associated with festivals; the malhar is sung in the rainy season; the shair is suitable for love themes, the ragni for ballads, and the bhajan for devotional songs. Villagers are primarily interested in the words

rather than the tune of a song. Lyrics are in fact composed for
special occasions. Villagers fail to understand, for example,
the fact that the anthropologist could enjoy a song without understanding its words. The function of the rag is to set the mood for the
story or to provide a clue about the nature of the information to be
conveyed by the words of the song.

The structure of dramatic performances and lectures is in
many ways similar to that of music. The main components are the
religious plot or story, prose dialogue, and the musical accompaniment. Chanting may or may not be used. The plot, the cast
of characters, and the music are fixed, but the prose dialogue
permits a great deal of improvisation. Subject matter of plots tends
to be limited to a finite number of themes drawn from the epics,
the Puranas, the Upanishads, or perhaps Rajput heroic tales. Since
most of these themes are a matter of common knowledge, they
convey little if any new information. Furthermore, the language
of the chants is, as a rule, unintelligible to uneducated members of
the audience. In information theory terms, we might say that the
message is conveyed through the prose dialogue. Plot, music,
and chant are part of what Hymes (1961:21) has called the form of
the message. Like the rag, they set the mood and provide advance
information about the message. Mythological themes can be
elaborated in certain limited directions. Stories from the Ramayana
provide scope for emphasizing the traditional martial values of the
Rajput; the stories of Nal and Damayanti from the Mahabharata are
suitable for domestic topics. Just as the musician is allowed to
perform variations on a rag, the individual actor is given a great
deal of freedom in prose dialogue, and this provides him with an
opportunity to put his message across.

There are several instances of performances in which the
message differs considerably from the overt religious theme. In
one performance a Doom actor inserted a long plea for Hindi-
Muslim amity into the mythological story of Nal and Damayanti.
Even as a government official, he would never have been accorded

the attention he received nor the audience, had he attempted to make a prose speech.

Another instance is the <u>Bhajan</u> group, sponsored by the Arya Samaj sect of reform Hinduism, in which a single lecturer performs while accompanied by a group of musicians. The message of one of these lectures concerned fixed prices and honesty in business, a subject intorduced in the guise of a story from the Upanishads. The lecturer started by telling of a sage who arrived at the home of a famous raja. The raja paid him respect and offered him food, but the sage refused, saying, "How do I know that your kingdom is not full of tightwads and profiteers?" The raja replied, "Sir, there are no sinners in my kingdom. All goods in my kingdom are sold at fixed prices." This last statement was repeated in song with musical accompaniment, using the Bhajan rag, a rag associated with devotional songs. The lecturer went on to tell how he met a sanyasi who had been in America who told him that goods are sold at fixed prices there and that Americans are so honest they leave money for their milk on their doorstep. This statment, accentuated by musical underscoring, was followed by a discussion on the need for more honesty in business dealing.

The intercaste audience listened to the lecture with seeming interest and several people later commented favorably on the honesty of Americans. This interest contrasts sharply with the reception accorded to a group of students from Merut who wrote a modern play dealing with village development. In spite of the fact that intermissions were filled with movie songs and other light entertainment, the attitude of the village audience remained negative and even hostile. Many of them walked away before the end of the performance, criticising the fact that the theme was from daily life and had no connection with mythology.

In at least one instance, the Bhajan party technique was adapted to village development propaganda. A traditional Arya Samaj singer was employed by the Community Development Block.

He collected a group of followers and lectures and sang about
village uplift, using the Bhajan rag for songs about public health,
the Japanese method for rice cultivation, etc. His activities have
been singularly effective——he has been known to hold an audience
of several hundred in bitter cold winter weather. Although a
carpenter by caste, his followers included young people from a
number of castes, including Tyagis and Brahmans. Caste status
does not seem to impede his effectiveness. His followers stay with
him for a while in a traditional teacher-disciple relationship and
then return to their villages where they continue singing his songs
to their own groups. If he were to attempt to disseminate propaganda
as a village level worker, his effectiveness would be severely
limited by his low caste.

The use of traditional performances as instruments of social
reform in Khalapur is by no means unknown or new in Indian society.
Medieval bhakti preachers like Kabir and the Virashaiva saints
were essentially social reformers who spend much of their time
preaching against the evils of caste. The evidence suggests that
the roles of the religious preacher and of the secular social and
economic reformer, which to some Westerners seem quite separate,
are closely associated within the Indian social system. This would
provide an explanation for the extrordinary popularity of individuals
like Tilak, Gandhi, and Vinoba Bhave (compared with secular
leaders like Gokhale, Rajendra Prasad, or even Pandit Nehru)
who associate their message of egalitarian social reform with
traditional symbolism, and thus at least assure it a hearing.

Marriott (1959) has recently suggested that traditional
channels of cultural transmission in India are changing. He notes
that the newer channels of radio, newspapers, and cinema are
beginning to carry more and more of the burden of mass communication. Even so, the most popular of these media, the cinema,
shows a high incidence of mythological themes performed in a
manner reminiscent of village drama. The change is thus neither
so fast nor so abrupt as one might imagine.

REFERENCES

Cohn, Bernard S. and McKim Marriott. 1958. Networks and centers
    in the integration of Indian civilization. Journal of Social
    Research, Ranchi Bihar.

Damle, Y. B. 1959. Harikatha—a study in communication. Bulletin,
    Deccan College Research Institute. S. K. De Felicitation
    Volume, Poona.

Gumperz, John J. 1958. Dialect differences and social stratification
    in a North Indian village. American Anthropologist. 60:668-
    682. [In this volume, pp. 25-47.]

Hein, Norvin. 1959. The Ram Lila. In: Singer, 1958: 279-304.

Hitchcock, John T. 1956. The Rajputs of Khalapur. A Study of
    Kinship, Social Stratification, and Politics. Ph. D. disser-
    tation. Cornell University.

_____ 1959. Leadership in a North Indian village: Two case
    studies. In: Leadership and Political Institutions in India,
    ed. by Richard L. Park and Irene Tinker. Princeton: Prince-
    ton University Press.

Hymes, Dell H. 1962. The ethnography of speaking. In: Anthropo-
    logy and Human Behavior, ed. by Thomas Gladwin and W. C.
    Sturtevant. The Anthropological Society of Washington.

Marriott, McKim. 1959. Changing channels of cultural transmission
    in Indian Civilization. In: Intermediate Societies, Social
    Mobility and Social Communication, Proceedings of the 1959
    Annual Spring Meeting of the American Ethnological Society,
    pp. 63-73.

McCormack, William. 1959. Forms of communication in Virashaiva
    religion. In: Singer, ed., 1958: 119-129.

Rowe, William L. 1960. The marriage network and structural change
     in a North Indian community. Southwestern Journal of Anthro-
     pology. 16:299-311.

Singer, Milton (editor). 1958. Traditional India: Structure and
     Change. Journal of American Folklore, Vol. 71
     No. 281.

_____ 1959. The Great Tradition in a metropolitan center: Madras.
     In: Singer, 1958: 347-388.

12 | Hindi-Punjabi Code-Switching in Delhi

This paper deals with a linguistic phenomenon which is characteristic of urban agglomerates in the so-called "plural societies" of the East. In these societies, groups of widely different regional and cultural background live together in close geographical proximity. They trade, exchange services and mingle freely in public places. They are subject to the same government and often attend the same schools. Yet regular and frequent interaction has not obliterated the most important cultural and linguistic differences among them. Each group continues to preserve its own separate traditions, values, and loyalties, often evident in differences in dress and diet. The result is a range and variety of behavioral norms which are considerably greater than those found in the more highly industrialized urban societies of the modern West.

Home, family and kindred continue to be at the center of the individual's life. Marriage alliances and the relaxation of informal friendships rarely transcend these boundaries. Contact with outsiders is a necessity of daily life, but behavior in these public situations is sharply distinct from the intimacy of the family circle or peer group. An individual may mingle freely with others of different background and even strive to imitate them in business, at public gatherings, or in school. But at home he is expected to revert to the pattern of his own group. The separation of private from public behavior thus serves to insulate the group by limiting the flow of innovations filtering in from the outside.

The presence in private life of many exclusive kin groups parallels the concentration of certain types of public activities in the hands of particular communities. Wholesale and retail trades and

crafts are parcelled out among many relatively exclusive groups.
Religious practitioners, lawyers, and administrators are drawn
from yet other groups. The number of public activities in which the
individual engages determines how many modes of public behavior
he must learn. While these inter-group barriers are now slowly but
steadily breaking down, we still have a society which tolerates and
keeps distinct a wide variety of diverse modes of behavior. Interaction is characterized by a high degree of what anthropologists have
called "role specificity" (Bruner, 1956)— that is, the round of daily
activity is segmented into a series of separate spheres governed by
distinct and ofteh conflicting norms.

Given a population with highly diverse linguistic backgrounds, the above social environment is one which would tend to
preserve pre-existing language and dialect differences to an extent
rarely found in Western societies. In fact, throughout India and
other parts of Asia we find immigrant groups who maintain their
linguistic identity for many centuries, even in relatively small
communities. The number and kind of linguistic codes employed in
a community and their genetic origin are matters of historical
accident; once a code is established it tends to become associated
with the behavior characteristic of the group that most frequently
employs it. The group's language then becomes the symbol of
group identity. But this does not necessarily mean that it is monolithic;
far from it. Special, formal styles of the group language may be used
for religious and/ or professional activities peculiar to the group.
Other styles influenced by surrounding codes are used by those
members of the group whose activities bring them into daily contact
with members of surrounding groups. These conditions insure that
to the extent that an individual participates in different aspects of
community life, he must control the codes associated with those
aspects of community life.

In contrast to Western society, therefore, where one
linguistic code or a set of closely related styles of what is popularly
considered to be the same language serves all requirements of the
daily routine, code diversity characterizes the plural societies of
the urban East. Multilingualism is an integral component of social

interaction and a requirement for full participation in community
life.

There is, however, a fundamental difference between
community multilingualism of this sort and the isolated bi- or multilingualism which occurs when individuals of exceptional educational
background living in an essentially monolingual society control
more than one language. The distinction is one which is not ordinarily
made in the literature on the subject. Psycholinguists distinguish
between "compound bilinguals" who alternately employ two different
languages, not always with equal competence but presumably in the
same social context, and "coordinate bilinguals" who have near-native
control of two languages which they employ in distinct social settings
(Ervin and Osgood, 1954). They have also presented some evidence
for the fact that the latter condition is a more stable one, but their
interest so far has concentrated on the bilingual as an individual
and not on the group.

Both isolated and community bilingualism may be coordinate.
They differ in the nature of the linguistic norms followed. Isolated
bilinguals follow the norms of pronunciation and grammar prevalent
among native speakers of both languages in question. Thus an
American bilingual in French will attempt to follow Parisian norms.
Multilingual societies, on the other hand, tend to create their own
norms which are often quite different from those prevailing in the
respective monolingual societies. An Indian may speak English with
near-native control; he may read it, write it and lecture in it with
great success. But when he uses English in India his speech will
share many of the features of the other Indian codes with which English
alternates in the daily round of activities. Indian English will thus
deviate considerably from the norms current among native speakers
of English in the American Midwest. This kind of deviation represents
not a failure to control English, but a natural consequence of the social
conditions in the immediate environment in which Indian English is
spoken.

The social conditions prevailing in multilingual societies
create a number of often conflicting tendencies. The need for

frequent code-switching on the part of a large number of individuals tends to reduce the language distance between codes. Linguistic overlap is greatest in those situations which favor intergroup contact. Here, as we will show later in this paper, borrowings may reach proportions hitherto associated only with pidgin languages. But, on the other hand, the need for maintenance of at least some symbols of role specificity acts as a deterrent to excessive borrowing and thus prevents complete merger of codes. Interference will be considerably less in those situations which are specific to a single group. The linguistic picture thus shows a range of situationally determined styles of what is popularly considered the same language. These styles may vary greatly in pronunciation, grammar and lexicon, but the linguistic differences among them are rarely reflected in the popular conception of the language — and hence not in the terminology popularly applied to the language.

The linguist studying this problem may take one of two approaches: he may, as in most existing literature on the subject, concentrate on those styles or codes which are popularly known by the same name. He will then analyze all forms of the language regardless of when and where they are spoken. In the case of Punjabi, the linguist's statement would cover varieties used in those regions where Punjabi is the dominant language as well as in Delhi and those other parts of India where it is a minority language.

Or the linguist may approach the problem by defining the bounds of his study in terms of the "speech economy" (Hymes, 1962) of a single community. In this case, he would study all the codes used there regardless of language names and genetic affiliation. He would, however, exclude those varieties which are spoken elsewhere and are not "functional" (Nadel, 1957) in the community. This approach, seldom adopted to date, seems a promising one, since it relates speech behavior to the extra-linguistic environment in which it operates and may thus provide an insight into the relationship between social factors and language change. For these reasons, this approach is followed in this paper.

We use the term "code matrix" to designate the totality of functionally important codes in a specific community. The components of such a code matrix may be dialects or styles of the same language or genetically related or even unrelated languages. In India, urban societies differ considerably in the components of the code matrix. In industrial centers established in former tribal areas, such as Jamshedpur in Bihar, the code matrix includes tribal languages of the Munda family, the local dialects of Bihari, standard Hindi and the English of the educated. It is not unusual even for a relatively uneducated tribals to control at least some styles of all these languages. In Delhi, the Hindi and Punjabi components of the matrix are more closely related, but regardless of actual language distance between codes, Delhi and Jamshedpur remain multilingual societies exhibiting similar social characteristics.

The present paper is a preliminary attempt to illustrate some aspects of community multilingualism as it occurs among speakers of Hindi and Punjabi in Delhi. Speakers of Punjabi, the largest of Delhi's linguistic minority groups, trace their origin to a broad region extending from the districts of Hisar and Patiala about 150 miles west of Delhi to Rawalpindi in the present West Pakistan. Their native idiom, although genetically a close relative of Hindi, is recognized as a distinct language in the Indian Constitution. It has its own literary tradition and grammatical norms and is considered by many to be mutually unintelligible with Hindi. Although most Punjabi families have come to Delhi since the turn of the century, the two languages have coexisted within the same linguistic area as part of the same cultural complex for several hundred years. Varieties of Hindi are commonly employed as trade media in most urban bazaars within the Punjab. They are also used as superposed literary codes by Muslims and Hindus and thus coexist with literary Punjabi, cultivated primarily by Sikhs. Residence in Delhi has not brought about any radical change in linguistic environment for most Punjabis. It has merely increased the number of bilinguals and has also increased the uses to which Hindi is put, so that both idioms now serve important functions in daily social interaction. Punjabi is thus spoken both inside and outside the home. The varieties of Delhi Punjabi, however, are by no means homogeneous. Reflections of many regional dialects occur alongside special urban styles showing the influence of the predominant Hindi. Natives recognize these

distinctions and use the term ţheţ to refer to styles with divergent
local color.

The present study concentrates on those situations in which
code-switching is normal. The principal informant is a college student
who speaks Hindi, Punjabi and English. Although his family came to
Delhi from Peshawar, he has spent most of his life in Delhi. In the
interviews he was confronted with certain well-defined social situations
and was asked to imagine himself conversing in these situations, first
with a Punjabi-speaking fellow student and then with a speaker of
Hindi. At a later time the informant was requested to give the ţheţ
equivalents for his urban Punjabi utterances. The data was compared
with field observations made during a three-month stay in Delhi and
with data from auxiliary informants and information from a standard
grammar of Punjabi (Bailey, 1961). The information thus obtained is,
of course, preliminary and will require checking in more carefully
controlled field observations, but the results seem significant enough
to merit a report at this time.

The prospects for structural comparison of linguistically
diverse materials have been considerably improved by recent advances
in theoretical linguistics. Theoretical models of language structure
have been proposed which provide analytical categories general
enough to apply to all types of linguistic systems. A grammar is not
considered as specific to a language, but is conceived as a set of
rules assigning a structural description to observed data at the various
levels or strata of language (Chomsky, 1961). These grammatical
rules are expressed in terms of formulaic symbols related one to
another by closely defined quasi-mathematical procedures, a fact
which lends the statement an amount of rigor and comparability
difficult to achieve in a traditional prose description. Since grammatical rules may be made arbitrarily abstract, there is no longer any
a priori reason why the same statement may not be made to apply to
different sets of data, even though these data may be popularly
considered parts of separate languages. We simply distinguish
between shared rules and those which are particular to a sub-system

within the same overall structure. The latter rules will then form
a measure of the language distance between the substructures
involved.

These characteristics apply to a number of recently
proposed models of language structure. The present comparative
analysis will follow the system recently proposed by Sidney M.
Lamb (Lamb, 1962). Lamb's method consists of an elaboration
and a refinement of the so-called "item and arrangement" approach
of Hockett and others. Language patterns are viewed as describable
by code-like systems patterning on each of a series of strata -
phonemic, morphophonemic, morphemic, sememic - which are
recognized as basic properties of language. The model recognizes
three kinds of relationships: that of a class to its members, that
of a combination to its components, and that of an eme to its allos.
These relationships are symbolized by a set of class symbols
specific to each stratum, a set of morphotactic rules describing
the combination of units within a stratum, and a set of representation
rules which serve to convert the units of one stratum into those
of another. A grammatical statement is complete if it assigns
to an utterance a description on all strata of linguistic structure.

Comparative analysis of the linguistic texts collected
from the principal informant reveals that the differences among
them are almost entirely grammatical. More than 90% of the
lexical items in the urban code-switching style are also Hindi
words. Many of those items that differ do so by regular phonological correspondences such as that between long -aa in Hindi
kaam (work) and short -a in Punjabi kam (work).

We begin our comparative grammatical analysis at the
morphemic stratum. Tactical rules on this stratum are expressed
in terms of general class symbols representing categories such
as form-class, case, gender, etc. These symbols are given
specific lexical content only at the lower, morphophonemic level.
The greater proportion of tactical morphemic rules are common

to both codes. Some illustrative examples are given below. [1]

An Indicative Clause (IC) is that portion of an utterance which remains after the intonation has been removed. It may represent a complete sentence or part of a sentence. An Indicative Clause may be generated by the following rule:

1) $[S_{12}]$ $[S:]$ V_{12} $< IC$

An Indicative Clause consists of a set of optional substantive constructions and a verb construction. The verb may show grammatica

---

1. Symbols are used with the following meanings unless otherwise defined in the text:

S	=substantive phrase,	V =verb phrase,	Pr =pronoun;
Nc	= noun construction,	A =adjective,	stN =noun stem;
stA	=adjective stem,	cn =case-number suffix	pp =postposition;
Aux	=auxiliary,	stAux=auxiliary stem,	D = demonstrative pronoun;
P	= personal pronoun,	I =interrogative pronoun	R = relative pronoun

Subscripts symbolize agreement, while : indicates that more than one item in a category may occur. Optional items are placed in square brackets, large form-class items in { } brackets. $<$ signifies inclusion of a construction in a class; parentheses ( ) and plus signs (+) are used as in algebra to indicate possible morpheme combinations.

In the representational rules, superscript ^{m} symbolizes rules converting morphemic into morphophonemic statements. Superscript ^{mp} indicates rules converting morphophonemic into phonemic representations.

In the phonemic transcription, length is symbolized by double vowels in the case of ii, uu, aa, and oo, e, æ, and ɔ are always phonetically long.

agreement in person, number and gender (symbolized by subscript) with one of the substantive constructions.

2) $\{$ Pr, Nc $\}$ < S

The class of substantive constructions includes pronouns and noun constructions.

3) $[A_1 :]$ N_1 < Nc

A noun construction is formed by one or more adjectives (optional) followed by a noun.

4)   (stN + stA)   -cn [-pp]   < N

A noun in turn is made up of a noun stem or of an adjective stem followed by one of a class of case-number suffixes and optionally by one of a class of post-positions.

5)   (stA + stN - cn - K) -cn$_1$ < A

An adjective may be made up either of an adjective stem or of a noun stem. Noun stems when part of an adjective construction are followed by case-number suffixes or a special morpheme K. The entire construction is followed by case-number suffixes agreeing with the following noun.

6) $\{$ D^1, D^2, P, I, R $\}$ < Pr
7)   Q D^1 < I
8)   J D^2 < R

The class of pronouns includes two classes of demonstratives, personal, interrogative and relative pronouns; interrogative and relative pronouns in turn are compounds of demonstratives with the morphemes Q and J respectively.

The structure of the verb may be summarized by the

chart below. A, B, C, and D are cover symbols for morpheme classes. C^1, D^1 and C^2, D^2 refer to the first and second items in each column respectively. The symbol Aux stands for the auxiliary.

A	B	C	D	Aux
stV	$\widetilde{uu}$	T	cn_1	
stAux	iye	n	aa	

Morpheme combinations possible in various types of verb construction may be symbolized by the rule given below, from which the individual possible sentences may be derived by multiplying out as in an algebraic formula.

9) $A(1+ B^1(1 + C^1D^1)) + B^2(1 + C^1D^2) + D^1(1 + C^1 + C^2)$

While the bulk of the morphemic rules are shared, differences between codes appear in the representational rules translating morphemic class-symbols to the morphophonemic stratum and in the representational rules converting the morphophonemic into phonemic symbols. These will be illustrated by concrete examples from the data, which for brevity's sake are given in phonemic transcription. (Double vowels indicate length.)

	Punjabi	Hindi

10)   oo na-ii khaa-nd-aa   woo na-ĩĩ khaa-t-aa
                        He doesn't eat.
11)   oo ghar-wic h æ -g-aa   woo ghar-mæ̃ẽ hæ
                        He is in the house.
12)   is-d-i k-ii kimat hæ -g-iii   is-k-ii k-yaa kimat hæ
                        What is the price of this ?
13)   tuhãã-nuu k-ii caa-iidaa   aap-koo k-yaa caa-iye
                        What do you require ?
14)   mæ̃ẽ khaa-wãã   mæ̃ẽ khaa-ũũ
                        I should eat.

In the above examples, note the similarity in the case-number suffixes -aa and -ee in item 10, and in the initial question morpheme k- of Punjabi k-ii and Hindi k-yaa (what), in items 12 and 13. Some important differences appear in the morphophonemic realization of shared morphemes. Thus Punjabi -d- and Hindi -k- in item 12 represent the morpheme K also shown in item 5 above. Similarly, Punjabi -nd- and Hindi -t- in item 10 represent the same morpheme. The code differences can be symbolized by representational rules such as those illustrated below.

15) K^m / / P, —— / d $\tilde{u}\tilde{u}^m$/ / P, —— / $\tilde{a}\tilde{a}$
     ^{m} / / H, ——/ k ^{m}/ / H, —— / $\tilde{u}\tilde{u}$

P and H in this formula stand for Punjabi and Hindi respectively. The rule states that the morphemes K and $\tilde{u}\tilde{u}$ are realized morphophonemically as k and $\tilde{u}\tilde{u}$ in Hindi and as d and $\tilde{a}\tilde{a}$ in Punjabi. Similar relations hold between Hindi -koo and Punjabi -nuu; and Hindi -m$\tilde{æ}$ and Punjabi -wic (in).

In other cases the identity of rules on the morphophonemic level is reflected in differences when these rules are translated to the phonemic level. This is the case for Hindi woo and Punjabi oo (that, he). Because of their phonological similarity, and since within Hindi w- is lost within compounds such as j-oo (who) (see item 8 above), the two segments may be assigned the same morphophonemic transcription in both codes. The difference is then expressed in representational rules converting the morphophonemic into phonemic transcription:

16) oo^{mp} / / P,   # —— / oo
     mp / / H,   # —— / woo

This rule states that morphophonemic oo after juncture (#) is realized phonemically as oo in Punjabi and woo in Hindi.

On the phonological stratum, no differences in phonemic inventory were found in the code-switching styles. Punjabi tone, which occurs in items where Hindi equivalents have voiced aspirates, as in ghar (house), seems to be lost in code-switching situations, although it does occur in other contexts. Many of the phonetic

characteristics of Punjabi are also shared by Delhi Hindi. This is
the case with / æ / and / ɔ/ , which appear as monophthongs in
Delhi Hindi and diphthongs in Eastern Hindi. Similarly, / ṭ/ and / ḍ/
in Delhi Hindi share the extreme retroflexion of Punjabi, while in
Eastern Hindi retroflexion is less pronounced.

When we move from the code-switching situations into
others more specific to Punjabi-speaking groups, additional
differences appear at all strata resulting in an increase in the Hindi-
Punjabi language distance. On the morphemic level, thet Punjabi
adjectives have special endings to show agreement with oblique
plural nouns. Furthermore, the present participle allomorph -d-
changes to -n- with first person subjects. A locative suffix is added
to the class of number suffixes.

Some additional phonemic and morphophonemic differences
are illustrated by the thet alternates of items 11 and 12 above:

11a)   oo kár-wic hæ -g-aa
12a)   ed-d-ii k-ii páuu hæ-g-ii

Here, kár (house) and páuu (price) show rising tones. Furthermore,
in item 12a the Hindi-like pronominal oblique is- (this) is replaced
by ed-.

Other morphophonemic differences are brought in by
alternations in postpositions such as those listed below:

Hindi	Punjabi (Code-switching)	Punjabi (ṭheṭ)	
-se	-se	-t̃õõ	(from)
-saat	-saat	-nal	(with)

Lexical differences between thet and code-switching styles include
a high proportion of common adverbs of time, place and manner
and many frequently-used adjectives and nouns. Some examples are:

Hindi	Punjabi (Code-switching)	Punjabi (ṭheṭ)	
ab	ab	hun	(now)
idhar	idar	edar	(here)
itn-aa	itn-aa	enn-aa	(this much)
æs-e	æs-e	edd-aa	(like this)
acch-aa	acch-aa	cang-aa	(good)
dukaan	dukaan	haṭṭii	(store)

Aside from the ṭheṭ variations, additional alternations are possible
in certain extreme situations which reduce rather than increase
the Hindi-Punjabi language distance. These may be illustrated by
the following alternates for items 11, 13 and 14 above:

11b)   oo ghar-mæ̃ hæ-g-aa
13b)   aap-koo k-ii caaiye
14b)   mæ̃ khaa-ũ̆ũ̆

Note the substitution of mæ̃ for wic in item 11 and of aap-koo and
caaiye for tuhãã-nũ̆ũ̆ and caa-iidaa in item 13. In item 14 the
substitution of the suffix -ũ̆ũ̆ for -ãã makes the utterance identical
with Hindi. This utterance would be identified as Punjabi only if it
occurred as part of a larger one with definite Punjabi features.

One striking linguistic aspect of the code-switching
situation is the fact that we find few of the strictures against
structural borrowing commonly reported in the linguistic literature.
Interference extends to all levels of the grammar - morphemic,
morphophonemic and phonological - as well as to the lexicon. It
almost seems as if the two languages were gradually merging.
This situation differs little from what occurs in pidgins. At the
extremes of the stylistic continuum, only a few items, such as the
Punjabi verbal suffix -nd- and the Punjabi question word k-ii (what),
do not seem subject to borrowing. This evidently suffices to preserve the necessary minimum of symbols of role specificity.

Viewed from the point of view of social prestige, the linguistic status of the code-switching style is uncertain. Our principal informant considers it part of Punjabi. Older natives of Punjab, however, tend to dismiss it, representing it as an attempt of an ignorant person to speak Hindi. This seems unlikely, since as a bilingual our informant could easily have dropped the few markers which separate his Punjabi from his Hindi. We must assume that, deviant though it is, this style fills a definite social function in at least some situations.

Because of its lack of prestige and the disagreement regarding its status, the code-switching style may or may not be included in a descriptive grammar of Punjabi for which data has been collected without control of situation. Its inclusion depends on the choice of informant and on the way in which the interviews are conducted. Standard normative grammars will certainly not include it. Similarly, the informant, when questioned about Punjabi, will respond in terms of those situations which are specific to speakers of Punjabi. This should not be taken to mean that styles such as the code-switching style are unanalyzable by traditional linguistic methods. Such styles show the same kind of patterning found in other linguistic data and could be recovered if proper situational controls were used.

One other conclusion that emerges from this study concerns the problem of structural borrowings and the differences between pidgins and other languages. It would seem that the occurrence or non-occurrence of structural borrowings is not solely a matter of linguistic fact but is at least in part dependent on the existence of social norms which may act to filter them out of descriptive grammars. Similarly, the high incidence of what has been called "language mixture" in the case of pidgins may be explained by the absence of feelings of group loyalty or fluidity of social norms governing the situations in which pidgins are used.

BIBLIOGRAPHY

Bailey, T. Graham. Punjabi Grammar, in Punjabi Manual and Grammars (Languages Department, Punjab, India, Patiala, 1961).

Bruner, Edward M. "Primary Group Experience and the Processes of Acculturation", American Anthropologist, 58 (1956), 605-623.

Chomsky, Noam, "Some Methodological Remarks on Generative Grammar", Word, 17 (1961), 219-239.

Ervin, Susan M., and Osgood, C. E. "Second Language Learning and Bilingualism", in C. E. Osgood and T. A. Sebeok (eds.), Psycholinguistics. Journal of Abnormal & Social Psychology, Supplement, 1954.

Hymes, Dell H. "The Ethnography of Speaking", in Gladwin, Thomas, & W. C. Sturtevant (eds.), Anthropology and Human Behavior (Anthropological Society of Washington, D. C., 1962).

Lamb, Sidney M. Outline of Stratificational Grammar (University of California, ASUC Bookstore, 1962).

Nadel, S. F. The Theory of Social Structure (London, Cohen & West Ltd., 1957).

13 | The Relation of Linguistic to Social Categories

Recent empirical investigations in sociolinguistics have provided important evidence on the effect of extralinguistic influences on language behavior and language acquisition. It has been shown that both the structure and the stylistic aspects of messages can be affected by a variety of environmental, social and psychological conditioning factors (Cazden, 1965; Ervin-Trip, 1964; Ferguson, 1959; Ferguson and Gumperz, 1960). Although there is little controversy about the evidence itself, the more general question of the relationship between linguistic and social facts has hardly begun to be studied and it will be a long time before we can expect a sociolinguistic theory as explicit as the present theory of language. Nevertheless since data collection always involves a degree of selectivity, it is incumbent on any field manual to make clear at least some of the criteria which underlie the selection process. Failure to do so will seriously affect the comparability of the results. Specifically the following questions need clarification: (1) How is social information coded linguistically? (2) What are the mechanisms by which social categories affect the communication process?

1.   The Linguistic Coding of Social Information

The basic position with respect to the coding of social information was stated by Hymes (1962), who asserts that both language and language usage are structured and suggests that it is language usage rather than grammatical categories per se which most closely reflect social influences. This implies that from the sociolinguistic point of view every utterance has both social and referential meaning. The French sentence "asseyez-vous," for example, can be interpreted on one level as a request to the addressee to assume a sitting position, but it also implies something about the addressee's status vis-à-vis the speaker.

Even a brief look at the literature shows that features of any component or stratum of language structure may carry social meaning. Considerably more elaborate morphological status markers than the Franch can be found in Javanese (Geertz, 1960), Korean (Howell, 1967; Martin, 1964), and in many Asian languages. A possible English equivalent for the French "asseyez-vous" is the syntactic expression "won't you have a seat" (as contrasted with "sit down"). Other socially significant linguistic features include the suffix "-in" (Fischer, 1958), or purely phonological features such as the degree of "r-lessness" and the relative vowel height in the New York pronunciation of words like "sure" or "more" (Labov, 1964). In bilingual societies, as Rubin (1962) has shown, social information is conveyed by the switch from one language to another. In other societies social conditions may require the use of dramatic perform- ance styles rather than prose for the transmission of certain types of information (Gumperz, 1964).

Although social meanings may be coded almost anywhere within the linguistic system, they always require the existence of one or more referentially equivalent synonyms. It is the speaker's selection among these variables, as Labov (1964) has called them, which conveys social information.

There is furthermore an increasing amount of evidence for the assumption that social variation is not simply a matter of variation among isolated alternates, but that social markers occur in clusters such that selection of one of a particular set of alter- nates in one part of an utterance restricts the freedom of selection among subsequent sets. Thus, if an American shows social vari- ation among more or less diphthongized realizations of the vowel cluster / ay/ and also varies between "-ing" and "-in," selection of the less dipthongized vowel in "nice looking" also implies selection of the latter suffix variant. Social variation is thus governed by certain co-occurrence or co-variation constraints (Gumperz, 1964). Since, as Joos (1960) has pointed out, these re-

strictions cut across the usual components of language, we have
some justification for speaking of social variation as a selection
among codes rather than a choice among individual variants. Such
distinctions among social codes are most clearly marked in what we
commonly recognize as bilingual societies; but even in monolingual
societies, where codes are to a large extent isomorphic, co-
occurrence constraints do operate and may be important.

    For the purposes of this manual, it must further be pointed
out that co-occurrence restraints are not ordinarily part of linguistic analysis. Where they are recognized, their existence seems to
be assumed, rather than studied empirically. Since they have not
been studied, control of the rules that govern them is not ordinarily
regarded as part of the speaker's linguistic competence. A study
of communicative competence, in the broader sense, however,
must take account of such matters.

    In addition to the questions raised in the sections on
phonology and grammer, therefore, a study of language socialization
should raise linguistic questions such as the following:

      What is the degree of code differentiation and of internal
      language distance within the repertoire ?
      What is the nature of internal co-occurrence restrictions ?
      At what age does code differentiation appear ?
      When are co-occurrence rules learned ?
      What social conditions favor their learning ?

2. The Social Input to Sociolinguistic Rules

    Most scholars visualize the relationship of linguistic to
social categories as a match between closely connected but nevertheless conceptually independent systems. Language is regarded as
a set of rules enabling speakers to process information from the
outside world or to relate sounds to information. Social categories
are seen as part of this outside world, along with physical surroundings, artifacts, beliefs, etc. Just as concrete objects are identifiable through physical properties like shape, color, texture and

weight, which are subject to independent measurements, so social facts are conceived as measurable by social indices independent of the communication process. Sociolinguistics as seen in these terms, is an attempt to delineate social structure and linguistic structure more clearly by correlating these independently measured variables; and to detect changes in these structures through changes in the correlated measures. The sociolinguist might thus take sociologically determined indices such as social class, educational background, rank, performance on attitude tests and attempt to establish statistically significant correlations between these and verbal behavior. Or he might study verbal performances of populations differing on any of these indices.

Correlation between speech and social categories has been well documented by many decades of research in dialectology, bilingualism, and language contact studies. In recent years, they have been validated by highly sophisticated statistical techniques. Correlations are our only means of generalizing about the behavior of large populations, and they have been useful in predicting such phenomena as short-term trends in language history. But they also leave a number of questions unanswered. Why, for example, so some socially highly differentiated societies show almost no detectable linguistic variation, while there are others in which such variation is very pronounced? Why does sociolinguistic variation correlate with socioeconomic status in some societies, with educational background in some, and with cultural background in others?

Perhaps the most important criticism of the correlation approach to sociolinguistics derives from Bernstein's discussion of "restricted" and "elaborated" codes (Bernstein, 1964). The linguistic features which mark Bernstein's distinction roughly correlate with differences in class; but his sociological analysis demonstrates important differences in the norms or social rules underlying the informants' communicative behavior, differences which affect their perceptions of social relationships. Bernstein goes on to show that although restricted code speakers are more frequently found among the lower strata, they are also found in certain upper-class groups. There is no means of explaining such subcultural differences by a correlational method.

An approach to social theory which is somewhat more in line with sociolinguistic findings is the interactionist approach as exhibited in the writings of Goffman (1963), Garfinkel (1956), and Cicourel (1968). Interactionists deny the parallelism between social and physical measurement. They point out that information on social categories is obtainable only through the use of languages. Sociological measurement, in their view, always involves both the informant's and the investigator's perception of the categories that are being measured. This perception is seen as subject to the same culturally determined cognitive processes that ethnographic semanticists have discovered as operative in human naming behavior. Just as the meaning of words is always affected by context, social categories must be interpreted in terms of situational constraints.

Concepts such as status and role are thus not permanent qualities of speakers; instead, they become abstract communicative symbols, somewhat like phonemes and morphemes. Like the latter, they can be isolated in the analyst's abstract model, but they are always perceived in particular contexts. The division between linguistic and social categories is thus obliterated. Communication is seen as a two step process in which the speaker first takes in stimuli from the outside environment, evaluating and selecting from among them in the light of his own cultural background, personal history, and what he knows about his interlocutors, in order to decide on the social norms that apply to the situation at hand. These norms then determine the speaker's selection from among the communicative options available for encoding his intent.

In analyzing the factors entering into the selection of communicative signs, it is important to distinguish between the perceptual clues and background information that serve as the input to the selection process, and the actual stages that the analyst must postulate as part of his explanatory theory. The former are like the acoustic signals through which speech is identified as speech, whereas the latter are equivalent to the linguist's abstract grammatical categories. We assume that a speaker begins with a certain communicative intent, conscious or subconscious. He may want to ask

for something specific: a favor, some information, or he may want
to change the other's opinions or simply talk to be sociable. One
of his first steps is to determine what, if any, limitations the
environment imposes on his choice of interactional strategies. Each
culture classifies its surroundings into a finite set of discrete
categories (Blom and Gumperz, 1971), e.g., home, church, public
square, classroom, etc. Such settings, like color categories, are
determined both by universal and by culturally specific criteria
(Berlin and Kay, 1969) and thus vary from group to group. The
speaker must scan his environment to decide which of these classifications applies. Simultaneously, the speaker utilizes his
knowledge of his audiences and their possible social identities
(Goodenough, 1965) to determine what identity relationship to assume,
i.e., whether he can treat them as equals, inferiors, superiors,
casual acquaintances, colleagues, close friends, etc.

    The above three factors—knowledge of communicative intent,
setting, and possible identity relationships, in turn, enter into the
choice of speech events to be enacted.

    The speech event is probably the most general and most
abstract category of verbal interaction. Speech events are bounded
by certain opening and closing routines and are associated with rules
allocating speaking roles and constraining choice of overt topic, message form code or speech variety to be used, and ultimately, the
grammatical and lexical variables that can be used.

    Recent work in the ethnography of communication has illus-
trated cross cultural variation in the definition of speech events and
in the communicative uses they serve (Hymes, 1967; Gumperz, 1965;
Albert, 1964), and has discussed in detail component factors such as
those listed above. There has been less emphasis on the fact that
these factors do not act as independent variables. The selection
process is at least partially ordered so that social knowledge of environmental categories and of possible identity relationships serves
as input to decision making rules constraining choice of speech event
and of linguistic form in somewhat the same way that grammatical
rules constrain the phonetic realizations of linguistic forms.

It must be understood, of course, that selection never completely determines the actual form of a message. It merely restricts
the speaker's choice among possible alternative modes of expression.
Further selection among socially permitted alternates may then serve
as a vehicle for the expression of individual meaning.

From the point of view of fieldwork, the significance of the
interactional approach lies in the fact that social relationships and
social categorization of environment become the major social determinants of verbal behavior. Outside factors such as ecology, rank,
and educational background significantly affect verbal behavior only to
the extent that they influence speakers' perception of their social relationships. The study of rules governing these relationships in social
organization becomes an important part of the sociolinguist's task.

In practical terms this means that if the sociolinguist wishes
to achieve explanation, he cannot merely confine himself to comparisons of verbal performances with behavioral observation. He must
employ all the ethnographer's methods for arriving at the underlying
rules governing these performances. Important among these are
participant observation, preferably by actually living in the community, the recording of life and family histories, and deep unstructured
interviews focusing especially on family relations. Rules of etiquette
specifying what is regarded as appropriate conduct within the family,
with relatives, friends and neighbors, and outsiders must be determined

Perhaps the most important, yet so far relatively little used,
source of relevant data is the analysis of tape recorded natural conversation. The analyst can test his understanding of cultural norms
by utilizing the knowledge he has gained through conventional ethnographic methods in decoding the motivations that underlie speakers'
statements. He can then compare his own interpretation of what goes
on with that of community members reacting to the same tapes.
Moerman (1969) provides an interesting discussion of the limits of
ethnography based on examples of dispute analysis, using such procedures. Sociolinguistic analysis when based on these assumptions
can thus serve as a useful and replicable source of ethnographic insight.

BIBLIOGRAPHY

Albert, E. M. 1964. "Rhetoric," "logic," and "poetics" in Burundi:
    culture patterning of speech behavior. American Anthropolo-
    gist 66:6(2). 35-44.

Berlin, Brent, and Paul Kay. 1969. Basic color terms: their univer-
    sality and evolution. Berkeley: University of California Press.

Bernstein, Basil. 1964. Elaborated and restricted codes: their ori-
    gins and some consequences. American Anthropologist 66:
    6(2). 55-69.

Blom, Jan-Petter and John J. Gumperz. 1971. Social meaning in
    linguistic structures: code-switching in Norway. Directions
    in Sociolinguistics, ed. by John J. Gumperz and Dell Hymes.
    New York: Holt, Rinehart and Winston. [In this volume,
    pp. 271-307.]

Cazden, C. B. 1965. Environmental assistance to the child's acqui-
    sition of grammar. Ph.D. dissertation, Harvard University.

Cicourel, A. 1968. The social organization of juvenile justice. Un-
    published paper.

Ervin-Tripp, Susan. 1964. An analysis of the interaction of language,
    topic, and listener. American Anthropologist, 66:6(2). 86-
    102.

Ferguson, C. A. 1959. Diglossia. Word 15. 325-40.

_____ and John J. Gumperz (Eds.). 1960. Linguistic diversity
    in South Asia. Bloomington, Indiana: Research Center in
    Anthropology, Folklore and Linguistics.

Fischer, J. L. 1958. Social influences on the choice of a linguistic
    variant. Word 14. 47-56.

Garfinkel, H. 1956. Some sociological concepts and methods for
   psychiatrists. Psychiatric Research Reports 6. 181-95.

Geertz, C. 1960. Linguistic etiquette. The religion of Java, ed. by
   C. Geertz. Glencoe, Illinois: Free Press.

Goffman, E. 1963. Behavior in public places. Glencoe, Illinois:
   Free Press.

Goodenough, W. H. 1965. Rethinking "status" and "role": toward a
   general model of the cultural organization of social relationships. The relevance of models for social anthropology, ed.
   by M. Banton. New York: Praeger.

Gumperz, John J. 1964. Linguistic and social interation in two communities. American Anthropologist 66:6(2). 137-53. [In
   this volume, pp. 151-176.]

_____1965. Language. Biennial review of anthropology, ed. by
   B. J. Siegel, pp. 84-120. Stanford: Stanford University
   Press.

Howell, R. W. 1967. Linguistic choice as an index to social change.
   Ph.D. dissertation, University of California, Berkeley.

Hymes, D. H. 1962. The ethnography of speaking. Anthropology and
   human behavior, ed. by T. Gladwin and W. C. Sturtevant,
   pp. 13-53. Washington, D. C.: Anthropological Society of
   Washington.

_____1967. Models of the interaction of language and social set-
   ting. Journal of Social Issues 33:2. 8-28.

Joos, M. 1960. The isolation of styles. Monograph Series on Languages and Linguistics: No. 12. Washington, D. C.:
   Georgetown University Press.

Labov, W. 1964. Phonological correlates of social stratification. American Anthropologist 66:6(2). 164-76.

Martin, S. 1964. Speech levels and social structure in Japan and Korea. Language in culture and society: a reader in linguistics and anthropology, ed. by D. Hymes, pp. 407-13. New York: Harper and Row.

Moerman, M. 1969. A little knowledge. Cognitive Anthropology, ed. by S. Tyler. New York: Holt, Rinehart and Winston.

Rubin, J. 1962. Bilingualism in Paraguay. Anthropological Linguistics 1. 52-58.

14 | Communication in Multilingual Societies

No one would claim that there is a one-to-one relationship between languages and social systems, yet we continue to think of speech communities as discrete, culturally homogeneous groups whose members speak closely related varieties of a single language. To be sure, no human group of any permanence can exist without regular and frequent communication. But such communication does not necessarily imply monolingualism. Recent ethnographic literature deals increasingly with stable multilingual societies, where populations of widely different cultural and linguistic backgrounds live in close geographic proximity. They are subject to the same political authority, attend the same schools, exchange services and cooperate in many other respects. But they carry out their joint activities by means of not one, but a variety of languages. (Leach 1954, Salisbury 1962, Ferguson 1964, Rice 1962). A major contemporary linguistic problem is the description of the verbal skills involved in speakers' concurrent use of the languages used in such communities.

Whenever all members of such a community do not have equal facility in all the languages in use there, language choice is, of course, determined by requirements of intelligibility. But we also have evidence to show that a majority, or at least a significant minority of residents, can frequently communicate effectively in more than one language, and that they alternate among languages for much the same reasons that monolinguals select among styles of a single language (Rubin 1961; Fishman 1965). That is to say, the same social pressures which would lead a monolingual to change from colloquial to formal or technical styles may induce a bilingual to shift from one language to another. Where this is the case, the difference between monolingual and bilingual behavior thus lies in the linguistic coding of socially equivalent processes. In one instance speakers select among lexical or phonetic variants of what they regard as the same language; in the other case, speakers choose between what they view as two linguistic entities. We shall now inquire into the special verbal skills required by interlanguage shift and what differentiates them from the skills needed to shift among styles of the same language.

Since the classification of speech varieties as belonging to the same or different languages is in fact determined largely on socio-political grounds (Ferguson and Gumperz 1960), it can easily be shown that the purely qualitative distinction between monolingualism and bilingualism is by no means adequate to answer our question. Language pairs like Serbian and Croatian in Yugoslavia, Hindi and Urdu in India, Bokmal and Nynorsk in Norway, all of which have figured prominently in recent accounts of language conflict, are, for example, grammatically less distinct than some forms of upper- and lower-class English in New York. An individual who shifts from one member of such a pair to the other is bilingual in a social sense only. On the other hand, colloquial and literary varieties of Arabic would be regarded as separate languages were it not for the fact that modern Arabs insist on minimizing the differences between them. Thus speakers' views of language distinctions may depart considerably from linguistic reality.

Even when two speech varieties are obviously grammatically distinct, convergence resulting from language contact over time materially affects their distinctness. Scholars working in the Balkans where multilingualism has long been widespread, have frequently noted considerable overlaps in lexicon, phonology, morphology, and syntax among local varieties of Slavic and adjoining dialects of Greek, Rumanian, and Albanian. They also point out that these relationships are independent of historical relatedness (Sandfeld 1931).

The effect of convergence on the structure of languages is often questioned. Structural linguists have tended to criticize

writings on convergence on methodological grounds. Edward Sapir's
view that the grammatical core of a language is relatively immune
to diffusion is still widely accepted. Nevertheless, more recent,
structurally-oriented studies by Weinreich (1952) and Emeneau (1962)
reveal a number of clear instances of grammatical borrowings.
Such borrowings are particularly frequent in those cases where we
have evidence of widespread multilingualism.

Ethnographically oriented work on bilingual behavior
further shows that not all varieties of a language are equally affected.
Casual styles of either language tend to be less distant than more
formal varieties. Diebold, for example, finds that phonological
interference is greatest in code switching situations (1963). The
colloquial Canadian French expression, Pourquoi tu l'a fait pour?
cited by Mackey (1965) is a close translation equivalent of the
English, What have you done that for? John Macnamara cites a
similar example from rural dialects of Irish English, where sentences
such as I have it lost for I lost it can be explained as direct
translation equivalents of Gaelic. Both formal Canadian French
and educated Irish English avoid such translation equivalents.
Charles Ferguson (1964) in his discussion of diglossia——the use of
grammatically separate varieties among educated residents of
several societies——states that the varieties concerned in each
case constitute a single phonological structure, in spite of their
grammatical differences.

There is ample reason to suppose, therefore that whenever two or more languages are regularly employed within the
same social system, they differ significantly from the same
languages as spoken in separate social systems. They are grammatically more similar and at the same time show greater intralanguage
differentiation. Language distance is not a constant but varies with
the intensity and quality of internal communication. Any answer
to our question about the skills required in language switching
therefore requires empirical investigation by methods, which do
not depend on any prior assumption about linguistic or social
reality on the part of the analyst.

Measures of Language Distance

      Much of the linguistic research on bilingualism to date relies on measures of interference, "the use of elements from one language while speaking or writing another" (Mackey 1965). The usual procedure is to search the bilingual performance for features of pronunciation, grammar and lexicon not present in the monolingual standard, which can be attributed to second language influence. Interference analysis has provided important insights into the more general processes of borrowing (Weinreich 1953) and its effect on linguistic change. It also serves as an important tool in language pedagogy, where the object is to study what is involved in the monolinguals' learning of a new language and acculturating to a different monolingual community. Interference measurements of all kinds however assume that the structure of the standard is known and that speakers have direct access to the standard and seriously attempt to imitate it. These assumptions are justified for the ordinary second language learner or for isolated speakers of minority languages, whose significant contacts are largely with the surrounding monolingual community and who can thus be expected to conform to its norms. They do not however, apply in our case. Members of stable bilingual communities interact largely with other bilinguals and it can be shown that such interaction generates its own norms of correctness (Ervin-Tripp 1964). Although learning through prestige imitation takes place in all societies, the particular linguistic object of this imitation in bilingual societies must be established through empirical research; it cannot be assumed.

      A second technique of interlanguage comparison is that of contrastive analysis, which finds extensive application in the preparation of pedagogical language texts (Kufner 1962, Moulton 1962, Stockwell and others 1965). This method consists of a direct point by point comparison of the two systems at each component of structure. Differences are evaluated according to their place within the respective system (whether they are phonetic, phonemic, syntactic, and so forth). They are then counted under the assumption that "what the student has to learn equals the sum of the differences established by this comparison" (Banathy, Trager and Waddle 1966).

Prediction of the hierarchy of difficulties is thus based on the linguist's analysis of their structural importance. For example, the fact that in Spanish the segments [d] and [ð] are in complementary distribution, with the former occurring initially in words like dar and the latter medially in words like lado, whereas they contrast in English words like dare and there, may lead to the diagnosis that the Spanish-speaking student has the problem of assigning phonemic status to two phonetic entities which are allophones and not phonemes in his own language (Banathy, Trager and Waddle 1966). But the assignment of phonemic status to a linguistic feature is generally based on the performance of "ideal speakers living in a homogeneous community" (Chomsky 1965). Since bilingual speakers are excluded from consideration here, ordinary structural categories can hardly be used to predict bilingual performance.

The fact that bilingual communities show more than the usual amount of intralanguage diversity also raises some doubt about the carry-over of traditional elicitation techniques into fieldwork in bilingual situations. If the linguist, as is commonly done, simply seeks out individuals who speak both languages well and asks them to repeat utterances in the two languages, he is likely to elicit largely formal (maximally distinct) styles. Colloquial expression like the French and Irish expressions cited above are quite likely to be suppressed as unsuitable as long as speakers themselves perceive of the interview situations as a formal encounter. Since the rules of language choice are largely beyond conscious control, even repeated requests to speak and behave informally are not likely to produce the desired results.

If instead of starting with the a priori assumption that two languages are distinct, we take the opposite view and treat them as part of a single whole, many of the difficulties cited above can be avoided. This means that in his fieldwork the linguist would disregard the speaker's view of the languages as distinct entities, and treat them as part of the same linguistic repertoire (Gumperz 1964). The distinction between grammars and languages current in recent linguistic theory provides some justification for this approach. A grammar is a theoretical construct, a set of rules

which underlie verbal performance. A language consists of the
set of utterances generated by the grammar. Implicit in the notion
of grammar is the assumption that some rules are universal, that
is, characteristic of human behavior as a whole, and others are
language specific. If we say that grammars may show varying
degrees of relatedness we are only carrying this notion a little bit
further. We then assume that bilingual behavior reflects both an
underlying set of general rules which apply to the entire linguistic
repertoire and lower order non-shared language specific rules.
It is the task of linguistic analysis to discover the dividing line
between these two sets of rules.

Recent work on machine translation provides a technique
for accomplishing this, which enables the investigator to focus
directly on the relationship between two sets of texts without
requiring any a priori linguistic or social assumptions. In some
earlier work in machine translation, it had in fact been assumed
that grammatical information could be disregarded. But this
assumption was soon proved wrong when it was shown that grammatical analysis is the most efficient way of organizing the information
required for translation so as to fit into a computer's storage
capacity (Lamb 1965). If we then ask what is the minimum coding
necessary to translate the speaker's performance in Language A
to the same speaker's performance in Language B we must in
fact do a linguistic analysis. But note that a grammar in these
terms is merely an information storage device; it is not an
independently patterned organic entity. Its categories are justified
only to the extent that they facilitate the translation process. The
best solution is simply that which provides the simplest translation
rules. Since the greater the grammatical overlap, the easier the
translation process, it is simplest to assume that there is a single
underlying system from which the differences of the two languages
can be derived. Language distance can than be measured as a
function of the number of nonshared rules.

If translatability measures are based only on a single
set of texts, the number of grammatical rules needed will be an
arbitrarily restricted selection. But the greater the number of

speakers measured, and the greater the variety of contexts in
which the texts are collected, the more complete will be the body
of rules. Translatability measures thus are akin to sociological
forms of measurement in that they depend for their validity on
sample size and on interaction processes and are therefore ideally
suited for socio-linguistic analysis where interspeaker variation is
the central problem.

Case Studies

        During the last few years, we have experimented with
translatability measures in several societies. Although our results
are still preliminary, they are of sufficient general interest to
warrant reporting here. The following data collection procedure
was employed. Conversational texts in two languages were
collected from bilingual speakers interacting in natural settings.
Texts in Language A were then translated into Language B, and texts
in Language B were rendered into Language A, by a second group
of bilinguals. We were interested in determining the minimum
number of differences necessary for utterances to be perceived as
distinct languages by their speakers. Translations were therefore
edited to maximize the number of translation equivalents and
minimize the language distance without destroying grammatically
in either language. A third group of bilinguals was therefore asked
to check each translated text individually to judge its acceptability.

        A preliminary study of Hindi-Punjabi bilingual college
students in Delhi shows that both languages are analyzable in terms
of a common set of grammatical categories, (Pronouns, Adverbs,
Inflectional Patterns, and so forth) and in terms of identical rules
for their combination in sentence structures. They furthermore
have the same articulatory base. Texts in the two languages differ
only in the morphophonemic rules which determine the phonetic
shape of relevant words and affixes. Here is an extreme example
(morpheme boundaries are indicated by a dash, word boundaries

by a space. The following abbreviations are used in these and other examples: Lit. E: literal English; H: Hindi; P: Punjabi; M: Marathi; K: Kannada; T: tense; ADJ: adjective; ADV: adverb; AGR: agreement; AUX: auxiliary; DAT: dative; GEN: genitive; OBL: oblique; N: noun; NP: noun phrase; PN: pronoun; PP: post position; S: sentence; VS: verb stem; VP: verb phrase; PART: particle; PPL: participial suffix).

1. "He doesn't eat."

P	oo	naii	khaa-	nd-aa
	PN	ADV	VS	T AGR
H	woo	naĩ̃	khaa	t aaa
Lit. E	he	not	eat-ing	

2. "He is in the house."

P	oo	kar-	wic	hæ	g-aa	
	PN	N	PP	AUX	PART	AGR
H	woo	ghar	mẽẽ	hæ		
Lit. E	he	house	in	is		

Note that in the above sentences even content words such as 'eat' and 'house' are identical. Differences lie primarily in the function words (i.e., words referring to grammatical relations such as 'in') and inflectional endings. The position of these items within the sentence is the same in each case. Only the Punjabi particle g-aa in sentence 2 does not have a direct Hindi equivalent in that context. However g-aa does occur elsewhere in Hindi (Gumperz 1964a).

An even more striking example of linguistic overlap is found among bilingual speakers of Kannada and Marathi, two genetically unrelated languages belonging to the Dravidian and Indo-Aryan stocks, respectively. Our data on these languages was collected in the course of some three months' fieldwork in a village in Sangli district of Maharashtra State, India. The village is located about seven miles from the border of Mysore State in an area where, according to historical records, Kannada and Marathi have been in contact for more than a thousand years. Both languages possess a standard literature and both have, at one time or another, served as the administrative language of the area and the religious language for various groups there. Since 1955, when the present boundaries between Mysore and Maharashtra were established, Marathi has become the main literary language of the region and the sole medium of primary and secondary education.

Approximately 70 percent of the population of our village are native speakers of Kannada. The majority of these are members of the dominant Jain caste, a group of cultivators and entrepreneurs. A significant minority of Muslim village residents, furthermore, speak a form of Deccani Hindi. There is also a small community of lower caste speakers of Telugu. A sizable group of untouchables speaks only Marathi. The linguistic repertoire thus includes local dialects of Kannada, Marathi, Telugu and Deccani Hindi. Telugu and Hindi, however, are spoken only by their native speakers. Marathi, and to a slightly lesser degree Kannada, serve as media of intergroup communication. Literacy is relatively widespread in the village, and the Jains and other higher castes, whatever their native language, have a good command of standard Marathi. With the exception of a few Jain priests, however, no one can read or write Kannada.

Since we were fortunate enough to obtain lodging in a village home and to participate in many activities, we were able to record natural speech in a wide variety of styles varying from formal recitations to unguarded chatter. All texts were transcribed and analyzed in terms of grammatical categories suitable for serving as input data for the machine translation program devised by Douglas Johnson (1965) and based on the work of Sydney Lamb (1965). Here are some sample sentences along with constituent structure diagrams:

3. "We told about our poverty."

Lit. E	this	us	of	poverty		told		we
K	id	nəm	də	gəribstiti	heḷ	Ø	dew	nawr
M	he	am	cə	gəribstiti	sahgit	l	ə	ami

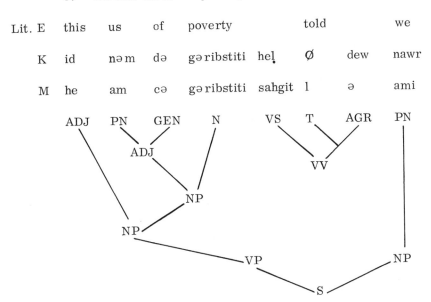

4. "I have a beedi (cigaret)."

Lit. E	me	of	near	beeḍi	is
K	nən	də	hatyag	biḍi	eti
M	majh	ə	jəwəḷ	biḍi	hay

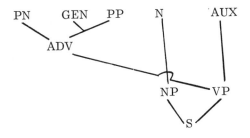

5. "I cut some greens and brought them."

Lit. E	greens	a little	having cut	having taken	[I] came
K	tepla	jera	khod i	tegond i bə	ø yn
M	pala	jera	kap un	ghe un a	l o

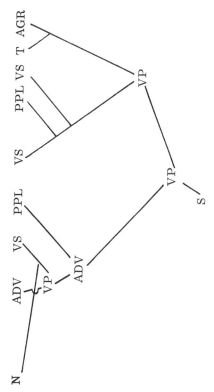

6. "He went some ten or twenty miles from here."

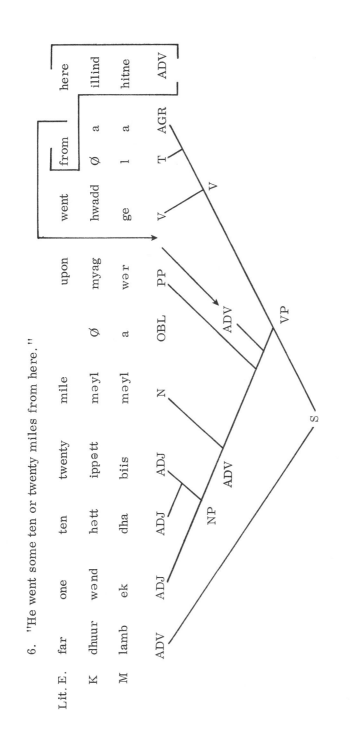

In contrast to the previous examples, the above sentences are lexically distinct in almost every respect. Yet they show identical grammatical categories and identical constituent structures. It is possible to translate from one to the other by a simple process of word for word or morph for morph substitution. The similarity is even more striking by comparison with the English which differs radically from the Indian languages, for example in the way in which possession in sentence five and the verbal action in sentence six are coded grammatically.

We were able to analyze our whole extensive corpus of bilingual texts without having to postulate grammatical categories or rules for one language which were not present in the other language. Independent phonetic perception tests further showed that native speakers were unable to keep the two languages apart on phonological grounds alone. The identity is furthermore not merely confined to grammatical form; it also extends to semantic domains relating to grammatical categories. Nouns in both languages appear in two numbers, singular and plural, and three case forms are oblique, one which carries little or no semantic load, a genitive and a dative which do. The local Kannada dialect has lost the objective case, which is characteristic of standard Kannada and of other Dravidian languages. There are two major gender-like categories: human and nonhuman. The latter is in turn subdivided into masculine and feminine. Here the local Marathi dialect seems to have lost the three gender distinction of standard Marathi by transferring all masculine and feminine nouns with nonhuman referents to the neuter category and thus merging with the Dravidian system.

The following lists of pronouns and common post-positions gives further evidence of the semantic identity of the two languages.

Pronouns:

M	K	E
mi	na	I
tu	ni	you (sing.)
apǝṇ	tan	reflexive
ami	nawr	we exclusive
apǝn	tawr	we inclusive
tumi	niwr	you (pl.)
hew	iiw	he, this one
tew	aw	he, that one
hi	iki	she, this one
he	id	it, this one
hyani	iwr	they (human)
kon	yar	who
kay	yan	what

Postpositions:

M	K	E
-la	-gi	to
-at	-ag	in
-mage	hindgi	behind
-wǝr	myag	on
-khali	tyag	under
-jǝwǝr	hǝtyag	near

Note that both languages share distinct reflexive and non-reflexive, inclusive and exclusive and proximate and nonproximate categories. Both pronouns and postpositions are furthermore exact translation equivalents, so that a Marathi item is always replaceable by its Kannada equivalent wherever it occurs.

It is interesting to note that, when examined separately by historical linguists specializing in South Asian languages, our texts are characterized as somewhat deviant but nevertheless easily identifiable specimens of Dravidian and Indo-Aryan, respectively. Genetic relationships among languages are established largely through a process of matching at the morphophonemic level. Since this is the area of structure where the two varieties differ most, it is not surprising that historical linguists in the past have failed to make systematic analyses of the underlying similarities.

To be bilingual in either Hindi-Punjabi or Kannada-Marathi——as these languages are spoken in our experimental community——a speaker simply needs to internalize two sets of terms for the same objects and grammatical relationships. He can switch from one language to the other by merely substituting one item in a pair for the other without having to learn any new grammatical rules other than the ones he already controls. If we contrast this form of bilingual communication with the rather complex selection among phonological, syntactic and lexical variables, which Labov's recent work in New York has revealed (1966), it seems clear that there are at least some circumstances where bilingualism may require less skills than the normal process of communication in some monolingual societies.

In evaluating the significance of the above data, it must be kept in mind, however, that our sample was somewhat biased when compared to what is normally understood as bilingual behavior. In attempting to see whether it is possible for one speaker to speak two languages using the same set of grammatical categories, we confined ourselves only to those speech varieties which are regularly used in bilingual interaction. If we take into account literary varieties or varieties used in religious ritual and other activities that are language specific, a number of new differences arise. In more formal Punjabi, for example, we would have to account for word tone at the phonetic level and for additional differences in lexicon and in the system of function words (Gumperz 1964b). In educated Marathi and Kannada, even when it is used among Marathi-Kannada bilinguals, differences in gender and in rules governing adjective-noun agreement not found in casual village speech will arise. Since the linguist's grammars rely heavily on educated speech, contrastive analysis based on these grammars will show considerably more language distance than our data reveal. The formal varieties concerned, however, are learned primarily through formal education; not all members learn them equally well. Translatability measures can account for this by successively sampling different groups of speakers in different settings. However, as we said before, language distance when measured in this way is not a constant. It varies both with social context and social class.

Because of the special circumstances of long and continuous contact between speakers of the languages concerned, our Indian examples are not likely to have too many parallels elsewhere. More recent work among Spanish-English bilinguals in New York shows somewhat different results. The two languages in this case are quite distinct phonetically. There are further more obvious differences in syntax. Where, for example, Spanish distinguishes between two verbs of "being" ser and estar, English has only one.

In the realm of verb tenses, Spanish has a number of special subjunctive forms and an inflected future which do not occur in English. It is interesting to note though that in the conversational speech of the uneducated the inflected future is dropped in sentences like "I will write" in favor of the periphrastic construction which, like the English, is formed with the verb ir "go" as the auxiliary. Similarly the only subjunctive form which occurs with any frequency is the conditional which serves as the direct translation equivalent of English constructions with "would." Social interaction seems to lead to increased translatability also with English and Spanish.

On the whole, however, the speech of the Spanish-English bilingual in New York approaches our usual image of bilingual behavior. In spite of some overlap, the systems concerned are distinct in every component. Nevertheless, even in this case, the translatability approach raises some new questions about the nature of bilingual skills. To give a phonological example, much of the difference between the two languages results from the presence in one language of articulations not occurring in the other. Thus

Spanish lacks the [š] of English <u>shoe</u> and English lacks the [ñ] of
Spanish <u>baño</u>. Further distinctions however emerge when we compare
the articulation of phonetically equivalent words. Thus the word
photo will be [fowtow] in English and [foto] in Spanish in the same
speaker's pronunciation. Whereas in Marathi-Kannada such pairs
would be undistinguishable. Spanish-English bilinguals maintain two
parallel sets of phonetically similar articulation ranges corresponding
to functionally equivalent phones.

It would seem that the necessity of keeping the above ranges
separate is an important problem in Spanish-English code switching.
Comparison of the formal speech of educated bilinguals with that of
uneducated bilinguals or with the same speakers in informal speech
shows in fact that these distinctions are frequently collapsed.

Some General Features of Bilingualism

Different as the above bilingual situations are, they nevertheless share certain common characteristics. All repertoires
maintain an unusually large number of variants at the morphophonemic
level. In actual sentences, moreover, the variants never appear in
all combinations. Regardless of how large or small the number of
nonshared rules, however, differences in the phonological realizations
of morphemes play an important part. Even in Hindi-Punjabi where
the list frequency of differences is relatively low, differences are
very noticeable because they affect affixes and common function
words with high text frequency. Variants furthermore never occur
in isolation, but in co-occurrent patterns, so that if a Hindi-Punjabi
bilingual begins a sentence with <u>oo</u> "he," he must also use the
participle affix <u>-nd-</u>. The alternate affix <u>-t-</u> does not co-occur
with <u>oo.</u> The rigidity of such co-occurrence rules reinforces the
perceptual distinctness of codes. In spite of the underlying grammatical similarities, therefore, the shift between codes has a quality of
abruptness which to some extent accounts for the speaker's view
of them as distinct languages. Such codes seem ideally suited for
communication in societies which stress cultural distinctions, while
at the same time requiring regular and frequent interaction. In

stylistic switching, co-occurrence rules also exist, but they seem less strictly defined, and transitions between styles are more subtle. Stylistic variation, furthermore, is signaled less by morphophonemic distinctions than by differences at the lexical level.

Conclusion

Our listing of the variant linguistic correlates of bilingualism was intended to be suggestive rather than exhaustive. Nevertheless the view that language distance is a function of social interaction and social context raises some interesting general problems. The common view that multilingualism, wherever it occurs, also reflects deep social cleavages is clearly in need of revision. If we wish to understand the social significance of language behavior, we must go beyond popular language names and simple language usage statistics. Furthermore, if in spite of surface appearances, as our Indian examples indicate, language is not necessarily a serious barrier to communication, why do such differences maintain themselves over long periods of time? What is it within the system of roles and statuses or in the norms of social interaction that favors the retention of such overt symbols of distinctness? Under what conditions do such symbols disappear?

Of more direct practical value is the question of the relative importance of social and language barriers to communication. Intralanguage variation clearly plays an important part in bilingual behavior, and measures of bilingual competence must account for it if they are to be socially realistic. Furthermore, the common assumption that uneducated speakers of minority languages learn better when instructed through the medium of their own vernacular is not necessarily always justified. Instructional materials in these vernaculars may rely on monolingual norms which are culturally quite alien to the student and linguistically different from his home speech. Considerably more research is needed on these and similar questions. We hope that our discussion highlights the importance of ethnographically oriented linguistic measurement in this task.

NOTE

The research reported herein was supported by grants from the National Science Foundation, Division of Social Science, and from the U.S. Office of Education. Thanks are due to Joshua A. Fishman and Roxana Ma for assistance and criticism. This paper is an expansion and revision of a previous paper: "On the Linguistic Markers of Bilingual Communication," The Journal of Social Issues, 1967, 23:48-57.

REFERENCES

Banathy, Bela, Trager, Edith, and Waddle, Carl D. 1966. The use of contrastive data in foreign language course development, pp. 35-56. In A. Valdman, ed., Trends in language teaching. New York, McGraw-Hill.

Chomsky, Noam. 1965. Aspects of the theory of syntax. Cambridge, MIT Press.

Ervin-Tripp, Susan. 1964. An analysis of the interaction of language, topic and listener. In John J. Gumperz and Dell Humes, eds., The ethnography of communication, American Anthropologist: 66, (6), Part 2:86-102.

Ferguson, Charles A., Gumperz, John J. 1960. Introduction. In Linguistic diversity in South Asia. Indiana University Publications in Anthropology, Folklore and Linguistics, 1960, Publication 13.

Ferguson, Charles A. 1964. Diglossia. In Dell Hymes, ed., Language in culture and society, pp. 429-439, New York, Harper.

Fishman, Joshua A. 1965. Who speaks what language to whom and when. La Linguistique, 2:67-88.

Gumperz, John J. 1964a. Linguistic and social interaction in two communities. In John J. Gumperz and Dell Hymes, eds., The ethnography of communication. American Anthropologist, 66 (6), Part 2:137-153. [In this volume, pp. 151-176.]

_____ 1964b. Hindi-Punjabi code-switching in Delhi. pp. 1115-1124. In Horace Lunt, ed., Proceedings of the ninth international congress of linguists. The Hague, Mouton. [In this volume, pp. 204-218.]

Johnson, Douglas. 1965. Memorandum on morphologies. Machine translation project. Berkeley, University of California. (Mimeograph).

Kufner, Herbert L. 1962. The grammatical structures of English and German. Chicago, University of Chicago Press.

Lamb, Sydney. 1965. The nature of the machine translation problem. Journal of Verbal Learning and Verbal Behavior, 4:196-210.

Leach, Edmond. 1954. Political systems of highland Burma. London, Harvard University Press.

Mackey, William F. 1965. Bilingual interference: its analysis and measurement. Journal of Communication, 15:239-249.

Moulton, William G. 1962. The sounds of English and German. Chicago, University of Chicago Press.

Rice, Frank A. 1962. Study of the role of second languages. Washington, D. C., Center for Applied Linguistics.

Rubin, Joan. 1961. Bilingualism in Paraguay. Anthropological Linguistics, 4:52-58.

Salisbury, Richard. 1962. Notes on bilingualism and linguistic change. Anthropological Linguistics, 4:1-13.

Sandfeld, K. 1930. Linguistique Balkanique. In Collection Linguistique de La Societé de Linguistique de Paris, 31.

Stewart, William. 1962. Functional distribution of Creole and French in Haiti. In E. P. Woodworth and R. J. DiPietro, eds., Linguistics and Language Study Monograph No. 15. Washington, D. C., Georgetown University.

Stockwell, Robert P., Bowen, J. Donald, and Martin, John W. 1965. The grammatical structures of English and Spanish. Chicago, University of Chicago Press.

Stockwell, Robert P., Bowen, J. Donald. 1965. The sounds of English and Spanish. Chicago, University of Chicago Press.

Weinreich, Uriel. 1953. Languages in contact. New York, Linguistic Circle.

15 | Convergence and Creolization: A Case from the Indo-Aryan/Dravidian Border in India

In Collaboration with Robert Wilson

Historical linguists frequently point to bilingualism as a major determinant of language convergence. It is assumed that the greater the number of individuals who control two or more of the varieties spoken in a linguistically heterogeneous region and who use them alternatively in the course of their daily routine, the greater the likelihood that features from one system will diffuse into another. Studies of such diffusion processes during the last few decades have revealed some striking cases of grammatical borrowing among otherwise unrelated languages, both in India and elsewhere around the world. Although lexical items are by far the most frequently borrowed, it seems clear that borrowing extends to all aspects of the grammatical systems. As Weinreich (1952) points out: 'language contact can result in such far reaching changes that the affected language assumes a different structural type'. There seems to be no reason therefore to draw an a priori distinction among pidginization, creolization and other diffusion processes; the difference may be merely one of degree.

Students of bilingualism and language contact so far, have concentrated primarily on the end effects of these diffusion processes. There has been almost no direct investigation of the actual mechanisms involved. The principal goal has been to explain the historical origin of particular items of lexicon, phonology or grammar. To this end texts or interview material in a given language are searched for deviant features. If these features cannot be explained on the basis of normal intra-language change and show similarities to a language with which the first is in contact, the deviant features are said to be the result of convergence. It is assumed, however, that the varieties involved are distinct systems and that apart from the convergent feature they will remain distinct.

The present paper takes a somewhat different approach. Rather than concerning ourselves with the historical origin of deviant features, we focus on interacting social groups, as they alternate among varieties in their linguistic repertoire (Gumperz 1964) in the course of natural conversation. The data derives from a study designed to specify some of the linguistic skills involved in this code-switching process. A model, based on recent work in machine translation, was constructed to simulate the operations performed by speakers in converting from one code into another (Gumperz 1967). In the present paper the local varieties are compared with the varieties of the standard language that are also used in the village. Our concern is essentially ethnographic, rather than historical: analytic, rather than normative. We start with the local varieties LV_1 and LV_2 and compare the corresponding St_1 and St_2 to them, rather than the reverse. Furthermore, we match sentences drawn from natural conversations rather than isolated forms. This procedure brings out similarities as well as differences and provides better insight into communication processes. We can of course lay no claim to reconstructing exactly what has happened. Our goal is to elucidate the sociolinguistic nature of the convergence processes.

Sociolinguistic setting

Kupwar village is located in Sangli district, Maharashtra, approximately seven miles north of the Mysore border. It has a population of 3,000 and four languages. Village lands are controlled largely by two land-owning and cultivating groups, Kannada-speaking Jains, who form the majority, and Urdu-speaking Muslims. There are furthermore, large contingents of Kannada-speaking Lingayats—largely craftsmen, Marathi-speaking untouchables and other landless laborers, as well as some Telugu-speaking rope makers.[1]

As Indian villages go, Kupwar is well integrated into the regional communication system. Sangli, the district capital, where Marathi is the dominant language, is only three miles away by a fairly good unpaved road. Kupwar has both a primary school and a junior high school, the latter founded and controlled by local Jains. Village milk and produce are regularly sold on the Sangli market. A number

of village leaders have been prominent in regional Congress politics
ever since the days of Indian independence and many Jain and Muslim
families have members who hold relatively high positions in State
service.

Marathi is the principal literary language. It is also spoken
in the neighboring urban bazaars as well as in many surrounding villages. In Sangli there is an Urdu medium high school controlled by
Muslims, but very few villagers attend it. With increasing education
during the last twenty years, literary forms of Marathi and Urdu
have become better known in the village. They are used in written
communication and increasingly also in conversation with educated
visitors. Although we have no exact figures literacy is almost certainly above the national average. Those who are literate tend to be
literate primarily in Marathi and secondarily in one of the several
varieties of Hindi-Urdu or in English. Only one or two Jain priests
read Kannada although Kannada is taught in schools across the Mysore
border, where many local residents have close relatives.

As far as can be determined, almost all local men are bi-
or multi-lingual. Marathi serves as the main local medium of intergroup communication. Jains, for example, use it in talking to their
Muslim or untouchable field hands. We furthermore have recorded
conversations where Jains discussing business affairs seem to be
switching freely between Kannada and Marathi.

There is every indication that the Kannada-speaking Jain
cultivators and the Marathi-speaking service castes have both been
in the region for more than six centuries. The Urdu-speaking Muslims date from the days of the Mughal domination three or four centuries ago. Bilingualism in Kupwar is therefore a long standing tradition. Why has it been maintained for so long? Why has regular and
frequent interaction among local residents not led to the 'triumph' of
one language?

Information obtained from living in the village over a period
of several months suggests that the major factor in language maintenance is that the local norms or values require strict separation be-

tween public and private (intra-kin group) spheres of activity. There is considerable interaction with members of other groups at work and in the public areas of the village, but a person's home is pretty much reserved for the members of his extended family and for close friends who tend also to be close relatives. Village residences are distributed in such a way that each major caste or group of castes such as the Jains, Muslims, Lingayats, Untouchables has its own neighborhood. During our residence in a village Jain home we observed few if any non-Jain visitors. Those strangers who did visit could immediately be distinguished from relatives by their stiff and somewhat distant demeanor. The separateness of the home environment and of the home-group is symbolized in dress and posture as well as in language. Speech in the home, especially speech to women and children, is exclusively in the home-group language.

There are also some communication situations outside the home in which code-switching is not common and in which only one language is appropriate. Religious rituals for Kannada speakers, for example, are conducted in Kannada, and for Marathi speakers in Marathi.

When a Kannada-speaking Jain employs Urdu and Marathi speakers in his work group, all three local varieties of these languages may be heard. Now, there is little reason to doubt that his non-Jain co-residents would understand directions given in Kannada. The extensive bilingualism among men and the intertranslability that has come about (see below) indicate as much. For the Jain to address one of these others in Kannada, however, would be tantamount to saying, I consider you a potential member of my home and friendship group. Marathi, the normal language for intergroup contact, does not carry such a connotation in work situations, and is therefore preferred in them. The fact that Marathi is not the home language of the vast majority of local residents, nor of either socially dominant group, makes it socially neutral. As long as ethnic separateness of home life is valued, then, and language remains associated with ethnic separateness, there is little reason to expect multilingualism to disappear.

Intertranslatability

The constant code-switching required by the daily interaction routine has had some far reaching effects on local grammatical systems. When considered alone, to be sure, each local variety seems distinct. A historical linguist would readily identify particular texts as from a deviant dialect of Kannada, Marathi or Urdu. What would be missed is that sentence-by-sentence comparison of natural conversation texts in all three main local varieties reveals an extraordinary degree of translatability from one local utterance to the other. This translatability can be illustrated by the following example, which is taken from a corpus of almost 10,000 words of text tape recorded in natural settings during a three-month period.[2]

(I) 'I cut some greens and brought them.'

a. KuU	pala	jera	kaṭ	ke	le	ke	a	∅	ya
b. KuM	pala	jera	kap	un	ghe	un	a	l	o
c. KuK	tapla	jera	khod	i	təgond	i	bə	∅	yn
	greens	a little	having	cut	having	taken		/I/	came

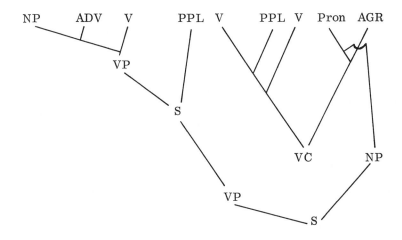

The sentences in this example are lexically distinct in almost every respect, yet they have identical grammatical categories and identical constituent structures (as shown in the rough constituent structure diagram above). It is possible to translate one sentence into the other by simple morph for morph substitution. Contrast the way in which predication is expressed in the English translation to the equivalent expressions in the three Indian languages. English is historically related to Indo-Aryan Marathi and Urdu and Kannada is not, but English is nevertheless radically different, and in the same way, from all three local varieties. So great is the similarity among Ku grammatical structures that we were able to analyse an extensive corpus of bilingual texts involving all three local varieties without having to postulate syntactic categories or rules for one language which were not present in the other language. We may say, therefore, that the codes used in code-switching situations in Kupwar have a single syntactic surface structure.

Work still in progress further indicates that the three local varieties are also identical in phonetics although they have different morphophonemic rules (Gumperz 1967). What seems to have happened in these informal varieties is a gradual adaptation of grammatical differences to the point that only morphophonemic differences (differences of lexical shape) remain.

Convergent changes

The co-existence within the same community of standard varieties not directly affected by convergence along with maximally similar local varieties presents a special opportunity to examine changes generated by code-switching.

The remainder of this paper will examine the most important of these changes as they are revealed in the syntax and semantic structure of Ku varieties. The emphasis will be on KuU since it has changed most radically. Relevant features of the standard languages will be discussed first, followed by Ku equivalents.

Gender

Urdu nouns and pronouns fall into two gender classes: masculine and feminine. Gender classification of nouns is based on (a) the phonological shape of plural suffix allomorphs, and (b) agreement markers (A) occurring in subject-verb constructions and elsewhere, which will be discussed further below. Most, but by no means all, animate nouns denoting females are feminine, and most nouns denoting males are masculine. Inanimate nouns are predictably assigned to either gender. Moreover, the masculine category is unmarked since it occurs in constructions where gender is otherwise unspecified or where agreement is blocked by syntactic rules. Urdu gender is therefore a syntactic category in spite of the fact that there is some correlation with sex. Marathi also has grammatical gender defined by similar criteria. There are, however, three gender categories: masculine, feminine and neuter, of which the latter is unmarked.

Kannada nouns fall into three gender-like classes characterized by the shape of plural suffix allomorphs and by agreement markers. Kannada gender, however, is semantically determined. All nouns denoting male humans are masculine, all nouns denoting female humans are feminine and all other animate and inanimate nouns are neuter.

The Ku gender systems are semantically based and closely resemble that of Kannada. KuK is identical with K. In KuM non-human nouns which correspond to M masculines or feminines appear as neuter. Only human males are masculine and human females feminine. The system has therefore become isomorphic with KuK and K. In KuU all U non-human nouns are merged into the unmarked masculine, so that only human females remain as a special gender category. Thus both KuM and KuU have enlarged their unmarked category, so as to make the remainder (one category, feminine, in Urdu; two categories, masculine and feminine, in Marathi) semantically determined, as are all gender categories in KuK.

(2) 'There was a flood'

a.	HU	wǝhã	nǝdii	a-ii
b.	KuU	hwa	nǝdi	ay-a
c.	KuM	tith	nǝdi	al-ǝ
d.	KuK	yǝlli	hwǝLi	bǝt tu
		there	river	came

Note that in HU the noun nǝdii takes feminine agreement -ii, KuU has the unmarked masculine agreement marker -a, and KuM the neuter marker -ǝ.

Agreement

HU verb constructions of the structure Vb-T-A Aux-T-A, containing a verb stem (Vb) inflected for tense (T) followed by a tense-inflected auxiliary (Aux) show agreement (A) in two positions. In all Ku varieties as in K there is only one agreement marker which occurs at the end of the verb phrase: Vb-T Aux-T-A.

(3) 'He went to graze the buffalo'

a.	HU	wo	[bhæs	cǝrane – ke	liye]	gǝya	th – a
b.	KuU	o	gǝe	t – a	[bhæs	carn – e – ko]	
c.	KuM	tew	gel	hot – a	[mhæs	car – ay la]	
d.	KuK	aw	hog	id – a	[yǝmmi	mes – ∅ – k]	
		he	go	past (A)	[buffalo	graze (obl) to]	

The verb complement phrase ['to graze the buffalo'] is included here primarily for the sake of meaning. In the text it is preceded by a slight pause and appears to be phonologically separate from the first. Note how KuU follows the common Ku work order (Subject Verb Phrase Complement) and thus contrasts with the normal HU order (Subject Complement Verb Phrase).

In HU the past auxiliary ('were') is marked for gender but not for person. KuU seems to have restructured the gender agreement into person agreement in this case.

(4) 'Where did you go'

a.	HU	kəhã̃	gə-ya	th-a	tu	(to a man)
			gə-ii	th-ii	tu	(to a woman)
b.	KuU	khã̃	gəe	te	tu	
c.	KuM	kəṭṭə	gel	hotas	twa	
d.	KuK	yəlli	hog	idi	ni	
		where	gone	were	you	

Note the KuU form <u>te</u> in agreement with the second person <u>tu</u> which contrasts with KuU <u>ta</u> in <u>o gəe ta</u> 'he was gone'.

In constructions of the type Vb Tp A the U future verb constructions show person agreement (Tp) where K has only the invariable tense marker. KuU in this case again follows K, as shown in the example below.

(5) 'I'll go tomorrow'

a.	HU	məy	kəl	ja	-ũg-	a	(man
					. . .	ii	(woman)
b.	KuU	məy	kəl	jya	-ẽg-	a	(man or woman)

Note the U first person future marker -<u>ug</u>- where KuU has invariable future marker -<u>ẽg</u>-.

In HU and in M in a sentence of the structure NP_1 NP_2 VP, if the verb is transitive and in the past tense, then NP_2 takes an agentive post-position (HU -<u>ne</u>, Marathi -<u>nə</u> or <u>ni</u> or zero). When NP_2 is human it takes the dative suffix and NP-VP agreement is blocked (i.e. the VP has no grammatical subject with which to show agreement). If NP_2 is not human, VP shows agreement with NP_2. In K, as elsewhere in Dravidian languages, the VP in NP_1 NP_2 VP constructions uniformly show agreement with NP_1 (when agreement mar-

kers are permitted by syntactic rules) regardless of the tense or
transitivity of the verb. KuU and KuM again follow K in this case.

(6) 'Hey, fellow, did you sell the mare'

a.	HU	kya	bhaii	ghoṛii	beč dii	kya
b.	KuU	kya	baba	ghoṛi	di-ya	kya
c.	KuM	kay	baba	ghoṛi	dil-as	kay
d.	KuK	yan	əppa	kudri	kwaṭṭ-i	yan
		what	fellow	horse	gave - you	what

The NP$_1$ is the optional pronoun 'you' which is deleted here. Note that
the HU verb shows agreement with NP$_2$ ghoṛii, while all Ku verbs
agree with the second person pronoun tu, as would be the case in K.

In HU variable adjectives, demonstratives, possessive forms
of pronouns and modifier constructions consisting of noun plus genitive
post-position all show agreement with the case number and gender of
the noun head. In K as well as in all Ku varieties this type of agreement does not occur. The relevant KuU forms show masculine suffix
allomorphs while KuM forms have neuter endings.

(7) 'The mare which was sent to the cultivated fields'

a.	HU	bag mẽ	dii huii	ghoṛii
b.	KuU	bag-mi	dieso	ghoṛi
c.	KuM	maḷi-aa	dilvaḷə	ghoṛi
d.	KuK	maḷi-ay	kwattind	kudri
		garden in	given	mare

Pronominal and Adjectival Use of Possessives and Demonstratives

In all languages concerned, demonstratives or possessives
may occur either as noun modifiers or in predicate position. In K as

in other Dravidian languages forms in predicate position show a
nominalizing suffix. In all Ku dialects, as in HU and Marathi, there
is no phonological difference between forms occurring in the two positions.

(8) 'This house is yours'   'This is your house'

a. K	ii	mǝne	nim-dǝ		i-du	nim	mǝnǝ	
b. KuK	id	mǝni	nim-d	eti	id	nim-d	mǝni	eti
c. KuM	he	ghǝr	tumc-ǝ	hay	he	tumc-ǝ	ghǝr	hay
d. KuU	ye	ghǝr	tumhar-a	hǝy	ye	tumhar-ǝ	ghǝr	hǝy
	this-one	house	yours	is	this-one	your	house	is

Note that in KuK it is the predicate form that is generalized and not
the adjectival form.

Dative and Accusative Post-Positions

          Standard Kannada along with other Dravidian languages has
a special accusative post-position contrasting with the dative. HU
and M both show only dative post-positions for a human object in sentences like those below. Ku dialects including KuK follow Urdu and
Marathi. This accusative post-position can on occasion be elicited
in Kupwar, but it is always substitutable with the dative.

(9) 'Seeing the poor man, he gave'

a.	HU	gǝriib	admi-ko	dekh-kǝr	diy-a	th-a
b.	KuU	gǝrib	manus-ko	dekh ke	die	ta
c.	KuM	gǝrib	mansa-la	bǝg un	dil	hota
d.	KuK	gǝrib	mansya-gǝ	noḍ i	kwaṭṭ	ida
		poor	man - to	having seen	he gave	

Non-Finite VP's and Compound Verbs

Standard Marathi and Kannada and other Dravidian languages have a non-finite verb form which we can call the past non-finite. It is used in two different types of sentence constructions which are sometimes difficult to distinguish. One is the very common pan-Indian sentence with one or more non-finite verb phrases ended by a finite verb phrase (e.g. 'Having done the work, having eaten, I'll go home.'); the other is the verb phrase ending with a compound verb, which serves about the same function as prefixing does in Indo-European languages. Compound verbs differ from the former type of construction because only a very small class of verbs can serve as the second (i.e. compounding) element.

Urdu has different verb forms here. In KuU, as in the other Kupwar languages, the past non-finite is usually used for both types of construction, as stated above for Marathi and Kannada.

(10) 'I cut some greens and brought them'

a.	HU	pala	jəra	kaṭ-kər	le a-ya
b.	KuU	pala	jəra	kaṭ ke	le - ke a-ya
c.	KuM	pala	jəra	kap un	ghe - un al-o
d.	KuK	təpla	jəra	khod i	təgond-i bə-yn
		leaves	a few	having cut	taking (I) came

Copula Constructions

In HU and M both 'NP - is - NP' constructions like 'That is a table' and 'NP exists' constructions like 'Is the table here?' contain a copula 'is'. In standard Kannada as in other Dravidian languages NP-NP constructions contain no copula. In 'NP exists' constructions there is a form of 'be'.

(11) 'Your house is big'

a.	HU	tumhar-a	ghər	bəɽ-a	hay
b.	K	nim	mæne	doḍdu	
c.	KuU	tumhara	ghər	beḍa	hay
d.	KuM	tumcə	ghər	moʈhə	hay
e.	KuK	nimd	mæni	dwædd	eti
		your	house	big	is

All Ku varieties including KuK show the HU, M pattern.

The Subordinating Conjunction ki and its Syntax

In Urdu and Marathi, direct quotations and quotations of
questions are introduced by the subordinating conjunction ki 'that' as
follows:

S₁	ki	S₂	He said	that	'I'm going now'
			I don't know		that 'Where is he?'

In Kannada the order in introducing quotations is the reverse
of that described above, and the conjoining element is a form of the
verb 'say':

S₂ conj S₁ 'I'm going now' so saying he said.

All Ku varieties show the HU, M pattern.

(12) 'Tell (us) where you went yesterday'

a.	HU	bol-o	ki	kəhã	gəy-a	tha	kəl
b.	KuU	bol o	ki	khã	gəe	te	kəl
c.	KuM	sang a	ki	kuʈʈə	gel	hota	kal
d.	KuK	heḷ ri	ki	yəlli	hog	idi	ninni
		tell	that	where	did (you)	go	yesterday

Interrogative Verbal Suffixes

    HU and Marathi form 'yes or no' questions with the interro-
gative 'what'. Kannada has a verb suffix -a which forms 'yes or no'
questions. In U 'what' can occur in several positions in the verb
construction. In Marathi 'what' is always final. All Ku dialects
(a) have 'what' and (b) have it in final position as in Marathi. Kupwar
Kannada speakers reject the -a suffix as ungrammatical.

(13) 'Did you sell the horse'

a.	HU	kya	ghorii	dii
b.	KuU	ghodi	di ya	kya
c.	KuM	ghodi	dil əs	kay
d.	KuK	kudri	kwatt i	yan
		the horse	gave (you)	what ?

Some Instances of Semantic Change

    In Marathi and Kannada the general meaning of V plus oblique
plus dative is 'for doing—in order to do—.' HU would use V plus
oblique plus ke liye in equivalent constructions. KuU follows M and
K here.

(14) 'He went to graze the buffalo'

a.	HU	wo	bhəys	car-n-e	ke	liye gəy-a
b.	KuU	o	gəe	ta	bhəys	car ne ko
c.	KuM	tew	gel	hota	mhays	car-ay-la
d.	KuK	aũ	hog	ida	yəmmi	mes ka
		he	go	did	buffalo	graze to

    In Marathi and Kannada the present verb stem plus genitive
suffix is used as a noun modifier. In HU this construction occurs as

a noun modifier and in negative constructions of the 'should not' type. KuU forms are structurally identical with KuM and KuK and follow Marathi and Kannada.

(15) 'What should (you) do'

a.	HU	kya	kərna		
b.	KuU	kya	kar	ne	ka
c.	KuM	kay	kar	ay	cə
d.	KuK	yan	maḍ	o	d
		what	to do		

Inclusive and exclusive 'we' pronouns: Kannada and Marathi have two Ist person pronouns each, one meaning 'we but not you' and the other 'we including you'. HU does not make this distinction. KuU uses apun as the inclusive and ham as the exclusive 'we'.

Borrowing

Our data on borrowing of morphs confirms the findings of Weinreich, Emeneau and other students of language contact who maintain that both lexical and grammatical items can be borrowed, and that content word borrowings are more frequent. Within the realm of borrowed grammatical items some further finer distinctions can be drawn. Next after content words in order of frequency are adverbs, conjunctions, post-positions and other similar function words. Derivative suffixes are third. Here are some striking examples of this.

Marathi has a verb suffix -u which is used in constructions like ja-u syək -t- o '(he) can go' or ja-u-n-ko 'Don't go'. The standard Urdu 'can + Vb' construction is the verb root plus sək-.

All four Kupwar languages have the construction Vb-u-syək(s)-. The -u suffix has clearly been borrowed from Marathi.

(16) 'I can go'

a.	HU	mey	ja	sək-t-a		
b.	M	mi	ja	u šək	t	o
c.	KuU	mey	jya	u syək	t	u
d.	KuM	mi	ja	u syək	t	o
e.	KuK	na	hog	u syəks	t	yən
		I	go	can		

Inflectional morphs forming part of closed paradigmatic sets such as person and gender agreement or tense markers are almost never borrowed. Only in one or two instances did such borrowings occur. Here is one example:

(17) 'He even said something'

a.	KuK	aw	bi	yanr	matad ya
		he	even	something	told

The Kannada past ending -da would be expected here; ya is a past marker in Kupwar Urdu and Telugu.

(18) 'Cousins came to call us from there'

    a. KuU hwa - si həm - na   bula ne - ko pewne ae

        there - from us- to   calling - for cousins came

In the above case the KuU dative suffix -ko would be expected; -na is one of the Marathi allomorphs of the dative suffix.

In contrast to other borrowings which were freely elicited, items like the above, when heard on tape, were regarded as wrong or funny by natives. They were not repeated voluntarily. Such paradigmatically structured inflectional morphs seem to be at the core of the native speakers perception of what constitute 'different languages'.

Compare the above with examples from another language contact situation where ethnic identity is similarly marked by language distinctions. The languages here are HU and Panjabi (P), which although historically and typologically quite closely related are, nevertheless, officially recognized as separate languages.

(19) 'He doesn't eat'

     a.   HU   wo   nəhii   kha-t̲-a

     b.   P   o   nəhi   kha-nd-a

Here, aside from minor features of phonology, the only difference lies in the phonological realizations of the participal endings respectively -t̲- and -nd-. It seems that in each of these cases, and quite possibly elseqhere, wherever social norms favor the maintenance of linguistic markers of ethnic identity, and where there are no absolute barriers to borrowing of lexicon and syntax, these morphophonemic features take on the social function of marking the separateness of two language varieties. In some cases they seem to remain as the last barriers to complete language shift or creolization.

Discussion

What can one say about the nature of the processes of language change illustrated in our case study ? It is obvious that it is KuU which has undergone the greatest changes. It has adapted its gender system and radically restructured its system of agreement markers, in some cases even to the point of reshaping gender agreement markers into person agreement markers. It has further given up such typical HU features as verb compounding and has also undergone a number of semantic changes including the creation of a new distinction between exclusive and inclusive personal pronouns. KuK has also changed considerably. It has adapted to Marathi in that it has lost the distinction between pronominal and adjectival possessives and dative and accusative post-positions. Copula constructions, interrogative suffixes, and sentences with subordinating conjunctions have been restructured. KuM by contrast has changed least, though with major changes in gender and in agreement markers.

In sum, KuU has changed altogether in 11 of the cases discussed, KuM and KuK in 6 each (taking 2 a—c to apply to Marathi in the same way as to Urdu). Conversely, there have been no changes toward KuU, 1 toward KuM, 6 toward KuK, 4 toward KuK, KuM jointly, and 5 toward KuU and KuM jointly. Thus, if we assume for the sake of argument that the varieties involved in the diffusion process can be treated as independent entities, change has been toward KuU altogether in 5 of the cases discussed, KuK in 10, and KuM in 10.

These relations among the languages can be summarized as follows:

$$\begin{array}{lll}
\text{HU, M} \rightarrow \text{K} & \text{1, 2a—e} & 6 \\
\text{K} \rightarrow \text{HU, M} & \text{3, 4, 6, 7, 8a} & 5 \\
\text{HU} \rightarrow \text{K, M} & \text{5, 9a—c} & 4 \\
\text{HU, K} \rightarrow \text{M} & \text{8b} & 1
\end{array}$$

While we have no way of weighting the relative significance of the changes, the rough numerical relationships themselves are revealing. There are 12 possible relations of change among the three varieties: each variety toward each of the other two, or toward the other two jointly ($3 \times 3 = 9$), and each pair toward the third (3). Of these 12 possibilities, only 4 are found. (See Table 1.) As noted, KuK and KuM do not change toward KuU, singly or jointly. There are in fact no instances of changes involving just two of the varieties to the exclusion of the third. All changes are convergences involving the three varieties as a set, being changes either of one toward the other two, or of two toward the other one. The largest number of changes, and the only major case of two adapting to one, are of KuU and KuM toward KuK in semantic determination of gender, and in surface structure syntactic agreement (1, 2a—e). With the exception of the position of the interrogative marker (8b), all other changes discussed are of KuU toward KuK, KuM, where those two agree, and of KuK toward KuM, KuU, where those two agree. (Not, notice, of KuM toward KuK and KuU where those two may agree).

That KuM has been much more changed toward (where it agrees with one of the other languages) than changed form, despite its home group of speakers being a subordinate minority in the village

Table I

	U	K	M	U, K	U, M	K, M
U	▨			▨	▨	4
K		▨		▨	5	
M			▨		▨	▨
U, K	▨	▨	1	▨	▨	▨
U, M	▨	6	▨	▨	▨	▨
K, M		▨	▨	▨	▨	▨

reflects the position of Kupwar within the regional communication network. Marathi is and has been for several centuries the dominant regional language, being spoken in Sangli, the district capital, as well as by the majority of cultivators in several adjoining villages. Since Kupwar residents are well integrated into the political and social life of the area there is no reason to treat the village as a self-contained isolate. On the contrary the Kupwar Jain's need for communicating with Marathi-speaking business men and neighboring cultivators provides the most reasonable explanation for the use of Marathi as a medium for inter group communication in the village also.

The pattern would appear to be striking indication that the changes are based in mutual adaptation within the village. The equivalent roles of the language of the large majority, and of a minority of untouchables, reflect no doubt the status of the language of the latter outside the village, but that status is itself involved in what is the key to the whole, the norms governing choice of alternative variety in social situations. To what extent the adaptation in each language has been initiated by its home-group speakers, under the influence of their knowledge of the languages of others, and to what extent adaptation has been initiated by others, using a language to its home-group speakers, or, in the case of Marathi, to others, we are not able to say.

The present-day conditions after all reflect processes which must have taken place over a period of several hundred years during which time there have also been deep changes in power and prestige relationships. Notice, however, that almost all the changes can be interpreted as reductions or generalizations that simplify surface structure in relation to underlying categories and relationships. The semantic convergences of 9a—c, to be sure, would seem to reflect simply joint pressure on Urdu of Marathi and Kannada, and 9c entails a new distinction. The change in gender categories, though, results in making gender form predictable semantically. (In KuU there is a binary choice: [+human, +female] or not; in KuM a ternary choice: [+human, +female], [+human, −female], [−human].) The other changes show reduction in number of positions in which a category is marked (2a, 8b); reduction of number of categories marked (2c, 2b (where implicit gender of addressee is replaced by redundant surface agreement), 2e, 3, 4, 5); generalization of a surface form (without addition of a contrast) (some of the preceding, and 6); and changes that arguably are toward simpler, or more 'natural' surface structure relationships (2d, 7, 8a).

The most striking result of the various changes the dialects have undergone is the creation of three parallel creole-like local varieties. This linguistic situation seems uniquely suited to the social situation discussed at the beginning of the paper. Speakers can validly maintain that they speak distinct languages corresponding to distinct ethnic groups. While language distinctions are maintained, actual messages show word-for-word or morph-for-morph translatability, and speakers can therefore switch from one code to another with a minimum of additional learning.

The trend towards word-for-word translatable codes also explains many of the syntactic changes that the languages concerned have undergone. There are several instances where two grammatical categories in one language correspond to a single category in the other languages, as for example with Kannada dative and accusative and where the marked category in the first language is lost and the unmarked category is generalized. This same pressure for translatability of local codes further explains the many instances of restructuring of phonological materials by loan translation-like processes to fill categories in other local varieties.

Historical linguists as well as students of creolization in the past have had a tendency to think of standard languages as basic and to regard pidgins as relatively marginal or impermanent phenomena. For Kupwar, at least, and possibly for elsewhere, our situation would suggest a reversal of emphasis. If there is anything about the Kupwar linguistic situation that all speakers share it is the common Ku syntax. It is this syntax which is learned in childhood and in playgroups. Standard languages are superimposed on this system through formal education and other forms of contact with the outside. Knowledge of these languages is unevenly distributed, and is a function of an individual's socio-economic position. For many Kupwar residents, especially men, a model of linguistic competence must comprise a single semological, a single syntactic, and a single phonetic component, and alternative set of rules for the relation of semantic categories to morphemic shapes.

The Kupwar varieties have processes of reduction and convergence suggestive of pidginization and creolization. To say that the varieties have in fact undergone those processes would of course be misleading, if creolization is defined as requiring a pidgin as its starting point. We have no evidence of a pidgin-stage in the history of the village, or reason to suspect one. The adaptations involved are the result of several centuries of language contact. The present state of the varieties is creole-like, in that one finds grammatical structure and lexical shape pointing to different sources, quite like the stereotype of a pidgin or creole as the words of one language used with the grammar of another. And in Kupwar, whatever the exact historical circumstances, clearly the social basis for such striking convergence has been an important part of the same type as that associated with the changes that create a pidgin and persist in a creole. The need for constant code-switching and for mutual adaptation within a situation in which home languages are maintained has led to reduction and adaptation in linguistic structure. Historically viewed, moreever, where one is used to thinking of grammar as most persistent, lexicon as most changeable, in the normal development of a language, in Kupwar it is grammar that has been most adaptable, lexical shape most persistent. Kupwar, by the way, is not unique in this respect.

Similar findings have been reported for other parts of India (Pandit in press). To be sure, while it has been proposed that the major process of change for pidgins in new settings has been re-lexification, the local Kupwar varieties might be said to have undergone 're-syntactification' (if the term may be excused for the sake of the contrast). On the other hand, if Kupwar Urdu were examined in isolation from other Kupwar varieties, and the identity and history of its speakers, and compared only to Standard Urdu, it might be thought that its deviance was due, not to adaptation by a continuous line of native speakers, but to a discontinuity, to 'substratum' or creolizing influence from a community to whom it was not at first a native language. Standard Urdu and Kupwar Urdu would stand in a relation analogous to that of Standard French and Haitian Creole, for those for whom the latter is a drastically reshaped French dialect.

That Kupwar Urdu might be suspected of having undergone pidginization and creolization indicates that these processes are not different in kind from other processes of language contact and adaptation. The main difference between KuU and a creolized language may be, as Hymes suggests, that its starting point was not a pidgin. The Kupwar situation points up the urgent need for direct investigation of actual mechanisms of linguistic change in their actual settings, leading to a theory of the relations between the two and their possible results.

NOTES

Field research and analysis of the data were financed by grants from the National Science Foundation, the U. S. Office of Education and the Institute of International Studies, University of California, Berkeley, whose support is gratefully acknowledged. We are grateful to Dell Hymes for extensive comments.
    [1]Kannada and Telugu are members of the Dravidian family of languages. Marathi and Urdu are members of the Indo-Aryan branch of the Indo-European family, but are not directly related. Urdu, now the national language of Pakistan, and Hindi, the national language of India, are distinct politically and culturally and have different scripts

but linguistically almost identical. Following recent scholarly practice we use the term Hindi-Urdu to rever to these common features,
while the term Urdu, as used here refers more specifically to the
speech of local Muslim groups.
    [2]The following abbreviations are used in this and all following
examples: Standard Hindi-Urdu, HU; Standard Marathi, M; Standard
Kannada, K. The corresponding local varieties of each language in
Kupwar are indicated by the prefix Ku, thus Kupwar Urdu, KuU; Kupwar Marathi, KuM; Kupwar Kannada, KuK. Each example is preceded by an idiomatic English equivalent in quotation marks. A literal English translation is given at the bottom.

REFERENCES

Gumperz, John. 1964. 'Linguistic and social interaction in two com-
        munities. The ethnography of communication', ed. by John
        Gumperz and Dell Hymes, American Anthropologist 66 (6),
        pt. 2, 137-54. [In this volume, pp. 151-76.]
_____. 1967. 'On the linguistic markers of bilingual com-
        munication. Problems of bilingualism,' ed. by J. Mac-
        Namara, Journal of Social Issues 23(2):48-57.

Pandit, P. B. 'The Grammar of Number Names in a Bilingual set-
        ting' (typescript).

Weinreich, Uriel. 1952. Languages in contact, New York, Linguistic
        Circle of New York (2nd printing, 1963).

16 | Social Meaning in Linguistic Structures: Code-Switching in Norway

In Collaboration with Jan-Petter Blom

In recent discussions of the problem of language and society, Bernstein (1961, 1964) explores the hypothesis that social relationships act as intervening variables between linguistic structures and their realization in speech. His formulation suggests that the anthropologists' analysis of social constraints governing interpersonal relationships may be utilized in the interpretation of verbal performances This paper attempts to clarify the social and linguistic factors involved in the communication process and to test Bernstein's hypothesis by showing that speaker's selection among semantically, grammatically, and phonologically permissible alternates occuring in conversation sequences recorded in natural groups is both patterned and predictable on the basis of certain features of the local social system. In other words, given a particular aggregate of people engaged in regular face to face interaction, and given some knowledge of the speaker's linguistic repertoire (Gumperz 1964), we wish to relate the structure of that repertoire to the verbal behavior of members of the community in particular situations.

Data on verbal interaction derives from approximately two months' field work in Hemnesberget, a small commercial and industrial town of about 1300 inhabitants in the center of the Rana Fjord, close to the Arctic circle in Northern Norway. The settlement owes its existence to the growth of local trade and industry following the abolition of government-sanctioned trade monopolies covering most of Northern Norway in 1858. Since the Middle Ages, these monopolies had kept the area's economy dependent upon a small elite of merchant and landholding families with connections to southern Norway, separated by great differences in wealth, culture, and education from

the tenant farmers, fishermen, estate laborers and servants who
formed the bulk of the populace. Apart from a few shop owners and
government officials, present-day Hemnesberget residents are mostly
descendants of these latter groups. They have been attracted to the
town from the surroundings by new economic opportunities there,
while a hundred years of relatively free economic development have
splintered the old ruling circles. Many of this former elite have
moved away, and the remainder no longer form a visible social
group in the region.

Present inhabitants of Hemnesberget earn their livelihood
mainly as craftsmen in family workshops or in the somewhat larger
boat-building and lumber-processing plants, all of which are locally
owned. The area serves as a major source of wood products and
fishing equipment for the northernmost part of Norway. A significant
group of merchant middlemen deal in locally produced boats and
other products, which they ship north for resale, and maintain sales
agencies for motors and other appliances and manufactured goods
from the South.

While at the beginning of the century, Hemnesberget was
the most important communications and commercial center in the
area, it has been eclipsed in recent years by government sponsored
economic development which has turned the town of Mo, at the mouth
of the Rana Fjord, into Norway's major iron and steel producing
center. The region of Mo has grown from about 1,000 inhabitants
in 1920 to almost 9,000 in 1960, largely through immigration from
the region of Trøndelag and southern Norway. It now boasts several
modern department stores, hotels, restaurants, and cinemas. The
railroad from Trondheim in the south through Mo and on north to
Bodø was completed shortly after the Second World War and the road
system is steadily improving. All these new communication arteries,
however, now bypass Hemnesberget, which has all but lost its
importance as a communication link for both land and sea traffic.

Although the immediate ecological environment has changed
greatly, Hemnesberget remains an island of tradition in a sea of
change. There is a regular once-a-day boat service to Mo, buses

leave for the railroad station twice a day, and a few people commute to Mo by private automobile or motorcycle. However, the bulk of the residents spend most of their working and leisure time in and around Hemnesberget. Those who can afford it build vacation cabins in the unsettled areas across the fjord a few miles away. Our interviews uniformly show that social events in Mo i Rana are only of marginal interest to local inhabitants.

The Community Linguistic Repertoire

Most residents of Hemnesberget are native speakers of Ranamål (R), one of a series of dialects which segment Northern Norway into linguistic regions roughly corresponding to other cultural and ecological divisions (Christiansen 1962). As elsewhere in Norway, where local independence and distinctness of folk culture are highly valued, the dialect enjoys great prestige. A person's native speech is regarded as an integral part of his family background, a sign of his local identity. By identifying himself as a dialect speaker both at home and abroad, a member symbolizes pride in his community and in the distinctness of its contribution to society at large.

Formal education, however, is always carried on in the standard, the language of official transactions, of religion and of the mass media. Norwegian law sanctions two standard languages: Bokmål (formally called Riksmål) and Nynorsk (formerly Landsmål), of which only Bokmål (B) is current in northern Norway.

Education is universal and, allowing for certain individual differences in fluency, all speakers of Ranamål also control the standard. Both Bokmål and Ranamål therefore form part of what we may call the community linguistic repertoire (Gumperz 1964), the totality of linguistic resources which speakers may employ in significant social interaction. In their everyday interaction, they select between the two as the situation demands. Members view this alternation as a shift between two distinct entities, which are never mixed. A person speaks either one or the other.

The fact the two varieties are perceived as distinct, however, does not necessarily mean that their separateness is marked by significant linguistic differences. Pairs such as Hindi and Urdu, Serbian and Croatian, Thai and Laotian, and many others which are regarded as separate languages by their speakers are known to be grammatically almost identical. The native's view of language distinctions must thus be validated by empirical linguistic investigation.

We began our analysis by employing standard linguistic elicitation procedures. A series of informants selected for their fluency in the dialect were interviewed in our office and were asked to produce single words, sentences, and short texts, first in the dialect and then in the standard for taping or phonetic recording by the linguist. These elicitation sessions yielded a series of dialect features which are essentially identical to those described by Norwegian dialectologists (Christiansen 1962).

The vowel system distinguishes three tongue heights. High: front unrounded i, front rounded y, central rounded u, back rounded o. Mid: front unrounded e, front rounded ö, back rounded å. Low: front unrounded æ, front rounded ø , back a.

Consonants occur either singly or as geminates. Vowels are phonetically short before geminates, consonant clusters, and palatalized consonants. There are two series of consonants: unmarked and palatalized. Unmarked consonants include: stops p, b, t, d, k, g; spirants f, v, s, š, j, ç; nasals m, n, ŋ; trill r, lateral l, and retroflex flap ḷ. The palatal series contains tj, dj, nj, lj. On the phonetic level, a set of cacuminal or retroflex allophones occur for the sequences rs [š], rd [ḍ], rt [ṭ] and rn [ṇ].

The local pronunciation of the standard differs from the 'pure' dialect as follows: Bokmal does not have the phonemic distinction between the palatalized and non-palatalized series of consonants. Only non-palatalized consonants occur. In addition, it does not distinguish between mid front rounded / ö/ and low

front rounded / ø /; only the former occurs. On the purely phonetic
level, dialect allophones of the phonemes / æ / and / a/ are
considerably lower and more retracted than their standard equivalents.
The dialect furthermore has a dark allophone [ɫ] of / l/ where the
standard has clear [l]. The cacuminal or retroflex allophones of
/ s/ , / d/, /t/ and / n/ , and the flap / ḷ / , however, which are
commonly regarded as dialect features, are used in both varieties,
although they tend to disappear in highly formal Bokmal.

   Morphological peculiarities of the dialect include the
masculine plural indefinite suffix -æ and the definite suffix -an,
e.g. , (R) hæ stæ (horses), hæ stan (the horses), contrasting with
(B) hester and hestene. In verb inflection the dialect lacks the
infinitive suffix -e and the present suffix -er of regular verbs.
Further differences in past tense and past participle markers and
in the assignment of individual words to strong or weak inflectional
classes serve to set off almost every dialect verb from its standard
Norwegian equivalent. Here are some examples of common regular
and irregular verbs and their standard equivalents:

Infinitive		Present		Past		Past Participle		
(R)	(B)	(R)	(B)	(R)	(B)	(R)	(B)	
finj	finne	finj	finner	fanj	fant	fønje	funnet	(find)
vara	væ re	e	ær	va	var	vøre	vært	(be)
or va								
få	fä	får	får	fekk	fikk	fått	fätt	(get)
stanj	stå	står	står	sto	sto	stie	stått	(stand)
jæ r	jøre	jæ r	jør	joḷ	jøre	jort	jort	(do)
læ s	lese	læ s	leser	læ st	leste	læ st	lest	(read)
ta	ta	tek	tar	tok	tokk	tatt	tatt	(take)
						or tiçe		

Other important dialect features appear in pronouns, common adverbs
of time, place and manner, conjunctions and other grammatically
significant function words. Here is a list of some of the most common
distinctive forms of personal pronouns and possessive pronouns:

(B)	(R)	
jæjj	og	(I)
mæjj	meg	(me)
dæjj	deg	(you)
hann	hanj	(he)
hunn	ho	(she)
hanns	hanjs	(his)
hennes	hinjers	(hers)
dere	dåkk	(you) [plural]
di	dæmm*	(theirs)

*Sometimes also di and deres

Interrogatives, relatives, and indefinites:

(B)	(R)	
såmm	să	(who, which [relative])
va	ke	(what [interrogative])
vemm	kem	(who)
noe	nåkka	(something)
vorfårr	kefør	(what for)
vilket	kefør nokka	(which [thing])
vilken	kefør nann	(which [person])
vær	kvar	(every)
en	ein	(one)

Adverbs and conjunctions:

(B)	(R)	
till	tell	(to, towards)
menn	mænn	(but)
hær	her	(here)
fra	ifra	(from)
mellåm	imeljæ	(in between)
vordan	kelesn	(how)
viss	vess	(if)

        The above data constitute empirical evidence to support the
view of the dialect as a distinct linguistic entity. By comparing
information collected in this manner with local speech forms elsewhere in Northern Norway, dialectologists interested in historical
reconstruction identify Ranamål as one of a series of Northern
Norwegian dialects set off from others by the fact that it shows
influences of Eastern Norwegian forms of speech (Christiansen
1962). In this paper, however, we are concerned with social interaction and not with history, and this leads us to raise somewhat
different problems.

        The elicitation sessions which provide the source data for
dialect grammars are conducted in the linguist's, and not in the
informant's, frame of reference. Although by asking speakers to
speak in the dialect, the linguist may be interested in purely
descriptive or historical information, the native speaker, mindful
of the association between dialect, local culture, and local identity,
is of course anxious to present his locality in the best possible light.
Consistency of performance in linguistic interview sessions might
well be the result of the interviewer's presence; it need not reflect
everyday interaction. Furthermore, when comparisons with other
forms of speech are made, it is the linguist's analysis which serves
as the basis for these comparisons, not the speaker's performance.

Ranamål and Bokmål as Codes in a Repertoire

        In order to understand how natives may perceive the dialect
standard language differences some further discussion of the way
in which distinctions between what are ordinarily treated as separate
linguistic systems may be manifested in everyday speech is necessary.
Thus if we compare a bilingual's pronunciation of the Norwegian
sentence vill du ha egg og beiken till frokast? with the same speaker's
pronunciation of the English equivalent "Will you have bacon and
eggs for breakfast?" the two utterances will show phonetic distinctions
in every segment. The Norwegian voiced spirant [v] has much less
spirantal noise than its English equivalent, the [i] is tense as compared
to the lax English [ɪ], the Norwegian [l] may be clear or dark but it

is phonetically different from English [1]. The Norwegian central rounded [u] in du has no direct English equivalent. In egg the Norwegian has a tense [e] and the [g] has an aspirate release whereas in English the vowel is lax and [g] has a voiced release. Similarly, the Norwegian has a stressed vowel [æi] in beiken whereas the English has [ey]. Bilinguals whose entire articulation shifts in this way can be said to have two distinct articulation ranges in addition to two sets of grammatical rules.

Analysis of recordings of Hemnesberget speakers' switching from the dialect to the standard reveals a different situation. In a sentence pair like hanj bor på nilsen 's paŋšonat and its Bokmål equivalent hann bor på nilsen's paŋšonat, "He lives in Nilsen's pensionat," only the realizations of / a/ , /ɬ/ , and /nj/ which appear in our list of dialect characteristics differ. In other relevant respects the two utterances are identical. Furthermore, even in the case of these dialect characteristics, speakers do not alternate between two clearly distinguishable articulation points; rather, the shift takes the form of a displacement along a scale in which palatalized consonants show at least three degrees of palatalization, strong [nj] , weak [nʲ], and zero [n] and / a/ and / æ / each show three degrees of retraction and lowering.

While the switch from Norwegian to English implies a shift between two distinct structural wholes, the Bokmål-Ranamål alternation, in phonology at least, seems more similar to conditions described by Labov (1966) for New York speech. A speaker's standard and dialect performance can be accounted for by a single phonetic system. The bulk of the constituent phones within this system are marked by relatively stable, easily identifiable points of articulation. The palatalized consonants and the vowels listed above differ in that they vary within a much greater articulation range. They are instances of what Labov has called variables (1964). It is the position of such variables along the scale of possible articulations which, when evaluated along with morphological information, signals dialect vs. standard speech.

Not all items identified in our elicitation sessions as Ranamål features function as variables, however. The contrast

between / ø / and / ð/ was never produced spontaneously. In
normal discourse only [ð] occurs. Furthermore, as we stated
above, the flap allophone / ļ / and the retroflex stop allophones
which find a prominent place in dialect grammars are also used in
local Bokmål as well as in eastern varieties of Standard Norwegian;
thus their status as dialect markers is doubtful.

Our texts also reveal some individual differences in the
pronunciation of the palatalized consonant and vowel variables.
While the normal dialect speech of most residents shows strong
palatalization of these consonants and extreme vowel retraction,
some of the more highly educated younger residents normally have
medium palatalization and medium vowel retraction. Regardless,
however, the direction of variation is the same for all individuals.

In the realm of morphology-syntax it is also possible to set
up a single set of grammatical categories to account for what on the
surface seem like striking differences between the two varieties.
All nouns, for example, appear in an indefinite form consisting of
the noun stem and in a definite form made up of stem plus suffixed
article, both of which are inflected for singular and plural. There
are three subcategories of noun gender: masculine, feminine, and
neuter, and the case categories are shared. Verbs appear in
imperative, infinitive, present, past, and past participle forms.
Basic function word categories, including pronouns, conjunctions,
and adverbs, are shared, etc.

Ranamål shows a few peculiarities in the order of pronouns
and verbs in sentences such as (R) ke du e ifrå, (B) vor æ r du fra,
"Where are you from?" But even without detailed analysis it is
obvious that these differences correspond to relatively low order
syntactic rules. The majority of the distinctions between the dialect
and the standard thus do not affect the basic grammar, but only
what we may call the morphophonemic realization of shared categories.

Even at the morphophonemic level, variation is not without
pattern. Examination of such alternates as (B) till, (R) tell, "to";
(B) fikk, (R) fekk, "received"; (B) hest, (R) hæ st, "horse"; (B)

menn, (R) mæ̱nn, "but", suggests a general process of lowering of
front vowels in the dialect. This lowering process is also found
elsewhere in Norway, although it may occur in different linguistic
forms. Similarly, other sets of alternates such as isse/ ikke,
"not"; dæ̱mm/ di, "they"; ifrå/ fra, "from", are common in other
Norwegian regions.

Leaving aside historical considerations, it is almost as if
all dialect variation within Norway were generated by selection of
different forms from a common reservoir of alternates. Ranamål
differs from other dialects not so much because it contains entirely
different features, but because of the way in which it combines
features already found elsewhere. Furthermore, Hemnesberget
pairs such as (B) læ̱rer, (R) lerar, and (B) hæ̱r, (R) her, which
conflict with the lowering process mentioned above, suggest that here
as elsewhere selection may at times be motivated by social pressures
favoring maintenance of distinctions (Ramanujan 1967). No matter
what the actual historical facts are, however, the narrow range of
variation we find lends support to our view of dialect features as
variables within a single grammatical system.

The effect of structural similarities on speakers' perception
of speech differences is somewhat counterbalanced by the fact that
choice among these variables is always restricted by sociolinguistic
selection constraints such that if, for instance, a person selects a
standard morphological variant in one part of an utterance, this
first choice also implies selection of pronunciation variables tending
towards the standard end of the scale. A speaker wishing to ask
for another's place of residence may, for example, start his
sentence either with (R) ke "where," or (B) vor. In the first case,
the rest of the sentence will read hanj e ifrå, "is he from?" In
the second case, it will be æ r hann fra; vor and hanj do not co-occur.
Similarly, selection of e, "is" requires dialect pronunciation; the
form æ r, "is" would sound odd if it appeared in the same sentence
with hanj.

It is the nature of these selection constraints and the manner
in which they cut across the usual boundaries of phonology and

morphology to generate co-occurrences among phonetic and allomorphic
and lexical variables, which lends the Ranamål-Bokmål variation its
peculiar stamp, and sets it off, for example, from the phonologically
similar situation in New York. Sociolinguistic selection rules also
account to some extent for the speaker's view of the two varieties as
separate entities.

Since the dialect and the standard are almost isomorphic
in syntax and phonetics and vary chiefly in morphophonemics, and
since most speakers control the entire range of variables, it would
be unreasonable to assume, as is frequently done wherever two
distinct dialects are spoken, that selection patterns affecting the above-
mentioned selection rules are motivated by considerations of
intelligibility. The most reasonable assumption is that the linguistic
separateness between the dialect and the standard, i.e. the maintenance
of distinct alternates for common inflectional morphemes and function
is conditioned by social factors.

Some idea of how this came about can be obtained by con-
sidering the conditions under which the two varieties are learned.
The dialect is acquired in most homes and in the sphere of domestic
and friendship relations. As a result, it has acquired the flavor of
these locally-based relationships. On the other hand, dialect
speakers learn the standard in school and in church, at a time when
they are also introduced to national Norwegian values. It has therefore become associated with such Pan-Norwegian activity systems.

Since the adult population has equal access to both sets of
variants, however, the developmental argument does not provide
sufficient explanation for the maintenance of distinctness. Immigrants
to urban centers around the world, for example, frequently give up
their languages after a generation if social conditions are favorable
to language shift. The hypothesis suggests itself, therefore, that
given the initial acquisition patterns, the dialect and the standard
remain separate because of the cultural identities they communicate
and the social values implied therein. It is this aspect of the
problem that we intend to explore in the remaining portions of the

paper. Before we proceed, however, something more needs to be said about the process of social symbolization.

Students of communication usually distinguish between semantics proper, or reference, and pragmatics (Ervin-Tripp 1964). Reference indicates verbal categorization of objects' actions and experience in terms of their objective properties; pragmatics deals with the effect of symbols of various kinds on speakers and listeners, i.e., with the significance of what is communicated for the actors involved. Most discussions of pragmatics ordinarily do not distinguish between individual intent and interpersonal significance of usage patterns, although it is evident that without such a distinction it would be impossible to explain the fact that the same message may indicate praise in some instances and disapproval in others. Effective communication requires that speakers and audiences agree both on the meaning of words and on the social import or values attached to choice of expression. Our discussions will be confined to the latter. We will use the term social significance or social meaning to refer to the social value implied when an utterance is used in a certain context.

In general, the assignment of value to particular objects or acts is as arbitrary as the referential naming of objects. Just as a particular term may refer to a round object in one group and a square object in another, so also the value of actions or utterances may vary. Thus the same term may indicate mere local distinctions in one community and symbolize social stratification elsewhere. Social meanings differ from referential meanings in the way in which they are coded. Whereas reference is coded largely through words, social meaning can attach not only to acoustic signs but also to settings, to items of background knowledge, as well as to particular word sequences. In Hemnes, for example, values attached to a person's family background or to his reputation as a fisherman are important in understanding what he says and influence the selection of responses to his actions.

It must also be pointed out that referential meanings are at least to some extent recoverable through the study of individual words, they are segmental to use Pike's term (1966), while social meanings are not. A sentence like ke du e ifrå, "Where are you from?" can be divided into units of reference like ke, "where"; du, "you"; e, "are"; ifrå, "from". Social significance attaches to the utterance as a whole; it is not segmentable into smaller component stretches. Sociolinguistic co-occurence patterns along with intonation contours enable the speaker to group language into larger pragmatic wholes and to interpret them in relation to signs transmitted by other communicative media.

Local Organization and Values

Social life in Hemnesberget shows a fluidity of class structure quite similar to that described for Southern Norway by Barnes (1954). Extremes of poverty and wealth are absent. Expressions of solidarity such as "We all know each other here in Hemnes," and "We are all friends here" recur in our interviews. The majority of those who claim local descent show a strong sense of local identification. To be a hæmnesværing, "Hemnes resident," in their view is like belonging to a team characterized by commonalty of descent. Members of this reference group act like kin, friends and neighbors cooperating in the pursuit of community ideals. In everyday behavior they symbolize this quality of their ties through greetings, exchanges of personal information and through general informality of posture towards fellow members. The dialect is an important marker of their common culture. Residents of neighboring settlements, of Mo i Rana, as well as other Norwegians, stand apart from this local community. They are potential competitors who must at least initially be treated with reserve. Their dialects are said to be different. The linguist interested in structural significance may wish to disregard such variation as minor. Nevertheless they have important social meanings for inter-community communication within the Rana region. They are constantly commented upon and joked about and seem to play an important role in the maintenance of local identity.

Despite the intense sense of local identification, perceptions of closeness within this local group are not everywhere the same

among Hemnes residents. More detailed interviews, observations
of visiting and recreational patterns and of the exchange of assistance
suggests a clear distinction between personal relations and the more
general local relations. The actual range of effective personal
relations for any single individual tends to be fairly small and stable
over time. For most people it includes only certain near kin, in-
laws, neighbors, or fellow workers. The community can thus be
described as segmented into small nuclei of personal interaction.
But since these groups are not marked linguistically, the behavioral
signs of friendliness and equality constitute a communicative idiom
which applies to both these nuclei and to other relations or shared
local identification.

        The meaning attached to local descent and dialect use—to
being part of the "local team"—is clearly seen when we consider those
members of the community who dissociate themselves from this
"team." Traditionally in Northern Norway the local community of
equals was separated from the landowning commercial and administrative elite by a wide gulf of social and judicial inequality. Since
the latter were the introducers and users of standard Norwegian,
the standard was—and to some extent still is—associated with this
inequality of status. Many of the functions of the former elite have
now been incorporated into the local social system. Individuals who
fill these functions, however, continue to be largely of non-local
descent. Although they may pay lip service to locally accepted rules
of etiquette and use the dialect on occasion, their experience elsewhere in Norway, where differences in education, influence and
prestige are much more pronounced, leads them to associate the
dialect with lack of education and sophistication. Therefore they
show a clear preference for the standard.

        Such attitudes are unacceptable to locals who view lack of
respect for and refusal to speak the dialect as an expression of
social distance and of contempt for the "local team" and its community
spirit. It is not surprising therefore that their loyalty to the dialect
is thereby reaffirmed. For a local resident to employ (B) forms
with other local residents is in their view to snakk fint or to
snakk jalat, "to put on airs."

Since the different social meanings which attach to the
dialect are regular and persistent, they must in some way be reinforced by the pattern of social ties. This relationship can best be
described if we consider the socio-ecological system which sustains
the community. There is a correlation between a person's regional
background, his reference group, and the niche he occupies in this
system (Barth 1964). This information enables us to segment the
local population into three distinct categories: 1) artisans,
2) wholesale-retail merchants and plant managers, and 3) service
personnel. Members of the first two categories are the basic
producers of wealth.

The more than fifty percent of the population which falls
into the first category includes draftsmen who may or may not own
their own shops, as well as workmen employed in the larger plants
and their dependents. Most of them are locally born or have been
drawn to Hemnes from the surrounding farms by the demand for
their skills. Since they live and work among their relatives and
among others of the same social background, they tend to choose
their friends and spouses from within their own reference group and
thus become strong supporters of local values.

Wholesale-retail merchants buy lumber products and finished
boats from producers in the Rana area, furnishing them with supplies
and gear and appliances in exchange. They sell boats, lumber
products and fishing supplies to customers all the way up to the
northernmost tip of Norway. Relationships between merchants and
their customers most commonly take the form of longterm credit
arrangements based on personal trust in which credit is given to
artisans against their future production. Also part of the second
category are the managers of large local enterprises who achieve
their position partly because of their special commercial and
managerial skills and partly through their ability to get along with
and keep the confidence of owners, workers and foremen.

Like artisans, members of category two are largely of
local descent. Although they tend to be in the higher income
brackets, they maintain kin and conjugal relationships among

craftsmen and fishermen-farmers. The fact that their livelihood
depends to a great extent on their standing within the system of
locally based relations leads them to associate more closely with
the local values. The circumstances of their commercial enterprises however, also take them outside this local network. They
must be able to act within the urban commercial ethic, and they
must also maintain personal ties with their customers in the North
and elsewhere. The range of their social connections includes both
local and supralocal ties, involving different and sometimes conflicting standards of behavior. The result is that while they maintain
strong loyalty to general local values they tend to avoid close personal
ties with their kin in the first category and confine their friendships
to others who are in similar circumstances.

The third category is a composite one, consisting of individuals whose position depends on the productivity of others. It
includes persons engaged in purely local services — private and
administrative — of all kinds such as salesmen, clerks, repairmen,
shopkeepers, professionals and those who are employed in repair
shops and in transportation. The sociocultural background of these
people varies. Those who perform manual labor tend to be of
local descent and are culturally indistinguishable from members of
the first category. The same is true for the lower echelons of
employees in stores and in administrative offices. Among the
owners of retail businesses, clothing, shoe, pastry and stationary
shops many belong to families who have moved to Hemnesberget
from other urban or semiurban centers in Northern Norway. Their
kin and friendship relations tend to be dispersed among these
communities, and this leads them to identify with the differentiated
non-local middle class value system. Shopowners of local background also aspire to these standards, at the same time trying to
maintain their position in the "local team" by showing loyalty to its
values. Professionals are similarly drawn to Hemnes from the
outside because of their technical expertise. The more stable
core of this group, the school teachers, tend to be of North
Norwegian background. Doctors, veterinarians, dentists and
priests frequently come from the South. Invariably their values are
those of the Pan-Norwegian elite.

Economic conditions in Hemnes leave little room for the academically trained and those with technical skills outside local niches. Consequently young people from all categories who aspire to higher education must spend much of their student years away from Hemnes and will eventually have to seek employment somewhere else. While they remain students, however, they are partly dependent on their families. They tend to return home during the summer vacation and seek local employment.

Contextual Constraints

Previous sections have dealt with the linguistic repertoire, internal cultural differences, and relevant features of social organization. We have suggested that linguistic alternates within the repertoire serve to symbolize the differing social identities which members may assume. It is, however, evident from our discussion that there is by no means a simple one-to-one relationship between specific speech varieties and specific social identities. Apart from the fact that values attached to language usage vary with social background, the same individual need not be absolutely consistent in all his actions. He may wish to appear as a member of the local team on some occasions, while identifying with middle class values on others. In order to determine the social significance of any one utterance, we need additional information about the contextual clues by which natives arrive at correct interpretations of social meaning.

Recent linguistic writings have devoted considerable attention to speech events as the starting point for the analysis of verbal communication. It has been shown that aside from purely linguistic and stylistic rules, the form of a verbal message in any speech event is directly affected by a) the participants (i.e., speakers, addressees, and audiences); b) the ecological surroundings; and c) the topic or range of topics (Hymes 1964, Ervin-Tripp 1964).

In visualizing the relationship between social and linguistic factors in speech events, it seems reasonable to assume that the former restrict the selection of linguistic variables in somewhat the same way that syntactic environments serve to narrow the broader dictionary meanings of words. For the purpose of our analysis, we can thus visualize verbal communication as a two-step process. In step 1, speakers take in clues from the outside and translate them into appropriate behavioral strategies. This step parallels the perceptual process by which referential meanings are converted into sentences. In step 2, these behavioral strategies are in turn translated into appropriate verbal symbols. The determinants of this communicative process are the speaker's knowledge of the linguistic repertoire, culture and social structure, and his ability to relate these kinds of knowledge to contextual constraints. For Hemnesberget, it seems useful to describe these constraints in terms of three concepts representing successively more complex levels of information processing.

We will use the term setting to indicate the way in which natives classify their ecological environment into distinct locales. This enables us to relate the opportunities for action to constraints upon action provided by the socially significant features of the environment. First and most important among local settings in Hemnesberget is the home. Homes form the center for all domestic activities and act as meeting places for children's peer groups. Houses are well built and provide ample space for all. Also, friends and kin prefer the privacy of meetings at home to restaurants or other more public places.

Workshops and plants where productive activity is carried on are separated for the most part from residential areas, although some families continue to live next to their workshops along the shore of the fjord. The work force normally consists of male members of the group of owners, whether managed by a single nuclear family or by a group of families connected by filial, sibling or in-law ties. Employees in the larger plants frequently also include groups of kin who work together as work teams. In view of the homogeneity of workers, it is not surprising that the place of work frequently forms the center for informal gathering among males. In offices, shops and merchant establishments, on the other hand, where the expertise requirements favor socially more differentiated personnel, work relations tend to be less colored by pre-existent social ties.

A second group of settings lacks the specific restrictions on personnel which mark those mentioned above. These include the public dock, where visiting boats and the steamer are moored, as well as a few of the larger stores, for example the co-operative society store located near the central square, the square itself, and the community park. Here all local residents may meet somewhat more freely without commitments, subject of course to the constraints imposed by lack of privacy. The primary school, the junior high school, the church and community meeting hall all form somewhat more restricted meeting grounds for more formal gatherings such as class room sessions, religious services, political meetings, meetings of various voluntary associations, and occasional movie performances. The church is used only for church services.

The socio-ecological restrictions on personnel and activities still allow for a wide range of socially distinct happenings. The school, for example, is used for class sessions during the day and for meetings of voluntary associations during the evening. Similarly in the town square, men gather for discussions of public affairs, women shoppers stop to chat with acquaintances, adolescent peer groups play their various games, etc. A closer specification of social constraints is possible if we concentrate on activities carried on by particular constellations of personnel, gathered in particular settings during a particular span of time. We will use the term social situation to refer to these. Social situations form the background for the enactment of a limited range of social relationships within the framework of specific status sets, i.e., systems of complementary distributions of rights and duties (Barth 1966).

Thus alternative social definitions of the situation may occur within the same setting, depending on the opportunities and constraints on interaction offered by a shift in personnel and/ or object of the interaction. Such definitions always manifest themselves in

what we would prefer to call a <u>social event</u>. Events center around
one or at the most a limited range of topics and are distinguishable
because of their sequential structure. They are marked by stereotyped and thus recognizable opening and closing routines. The
distinction between situation and event can be clarified if we consider
the behavior of Hemnes residents who are sometimes seen in the
community office, first transacting their business in an officially
correct manner, and then turning to one of the clerks and asking
him to step aside for a private chat. The norms which apply to the
two kinds of interaction differ; the break between the two is clearly
marked. Therefore they constitute two distinct social events although
the personnel and the locale remain the same.

The terms setting, social situation, and social event as used
here can be considered three successively more complex stages in
the speaker's processing of contextual information. Each stage
subsumes the previous one in such a way that the preceding one is
part of the input affecting the selection rules of the next stage. Thus,
a speaker cannot identify the social situation without first having
made some decision as to the nature of the setting. To demonstrate
how these factors influence language usage in Hemnesberget, we
turn now to some examples drawn from participant observation.

The fact that the dialect reflects local values suggests
that it symbolizes relationships based on shared identities with
local culture. Casual observations and recording of free speech
among locals in homes, workshops, and in the various public
meeting places where such relationships are assumed, do indeed
show that only the dialect is used there. On the other hand, statuses
defined with respect to the superimposed National Norwegian system
elicit the standard. Examples of these are church services, presentation of text material in school, reports and announcements—but
not necessarily informal public appeals or political speeches—at
public meetings. Similarly, meetings with tourists or other strangers
elicit the standard at least until the participants' identity becomes
more clearly known.

Situational and Metaphorical Switching

When within the same setting the participants' definition of
the social event changes, this change may be signalled among others
by linguistic clues. On one occasion, when we, as outsiders,
stepped up to a group of locals engaged in conversation, our arrival
caused a significant alteration in the casual posture of the group.
Hands were removed from pockets, and looks changed. Predictably
our remarks elicited a code switch marked simultaneously by a
change in channel cues (i. e. sentence speed, rhythm, more hesitation
pauses, etc.) and by a shift from (R) to (B) grammar.

Similarly teachers report that while formal lectures —
where interruptions are not encouraged - are delivered in (B), they
will shift to (R) when they want to encourage open and free discussion
among students.

Each of these examples involves clear changes in the
participants' definition of each others rights and obligations. We
will use the term <u>situational switching</u> to refer to this kind of a
language shift.

The notion of situational switching assumes a direct relationship between language and the social situation. The linguistic
forms employed are critical features of the event in the sense that
any violation of selection rules changes members' perception of the
event. A person who uses the standard where only the dialect is
appropriate violates commonly accepted norms. His action may
terminate the conversation or bring about other social sanctions.
Furthermore situations differ in the amount of freedom of choice
allowed to speakers. Ritual events, like the well known Vedic
ceremonies of South Asia, constitute an extreme example of determination, where every care is taken to avoid even the slightest
change in pronunciation or rhythm lest the effectiveness of the
ceremony be destroyed. The greetings, petitions, and similar
routines described by Albert (1964) similarly seem strictly determined.

In Hemnesberget, as our example will show later on, speakers are given relatively wide choice in vocabulary and some choice in syntax. Selection rules affect mainly the variables discussed above. Values of these variables are sociolinguistically determined in the sense that when we speak of someone giving a classroom lecture or performing a Lutheran church service or talking to a tourist we can safely assume that he is using (B) grammatical forms. On the other hand two locals having a heart to heart talk will presumably speak in (R). If instead they are found speaking in (B) we conclude either that they do not identify with the values of the local team or that they are not having a heart to heart talk.

In contrast with those instances where choice of variables is narrowly constrained by social norms, there are others in which participants are given considerably more latitude. Thus official community affairs are largely defined as non-local and hence the standard is appropriate. But since many individuals who carry out the relevant activities all know each other as fellow locals, they often interject casual statements in the dialect into their formal discussions. In the course of a morning spent at the community administration office, we noticed that clerks used both standard and dialect phrases, depending on whether they were talking about official affairs or not. Likewise when residents step up to a clerk's desk, greeting and inquiries about family affairs tend to be exchanged in the dialect, while the business part of the transaction is carried on in the standard.

In neither of the above cases is there any significant change in definition of participants' mutual rights and obligations. The posture of speakers and channel clues of their speech remain the same. The language switch here relates to particular kinds of topics or subject matters rather than to change in social situation. Characteristically the situations in question allow for the enactment of two or more different relationships among the same set of individuals. The choice of either (R) or (B) alludes to these relationships and thus generates meanings which are quite similar to those conveyed by the alternation between t̲y̲ or v̲y̲ in the examples from Russian literature cited by Friedrich (1966).

We will use the term metaphorical switching for this phenomenon.

The semantic effect of metaphorical switching depends on the existence of regular relationships between variables and social situation of the type discussed above. The context in which one of a set of alternates is regularly used becomes part of its meaning so that when this form is then employed in a context where it is not normal, it brings in some of the flavor of this original setting. Thus a phrase like 'April is the cruelest month' is regarded as poetic because of its association with T. S. Eliot's poetry. When used in natural conversation it gives that conversation some of the flavor of this poetry. Similarly when (R) phrases are inserted metaphorically into a (B) conversation this may, depending on the circumstances, add a special social meaning of confidentiality or privateness to the conversation.

The case of the local who after finishing his business in the community office turns to a clerk and asks him to step aside for a private chat further illustrates the contrast between metaphorical and role switching. By their constant alternation between the standard and the dialect during their business transaction, they alluded to the dual relationship which exists between them. The event was terminated when the local asked the clerk in the dialect whether he had time to step aside to talk about private affairs suggesting in effect that they shift to a purely personal, local relationship. The clerk looked around and said, "Yes, we are not too busy." The two then stepped aside although remaining in the same room, and their subsequent private discussion was appropriately carried on entirely in the dialect.

The Experiment

Our discussion of verbal behavior so far has relied largely on deductive reasoning supported by unstructured ethnographic observation. Additional tests of our hypothesis are based on controlled text elicitation. We have stated above that gatherings

among friends and kin implying shared local identities must be
carried on in the dialect. If we are correct in our hypothesis, then
individuals involved in such friendly gatherings should not change
speech variety regardless of whether they talk about local, national
or official matters.

In order to test this, we asked local acquaintances whom we
knew to be part of the network of local relationships to arrange a
friendly gathering at which refreshments were to be served and to
allow us to record the proceedings as samples of dialect speech.
Two such gatherings were recorded, one in the living room of our
local hosts, and the other in the home of an acquaintance. The fact
that arrangements for the meeting were made by local people means
that the groups were self-recruited. Participants in the first group
included two sisters and a brother and their respective spouses.
One of the men was a shopkeeper, one of the few in this category
who claims local descent, his brothers-in-law were employed as
craftsmen. All three men are quite literate compared to workmen
elsewhere in the world and well read in public affairs. They are
active in local politics and experienced in formal committee work.
The second group included three craftsmen, friends and neighbors
who worked in the same plant, and their wives. One of these had
served as a sailor on a Norwegian merchant vessel for several
years and spoke English. Participants were all quite familiar with
standard Norwegian, and our recorded conversations contain several
passages where the standard was used in quoting non-local speech
or in statements directed at us.

Methodologically, self-recruitment of groups is important
for two reasons. It insures that groups are defined by locally
recognized relationships and enables the investigator to predict
the norms relevant to their interaction. Furthermore, the fact
that participants have preexisting obligations towards each other
means that, given the situation, they are likely to respond to such
obligations in spite of the presence of strangers. Our tape recording
and our visual observations give clear evidence that this in fact
was what occurred.

Our strategy was to introduce discussion likely to mobilize obligations internal to the group, thus engaging members in discussion among themselves. This proved to be relatively easy to do. When a point had been discussed for some time, we would attempt to change the subject by injecting new questions or comments. In doing this, we did not of course expect that our own interjections would predictably affect the speakers' choice of codes. Participants were always free to reinterpret our comments in any way they wished. Nevertheless, the greater the range of topics covered, the greater likelihood of language shift.

As a rule, our comments were followed by a few introductory exchanges directed at us. These were marked by relatively slow sentence speeds, many hesitation pauses, and visual clues indicating that people were addressing us. Linguistically, we noted some switching to the standard in such exchanges. After a brief period of this, if the topic was interesting, internal discussion began and arguments that referred to persons, places, and events we could not possibly be expected to have any knowledge about developed. The transition to internal discussion was marked by an increase in sentence speed and lack of hesitation pauses and similar clues. The tape recorder was running continuously during the gatherings, and after some time participants became quite oblivious to its presence.

Only those passages which were clearly recognizable as internal discussion were used in the analysis; all others were eliminated. The texts obtained in this way consist of stretches of free discussion on diverse topics. The following passages show that our hypothesis about the lack of connection between code switching and change in topic was confirmed.

Group I: Topic: Chit chat about local events.

Gunnar: ja de va ein så kåmm idag--ein så kåmm me mælka--
            så sa hanj de va så varmt inj på mo i går--ja, sa eg,
            de va no isse vent anjæ dåkk må no ha meir enn di anjrann
            bestanjdi.

Yes, there was one who came today—one who came with
milk— so he said it was so warm in Mo yesterday. Yes,
I said, there is nothing else to be expected, you people
must always have more than anybody else.

Topic: Industrial planning.

Alf: her kunj ha vøre eit par sånn mellomstore bedreftæ på
             ein førti-fæmti manu so ha bešæftigæ denna falke detta
             sa ha gadd ledi amm vinjtæ rn.

             There might have been here some medium-size plants
             employing forty to fifty men which then could offer work
             to those we have nothing to do in winter.

Topic: Governmental affairs.

Oscar: vi jekk inj før denn første injstiljingæ ifrå šeikommitenn.

             We supported the first proposal made by the Schei
             Committee.

        Item one deals with a local topic in a somewhat humorous
way; items two and three concern planning and formal governmental
affairs. All these passages are clearly in the dialect. Of the
phonological variables, [nj] and [lj] show the highest degree of
palatalization and [a] and [æ] the highest degree of retraction throughout. Morphophonemic dialect markers are (R) ein, "one"; så,
"who"; isse, "not"; dåkk, "you"; meir, "more"; her, "here";
jekk, "went"; ifrå, "from". Even lexical borrowings from the
standard such as injstiljing, "proposal" and bedreftæ "plants" are
clearly in dialect phonology and morphology. We find one single
instance of what seems to be a standard form: (B) mellom/ (R)
imelja, "middle." But this only occurs as part of the borrowed
compound mellomstore "medium-size." In several hours of
conversation with both groups, marked by many changes in topic,

we have found a number of lexical borrowings but not one clear instance
of phonological or grammatical switching, in spite of the fact that all
informants clearly know standard grammar.

      While our hypothesis suggests that switching is constrained
in those situations which allow only local relationships to be enacted,
it also leads us to predict that whenever local and non-local relationships are relevant to the same situation, topical variation may elicit
code switching. To test this, we selected members of a formerly
quite active local peer group. For the last few years these individuals
have all been at universities in Oslo, Bergen, and Trondheim. They
return home in the summer either for vacation or to take up local
employment. In conventional interview sessions, all participants
claimed to be pure dialect speakers and professed local attitudes
about dialect use. They thus regard themselves as members of the
local "team". As fellow students, however, they also share statuses
that are identified with Pan-Norwegian values and associated with
the standard. Our assumption, then, is that if topical stimuli are
introduced which elicit these values, switching may result.

      Three gatherings were arranged in the home of one of our
informants. Refreshments were again served. Elicitation strategies
were similar to those employed with the first two groups and similar
ranges of topics were covered. The examples cited below show that
our hypothesis was again confirmed.

Group III Topic: Chit chat about drinking habits.

Berit: ja, ja mæn vi bjynjt anjer veien du—vi bjynjt i barnelošen—
           så vi har de unjajort.

           Yes, yes, we started the other way, we started in the
           children's anti-alcoholic league. So we have finished
           all that.

           Topic: Industrial development.

Berit: jo da viss di bare fikk de te lønn seg—så e i værtfall

prisnivåe hær i Rana skrudd høger enn de e vanligvis
anner stann i lanne.

Yes, if they could only manage to make it profitable—
so in any case the prices tend to be higher here in Rana
than is common in other places in the country.

Topic: Informal statement about university regulations.

Ola: mænn no ha dæmm læmpæ på de.

But now they have relaxed that.

Topic: Authoritative statement about university regulations.

Ola: de væl du mellom en fæmm sæks.

You choose that from among five or six.

     Comparison of Berit's and Ola's first statement with their
second statements shows considerable shifting in each case. Thus
Berit's second utterance has such unpalatalized forms as <u>anner</u> (versus
<u>anjer</u> above), and raised and less retracted [a] in <u>da</u>. She also uses
standard variables (B) <u>fikk</u>/ (R) <u>fekk</u>, (B) <u>viss</u>/ (R) <u>vess</u>, (B) <u>værtfall</u>/
(R) <u>kvart fall</u>, (B) <u>hær</u>/ (R) <u>her</u>, etc. Ola's second statement is
characterized by (B) <u>mellom</u>/ (R) <u>imelja</u> and (B) <u>en</u>/ (R) <u>ein</u>. Similarly
his [æ] in <u>fæm</u> and <u>sæks</u> is raised and fronted. In neither case is
the shift to the standard complete—after all the situation never lost
its informality. Berit's statement still contains dialect words like
the (R) <u>lønn</u>/ (B) <u>lønne,</u> "to be profitable"; (R) <u>stan</u>/ (B) <u>steder,</u>
"places"; and Ola has (R) <u>væl</u>/ (B) <u>velger,</u> "to choose." What we
see then is a breakdown of co-occurrence rules, an erosion of the
linguistic boundary between Ranamål and Bokmål. The tendency is
to switch towards standard phonology while preserving some
morphophonemic and lexical dialect features of (R). Features
retained in this manner are largely those which also occur in other
local dialects and to some extent also in Nynorsk. They have thus
gained some acceptance as proper dialect forms. Those characteristics

which locals refer to as broad speech, i.e., those that are known as
purely local peculiarities, tend to be eliminated.

It must also be noted that Berit and Ola also differ in their
pronunciation of the phonological variables. Ola's normal pronunciation shows the strong palatalization of consonants and extreme
vowel retraction characteristic of most residents. Berit's normal
pronunciation has medium palatalization and medium retraction.
Both, however, switch in the same direction, in response to similar
situational and topical clues, and this agreement on the rules of
stylistic manipulation is clearly more important in this case than the
mere articulatory difference in Berit's and Ola's speech.

The social character of the style switch was clearly revealed
when the tape recorded conversations were played back to other Hemnes
residents. One person who had been working with us as a linguistic
informant at first refused to believe that the conversations were
recorded locally. When he recognized the voices of the participants,
he showed clear signs of disapproval. Apparently he viewed the
violation of co-occurrence rules as a sign of what is derogatorily
called knot, "artificial speech" in colloquial Norwegian. Some of the
participants showed similar reactions when they heard themselves on
tape. They promised to refrain from switching during future discussion
sessions. Our analysis of these later sessions, however, revealed
that when an argument required that the speaker validate his status
as an intellectual he would again tend to use standard forms in the
manner shown above by Berit and Ola. Code selection rules thus
seem to be akin to grammatical rules. Both operate below the level
of consciousness and may be independent of the speaker's overt
intentions.

Additional information about usage patterns in group three
was provided through a fortunate accident. One of our sessions with
this group was interrupted by a somewhat mentally retarded young
person, who has the habit of appearing in peoples' homes to solicit
assistance for his various schemes. Here are some examples of
remarks addressed to him by Berit and Solveig, of all members
of the group the most prone to use standard forms. Her normal

pronunciation shows the least amount of consonant palatalization. She is socially more marginal to Hemnes than other members of the group.

Group III Topic: Talking to a retarded local youth.

Berit: e de du så vikarier førr hanj no.

              Are you a stand in for him now?

Solveig: hanj kanj jo jett gåte, hanj kanj no va me.

              He is good at word games, he should participate.

        Both Berit and Solveig's pronunciation in the above examples become identical with the ordinary speech of Ola and of the members of group one. The extreme palatalization of [nj] and the lowering of [a] is not normal for them; they clearly are talking down in this case. Their stylistic range, as well as their facility in switching, seems to be greater than those of the others.

        In comparing the behavior of the first two groups with that of group three, we find two different kinds of language usage patterns. All three groups speak both the dialect and the standard. Groups one and two, however, only show situational switching. When members talk to each other, differences of formality or informality of topics are reflected only in the lexicon. Pronunciation and morphology do not change. Those groups shift to (B) phonology and grammar only when remarks are addressed directly to us, who count as outsiders, or in indirect quotes of such matters as government rules, officials' statements, etc. In such instances of situation switching therefore, Ranamål and Bokmål are kept separate throughout by strict co-occurrence restrictions. In group three, on the other hand, deviation from the dialect results both from metaphorical and situation switching. Metaphorical switching furthermore involves a breakdown of the co-occurrence restrictions characteristic of situational shifts.

The dialect usage of locals corresponds to their view that the two varieties are distinct, and to their insistence on maintaining the strict separation of local and non-local values. For the students, on the other hand, the distinction between dialect and standard is not so sharp. Although they display the same general attitudes about the dialect as the team of locals, their behavior shows a range of variation rather than an alternation between distinct systems. It reflects a de facto recognition of their own non-local identification.

A fourth conversational group further illustrates the internal speech diversity in the community. The principal speakers here are two men, A and B, and C, who is A's wife. All come from families who tend to dissociate themselves from the egalitarian value system of the local team. Their normal style of speech for remarks directed at us, as well as for in-group speech, was Bokmål(B). Only in the few instances when A began telling local anecdotes did he lapse into Ranamål.(R) forms were introduced as metaphorical switches into what were basically (B) utterances to provide local color, indicate humor, etc. in somewhat the same way that speakers in group III had used (B) forms in (R) utterances.

In the course of the evening, A and B's teenage daughter joined the conversation. She expressed attitudes towards the dialect which are quite similar to those of the students in group three and thus are somewhat different from those of her parents. The few samples we have of her speech show (R) phonology similar to that of Berit and Solveig in group three.

Although the picture of language usage derived from the above four groups seems at first highly complex, it becomes less so when viewed in relation to speakers' attitudes, interactional norms, and local values. All Hemnes residents have the same repertoire. Their linguistic competence includes control of both (R) and (B) rules. They vary in the way in which they use these rules. Expressed attitudes towards (R) and (B) do not provide an explanation for these differences in speech behavior. The most reasonable explanation of the ways in which these groups differ seems to be that the dual system of local values, differences in individual

background, and the various social situations in which members find
themselves operate to alter their interpretation of the social meaning
of the variables they employ.

Conclusion

Our analysis in this paper is based on the assumption that
regularities in behavior can be analyzed as generated from a series
of individual choices made under specifiable constraints and
incentives (Barth 1966). This position implies an important break
with previous approaches to social structure and to language and
society. Behavioral regularities are no longer regarded as reflections
of independently measurable social norms; on the contrary, these
norms are themselves seen as communicative behavior. They are
reflected in what Goffman (1959) calls the rules of impression
management or, in our terms, in the social meanings which constrain
the actor's adoption of behavioral strategies in particular situations.

In interactional sociolinguistics, therefore, we can no
longer base our analyses on the assumption that language and society
constitute different kinds of reality, subject to correlational studies.
Social and linguistic information is comparable only when studied
within the same general analytical framework. Moving from statements of social constraints to grammatical rules thus represents
a transformation from one level of abstraction to another within a
single communicative system.

As Bernstein (1961) has pointed out, verbal communication
is a process in which actors select from a limited range of alternates
within a repertoire of speech forms determined by previous learning.
Although ultimately this selection is a matter of individual choice,
our paper shows that the rules of codification by which the deep
structure of interpersonal relations is transformed into speech
performances are independent of expressed attitudes and similar in
nature to the grammatical rules operating on the level of intelligibility.
They form part of what Hymes (1970) has called the speaker's
communicative competence. Sociolinguistic constraints on the

selection of variables seem to be of central importance in this codification process. We argued that they determine the speaker's perception of the utterances as a unit of social meaning. By accepting the native's view of what is and what is not properly part of a dialect or language, linguists have tended to assume these co-occurrences rather than investigate them empirically. We have attempted to develop descriptive procedures suitable for the empirical investigation of these rules by combining various ethnographic field techniques with conventional linguistic elicitation methods.

In Hemnes, where Ranamål and Bokmål communicate the same objective information, we were led to ask how the apparent separateness of the dialect and the standard can exist and be maintained. Ethnographic investigation suggests the hypothesis that Ranamål has social value as a signal of distinctness and of a speaker's identification with others of local descent. This social significance of the dialect can only be understood by contrast with the meanings which locals assign to the standard, the language of non-local activities. The standard is associated with education and power on the national scene and carries connotations of differences in rank which are unacceptable in the realm of informal local relations. When used casually among Hemnes residents, therefore, it communicates dissociation from the "local team."

Since most Hemnes natives live, marry, and earn their livelihood among others of their own kind, their values are rarely challenged. Their personal relations have all the characteristics of network closure (Barnes 1954). On the other hand, those with non-local background and who maintain significant ties in other communities tend to seek their friends among those in similar circumstances, even though they may have resided in Hemnes for more than a generation. Their contacts with members of the "local team" remain largely non-personal, focusing around single tasks, and thus similar in kind to non-local contacts. This lack of personal ties between individuals of dissimilar backgrounds and cultural identification reinforces the general social meanings ascribed to the dialect by those who share local background and identity, and thus contributes to maintaining the separateness of dialect and standard.

While this information provides the background for our study, it does not explain the fact that all residents frequently switch between the dialect and the standard. This can only be explained through the analysis of particular speech events. The concepts of setting, social situation, and social event represent an attempt to explain the natives' conception of their behavioral environment in terms of an ordered set of constraints which operate to transform alternative lines of behavior into particular social meanings. Our distinction between metaphoric and role switching shows how constraints at different levels of inclusiveness produce appropriate changes in the way speech performances are interpreted.

Although locals show an overt preference for the dialect, they tolerate and use the standard in situations where it conveys meanings of officiality, expertise, and politeness toward strangers who are clearly segregated from their personal life. In private gatherings where people meet as natives and equals, a speaker's use of standard variables suggests social dissociation, an attitude which is felt to be out of place. Although the students in our experimental sessions meet as locals and friends, they differ from other members of the local team because they share the additional status of intellectuals. This fact modifies the social meaning of standard forms when they are used among the students. To refrain from using standard forms for those topics which elicit particpants' shared experience as intellectuals would constitute an unnatural limitation on their freedom of expression. Group four demonstrates the effect of intra-community differences in value systems on language usage patterns. Because of this identification with the urban middle classes the adult members of this group use (B) as their normal form of speech while employing (R) only for special effect. Such usage distinctions however are not necessarily very stable. The teenage daughter of the adult members seems to follow local usage thus symbolizing her identification with her peer group, rather than with her family.

Our experiments, and the analysis presented in this paper, demonstrate the importance of social or non-referential meaning for the study of language in society. Mere naturalistic observation of speech behavior is not enough. In order to interpret what he hears, the investigator must have some background knowledge of the local culture of the processes which generate social meaning. Without this it is impossible to generalize about the social implication of dialect differences. The processes studied here are specific to particular small communities. Predictions of language maintenance or language shift in larger societies will of course have to depend on statistical generalizations. More studies along the lines suggested here, however, should materially improve the validity of such generalizations. For Hemnesberget, the fate of the dialect seems assured as long as local identification maintains its importance, and the socio-ecological system continues to prevent any significant accumulation of individuals who, like the students, fail to maintain the situational barrier between the dialects and the standard.

NOTE

Some of the data cited in this study were given in preliminary form in previous publications (Gumperz 1964 and Gumperz 1966). The authors are grateful to Einar Haugen, Aaron Cicourel, and Richard Howell for their comments. Field work for the study was sponsored by the Institute of Sociology, University of Oslo, Norway. We are grateful to Professor Sverre Holm of that institution for support and encouragement. Mr. Gumperz' stay in Norway was made possible through a senior post-doctorate fellowship from the National Science Foundation.

REFERENCES

Albert, Ethel. 1964. "Rhetoric", "logic", and "poetics" in Burundi: culture patterning of speech behavior. The ethnography of communication, ed. by John Gumperz and Dell Hymes. American Anthropologist 66:6, part 2, 35-54.

Barth, Fredrik (ed.) 1963. The role of the entrepreneur in social change in northern Norway. Bergen: Norwegian Universities Press.

_____ 1964. Ethnic processes in the Pathan-Baluchi boundary in Indo-Iranica: melanges présenté a Georg Morgenstierne a l'occasion de son soixante dixième anniversaire. Wiesbaden: Otto Harrassowitz.

_____ 1966. Models of social organization. London: Royal Anthropological Institute of Great Britain and Ireland.

Barnes, John A. 1954. Class and committees in a Norwegian island parish. Human Relations 8.39-58.

Bernstein, Basil. 1961. Social structure, language and learning. Educational Research 3.163-76.

_____ 1964. Elaborated and restricted codes: their social origins and some consequences. The ethnography of communication, ed. by John Gumperz and Dell Hymes. American Anthropologist 66:6, part 2, 55-69.

Christiansen, Hallfried. 1962. Malet i Rana. Oslo: Institut for Sociologi, Universitetet i Oslo.

Coldevin, Axel. 1958. Et bidrag til Rana-bygdens Socialhistorie. Oslo: Institut for Sociologi, Universitetet i Oslo.

Ervin-Tripp, Susan. 1964. An analysis of the interaction of language, topic, and listener. The ethnography of communication, ed. by John Gumperz and Dell Hymes. American Anthropologist 66:6, part 2, 86-102.

Goffman, Erving. 1959. The presentation of self in everyday life. New York: Doubleday.

Goffman, Erving. 1964. The neglected situation. The ethnography of communication, ed. by John Gumperz and Dell Hymes. American Anthropologist 66:6, part 2, 133-37.

Gumperz, John J. 1964. Linguistic and social interaction in two communities. The ethnography of communication, ed. by John Gumperz and Dell Hymes. American Anthropologist 66:6, part 2, 137-53. [In this volume, pp. 151-76.]

_____ 1966. On the ethnology of linguistic change. Sociolinguistics, ed. by William Bright, 27-49, The Hague: Mouton and Co.

Hymes, Dell. 1964. Introduction: toward ethnographies of communication. The ethnography of communication, ed. by John Gumperz and Dell Hymes. American Anthropologist 66:6, part 2, 1-35.

_____ 1970. On communicative competence. Philadelphia: University of Pennsylvania Press.

Labov, William. 1964. Phonological correlates of social stratification. The ethnography of communication, ed. by John Gumperz and Dell Hymes. American Anthropologist 66:6, part 2, 164-76.

_____ 1966. The social stratification of English in New York City. Washington, D.C.: Center for Applied Linguistics.

Ramanujan, A. K. 1967. The structure of variation: a study of caste dialects. Social Structure and Social Change in India, ed. by Bernard Cohn and Milton Singer. Chicago: The University of Chicago Press.

17 | Bilingualism, Bidialectalism, and Classroom Interaction

In Collaboration with Eduardo Hernández-Ch.

Recent systematic research in the inner city has successfully disproved the notions of those who characterize the language of low income populations as degenerate and structurally underdeveloped. There is overwhelming evidence to show that both middle class and non-middle class children, no matter what their native language, dialect, or ethnic background, when they come to school at the age of five or six, have control of a fully formed grammatical system. The mere fact that their system is distinct from that of their teacher does not mean that their speech is not rule-governed. Speech features which strike the teacher as different do not indicate failure to adjust to some universally accepted English norm; rather, they are the output of dialect or language-specific syntactic rules which are every bit as complex as those of standard English (Labov, 1969).

It is clear furthermore that the above linguistic differences also reflect far-reaching and systematic cultural differences. Like the plural societies of Asia and Africa, American urban society is characterized by the coexistence of a variety of distinct cultures. Each major ethnic group has its own heritage, its own body of traditions, values and views about what is right and proper. These traditions are passed on from generation to generation as part of the informal family or peer group socialization process and are encoded in folk art and literature, oral or written.

To understand this complex system, it is first of all necessary to identify and describe its constituent elements. Grammatical

analysis must be, and has to some extent been, supplemented by
ethnographic description, ethnohistory, and the study of folk art
(Hannerz, 1969; Stewart, 1968; Abrahams, 1964; Kochman, 1969).
But mere description of component sub-systems is not enough if
we are to learn how the plurality of cultures operates in everyday
interaction and how it affects the quality of individual lives. Minority
groups in urbanized societies are never completely isolated from
the dominant majority. To study their life ways without reference
to surrounding populations is to distort the realities of their everyday lives. All residents of modern industrial cities are subject
to the same laws and are exposed to the same system of public
education and mass communication. Minority group members, in
fact, spend much of their day in settings where dominant norms
prevail. Although there are significant individual differences in
the degree of assimilation, almost all minority group members, even
those whose behavior on the surface may seem quite deviant, have
at least a passive knowledge of the dominant culture. What sets them
off from others is not simply the fact that they are distinct, but the
juxtaposition of their own private language and life styles with that
of the public at large.

        This juxtaposition, which is symbolized by constant alterna-
tion between in-group and out-group modes of acting and expression
has a pervasive effect on everyday behavior. Successful political
leaders such as the late Martin Luther King and Bobby Seale rely on
it for much of their rhetorical effect. C. Kernan in her recent
ethnographic study of verbal communication in an Afro-American
community reports that her informants' everyday conversation
reveals an overriding concern — be it positive or negative —with
majority culture (Kernan, 1969).

        Majority group members who have not experienced a similar
disjuncture between private and public behavior frequently fail to
appreciate its effect. They tend merely to perceive minority group
members as different, without realizing the effect that this difference
may have on everyday communication. This ignorance of minority
styles of behavior seems to have contributed to the often discussed

notion of "linguistic deprivation." No one familiar with the writings of Afro-American novelists of the last decade and with the recent writings on black folklore can maintain that low income blacks are non-verbal. An exceptionally rich and varied terminological system, including such folk concepts as "sounding," "signifying," "rapping," "running it down," "chucking," "jiving," "marking," etc., all referring to verbal strategies (i.e., different modes of achieving particular communicative ends), testifies to the importance which Afro-American culture assigns to verbal art (Kochman, 1969; Kernan, 1969). Yet, inner city black children are often described as non-verbal, simply because they fail to respond to the school situation. It is true that lower class children frequently show difficulty in performing adequately in formal interviews and psychological tests. But these tests are frequently administered under conditions which seem unfamiliar and, at times, threatening to minority group children. When elicitation conditions are changed, there is often a radical improvement in response (Labov, 1969; Mehan, 1970).

The fact that bilingualism and biculturalism have come to be accepted as major goals in inner city schools, is an important advance. But if we are to achieve this goal we require at least some understanding of the nature of code alternation and its meaning in everyday interaction. Bilingualism is, after all, primarily a linguistic term, referring to the fact that linguists have discovered significant alternations in phonology, morphology, and syntax, in studying the verbal behavior of a particular population. While bilingual phenomena have certain linguistic features in common, these features may have quite different social significance.

Furthermore, to the extent that social conditions affect verbal behavior, findings based on research in one type of bilingual situation may not necessarily be applicable to another socially different one.

Sociolinguistic studies of bilingualism for the most part focus on the linguistic aspects of the problem. Having discovered that speakers alternate between what, from a linguistic point of view, constitute grammatically distinct systems, investigators then proceed to study where and under what conditions alternants are employed, either through surveys in which speakers are asked to report their own language usage (Fishman, 1965) or by counting the occurrence of relevant forms in samples of elicited speech. The assumption is that the presence or absence of particular linguistic alternates directly reflects significant information about such matters as group membership, values, relative prestige, power relationships, etc.

There is no doubt that such one-to-one relationships between language and social phenomena do exist in most societies. Where speakers control and regularly employ two or more speech varieties and continue to do so over long periods of time, it is most likely that each of the two varieties will be associated with certain activities or social characteristics of speakers. This is especially the case in formal or ceremonial situations, such as religious or magical rites, court proceedings, stereotyped introductions, greetings or leavetakings. Here language, as well as gestures and other aspects of demeanor, may be so rigidly specified as to form part of the defining characteristics of the setting — so much so that a change in language may change the setting.

There are, however, many other cases where such correlations break down. Consider the following sentences cited in a recent study of bilingualism in Texas (Lance, 1969:75-76):

1. Te digo que este dedo (I TELL YOU THAT THIS FINGER) has been bothering me so much.

   Se me hace que (IT SEEMS THAT) I have to respect her porque 'ta (BECAUSE SHE IS)

   But this arthritis deal, boy you get to hurting so bad you can't hardly even... 'cer masa pa tortillas (MAKE DOUGH FOR TORTILLAS).

Similar examples come from a recently recorded discussion between
two educated Mexican Americans.

    2a. W.   Well, I'm glad that I met you. O. K. ?

     b: M.   Andale pues (O. K. SWELL) and do come again. Mm.

     c: M.   Con ellos dos (WITH THE TWO OF THEM). With
                 each other. La señora trabaja en la canería orita,
                 you know? (THE MOTHER WORKS IN THE
                 CANNERY RIGHT NOW). She was...con Francine
                 jugaba...(SHE USED TO PLAY WITH FRANCINE...)
                 with my little girl.

     d: M.   There's no children in the neighborhood. Well...
                 sí hay criaturas (THERE ARE CHILDREN).

     e: M.   ...those friends are friends from Mexico que
                 tienen chamaquitos (WHO HAVE LITTLE
                 CHILDREN).

     f: M.   ...that has nothing to do con que le hagan esta...
                 (WITH THEIR DOING THIS).

     g: M.   But the person...de...de grande (AS AN ADULT)
                 is gotta have something in his mouth.

     h: M.   And my uncle Sam es el mas agabachado (IS THE
                 MOST AMERICANIZED).

    It would be futile to predict the occurrence of either English
or Spanish in the above utterances by attempting to isolate social
variables which correlate with linguistic form. Topic, speaker,
setting are common in each. Yet the code changes sometimes in
the middle of a sentence.

    Language mixing of this type is by no means a rarity.
Linguists specializing in bilingualism cite it to provide examples

of extreme instances of interference (Mackey, 1965). Some native
speakers in ethnically diverse communities are reluctant to admit
its existence. It forms the subject of many humorous treatises. In
Texas it tends to be referred to by pejorative terms such as Tex-
Mex. Yet in spite of the fact that such extreme code switching is
held in disrepute, it is very persistent wherever minority language
groups come in close contact with majority language groups under
conditions of rapid social change.

One might, by way of an explanation, simply state that
both codes are equally admissible in some contexts and that code
switching is merely a matter of the individual's momentary inclina-
tion. Yet the alternation does carry meaning. Let us compare
the following passage from a recent analysis of Russian pronominal
usage (Friedrich, 1966) with an excerpt from a conversation.

> 3. An arrogant aristocratic lieutenant and a grizzled,
>   older captain find themselves thrust together as the
>   only officers on an isolated outpost in the Caucasus.
>   Reciprocal formality at first seems appropriate to
>   both. But while the latter is sitting on the young
>   lieutenant's bed and discussing a confidential matter
>   he switches to ty (tu). When the lieutenant appears
>   to suggest insubordination, however, the captain
>   reverts to vy (vous) as he issues a peremptory
>   demand... (p. 240).

> 4. M. I don't think I ever have any conversations in
>   my dreams. I just dream. Ha. I don't hear
>   people talking: I jus' see pictures.
>
>   E. Oh. They're old-fashioned, then. They're not
>   talkies yet, Huh?
>
>   M. They're old-fashioned. No. They're not talkies,
>   yet. No. I'm trying to think. Yeah, there too
>   have been talkies. Different. In Spanish and
>   English both. An' I would't be too surprised if
>   I even had some in Chinese. (Laughter). Yeah,

> Ed. Deveras (REALLY). (M. offers E. a
> a cigarette which is refused). Tú no fumas,
> ¿verdad? Yo tampoco. Dejé de fumar.

The two societies, the social context and the topics discussed differ, yet the shift from English to Spanish has connotations similar to the alternation between the formal (second person pronoun) vy (vous) and the informal ty (tu). Both signal a change in interpersonal relationship in the direction of greater informality or personal warmth. Although the linguistic signs differ, they reflect similar social strategies. What the linguist identifies as code switching may convey important social information. The present paper is an attempt to elucidate the relationship between linguistic form, interactional strategies and social meaning on the basis of a detailed study of a natural conversation, and to suggest implications for understanding language use in the culturally diverse classroom.

The conversation cited in Items 2 and 4 was recorded in an institution specializing in English instruction for small Mexican immigrant children. The staff, ranging in age from recent high school graduates to persons in their middle fifties, includes a large number of people of Mexican or Mexican-American descent as well as some English speaking Americans. Of the latter group, several speak Spanish well. The recording was made by a linguist (E), a native American of Mexican ancestry who is employed as an advisor for the program. His interlocutor (M) is a community counselor employed in the program. She is a woman without higher education who has been trained to assist the staff in dealing with the local community. She has had some experience in public affairs. In spite of the difference in education and salary, both participants regard each other as colleagues within the context of the program. When speaking Spanish they address each other by the reciprocal tú. The program director or a Spanish-speaking outsider visitor would receive the respectful "usted." Conversations within the office are normally carried on in English although, as will be seen later, there are marked stylistic differences which distinguish interaction among Mexican-Americans from interaction across ethnic boundaries.

For analysis the taped transcript was roughly divided into episodes, each centering around a single main topic. Episodes were then sub-divided into 'turns of speaking' (i.e., one or more sentences reflecting a speaker's response to another's comment). The author and the interviewer cooperated in the analysis of social meaning. Two types of information were utilized. Turns containing a code switch were first examined as to their place within the structure of the total conversation in terms of such questions as: what were the relevant antecedents of the turn and what followed? what was the turn in response to, either in the same or preceding episodes? The purpose here was to get as detailed as possible an estimation of the speaker's intent. In the second stage the switched phrase would be substituted with a phrase from the other language in somewhat the same way that a linguistic interviewer uses the method of variation within a frame in order to estimate the structural significance of a particular item. By this method it was possible to get an idea of what the code switch contributed to the meaning of the whole passage.

Before discussing the social aspects of code switching, some discussion of what it is that is being switched is necessary. Not all instances of Spanish words in the text are necessarily instances of code switching. Expressions like ándale pues (Item 2) dice (he says) are normally part of the bilingual's style of English. Speakers use such expressions when speaking to others of the same ethnic background in somewhat the same way that Yiddish expressions like nebbish, oi gewalt, or interjections like du hoerst characterize the in-group English style of some American Jews. They serve as stylistic ethnic identity markers and are frequently used by speakers who no longer have effective control of both languages. The function of such forms as an ethnic identity marker becomes particularly clear in the following sequence between M. and a woman visitor in her office.

> 5. Woman: Well, I'm glad that I met you. O.K. ?
> M. : Andale, pues. (O.K. SWELL) And do come again, mmm?

The speakers, both Mexican-Americans, are strangers who have met for the first time. The ándade pues is given in response to the woman's O.K., as if to say: 'although we are strangers we have the same background and should get to know each other better. '

Aside from loan word nouns such as <u>chicano</u>, <u>gabacho</u>, or <u>pocho</u>, the ethnic identity markers consist largely of exclamations and sentence connectors. For example:

6. M: I says Lupe no hombre (WHY NO) don't believe that.
7. M: Sí (YES) but it doesn't.
8. M: That baby is...pues (THEN).

Mexican-Spanish is similarly marked by English interjections. Note for example the <u>you know</u> in the sentence:

9. M: Pero como, you know...la Estela...

The English form here seems a regular part of the Spanish text, and this is signalled phonetically by the fact that the pronunciation of the vowel <u>o</u> is relatively undipthongized and thus differs from other instances of <u>o</u> in English passages. Similarly, words like <u>ice cream</u> have Spanish-like pronunciations when they occur within Spanish texts, and English-like pronunciations in the English text.

The greater part of the instances of true code switching consist of entire sentences inserted into the other language text. There are, however, also some examples of change within single sentences, which require special comment. In the items below, the syntactic connection is such that both parts can be interpreted as independent sentences.

10. M: We've got all these kids here right now, los que están ya criados aquí (THOSE THAT HAVE BEEN RAISED HERE).

This is not the case with the noun qualifier phrase in Item (4) and the verb complement in (5). Other examples of this latter type are:

11. M: But the person...de...de grande (AS AN ADULT)
       is gotta have something in its mouth.
12. M: ci Será que quiero la tetera? para pacify myself.
       (IT MUST BE THAT I WANT THE BABY BOTTLE
       TO...)
13. M: The type of work he did cuando trabajaba (WHEN
       HE WORKED) he...what...that I remember, era
       regador (HE WAS AN IRRIGATOR) at one time.
14. M: An' my uncle Sam es el mas agabachado (IS THE
       MOST AMERICANIZED).

Noun qualifiers (2e), verb complements (2f), parts of a
noun phrase (13), the predicate portion of an equational sentence
(14) all can be switched. This does not mean, however, that there
are no linguistic constraints on the co-occurrence of Spanish and
English forms. The exact specification of these constraints will,
however, require further detailed investigation. Clearly, aside
from single loan words, entire sentences are most easily borrowed.
Sentence modifiers or phrases are borrowed less frequently. And
this borrowing does seem to be subject to some selection constraints
(Blom and Gumperz, 1970). But some tentative statements can
be made. Constructions like:

              *que have chamaquitos (WHO HAVE BOYS)

or,

              *he era regador (HE WAS AN IRRIGATOR)

seem impossible.

The Social Meaning of Code Switching

         When asked why they use Spanish in an English sentence or
vice-versa, speakers frequently come up with explanations like the
following taken from our conversation:

15. If there's a word that I can't find, it keeps comin' out in Spanish.
16. I know what word I want and finally when I...well bring it out in Spanish, I know the person understands me.

Difficulty in finding the right word clearly seems to account for examples like: para pacify myself (Item 17). In other instances, some items of experience, some referents or topics are more readily recalled in one language than in another, as in:

17. M: I got to thinking vacilando el pun to este (MULLING OVER THIS POINT).
18. M: They only use English when they have to...like for cuando van de compras (WHEN THEY GO SHOPPING).

Linguistically motivated switches into English occur when the discussion calls for psychological terminology or expressions, e.g., 'pacify,' 'relax,' 'I am a biter.' Such expressions or modes of talking seem rarely used in typically Mexican-American settings. On the other hand, ideas and experiences associated with the speaker's Spanish-speaking past such as Items (20) and (21) trigger off a switch into Spanish.

In many other instances, however, there seems to be no linguistic reason for the switch. Si hay criaturas (Item 3) is directly translated without hesitation pause in the following sentence. Many other Spanish expressions have English equivalents elsewhere in the text. Furthermore, there are several pages of more general, abstract discussion which contain no Spanish at all.

One might hypothesize that codes are shifted in response to E's suggestion and that M answers him in whatever language he speaks. This is clearly not the case. Several questions asked in English elicit Spanish responses and vice-versa.

In discussing the social aspects of switching, it is important to note that while the overt topic discussed is the use of English and

Spanish, much of the conversation is dominated by a concern with Mexican versus non-Mexican, i. e., common middle-class values or group membership. Spanish occurs most in episodes dealing with typically Mexican-American experiences. In several places fears are expressed that Mexican-American children are losing their language and thus, by implication, denying their proper cultural heritage. To some extent the juxtaposition of English and Spanish symbolizes the duality of value systems evidenced in the discussion.

At the start of the conversation several exchanges dealing with the mechanics of tape recorded operation are entirely in English. Code shifts begin with a sequence where M. asks E. why he is recording their talk and E. responds:

> 19. E: I want to use it as a...as an example of how chicanos can shift back and forth from one language to another.
>
> 20. M: Ooo. Como ándabamos platicando (OH. LIKE WE WERE SAYING).

M's switch to Spanish here is a direct response to his (E.'s) use of the word chicanos. Her statement refers to previous conversations they have had on related subjects and suggests that she is willing to treat the present talk as a friendly chat among fellow chicanos rather than as a formal interview.

Codes alternate only as long as all participants are chicanos and while their conversation revolves around personal experiences. Towards the end of the recording session, when a new participant enters, talk goes on. The newcomer is an American of English-speaking background who, having lived in Latin America, speaks Spanish fluently. Yet in this context she was addressed only in English and did not use her Spanish. Furthermore, in the earlier part of the session, when E. and M. were alone, there was one long episode where M. spoke only English even when responding to E's Spanish questions. This passage deals with M's visit to San Quentin prison, to see an inmate, and with prison conditions. The inmate was referred to only in English and the conversation contained

no overt reference to his ethnic background. Further inquiries made
while analysis was in progress revealed that he was a non-chicano.
It is evident from the first example that it is social identity and
not language per se which is determinant in code selection.   The
second example indicates when conversations have no reference to
speakers or their subjects' status as chicanos and when as in the
present case a subject is treated in a generally detached manner
without signs of personal involvement, code switching seems to be
inappropriate.

On the whole, one has the impression that except for a few
episodes dealing with recollections of family affairs, the entire
conversation is basically in English. English serves to introduce
most new information, while Spanish provides stylistic embroidering
to amplify the speaker's intent. Spanish sentences frequently take
the form of pre-coded, stereotyped or idiomatic phrases.

While ethnic identity is important as the underlying theme,
the actual contextual meanings of code alternation are more complex.

Turning to a more detailed analysis, many of the Spanish
passages reflect direct quotes or reports of what M. has said in
Spanish or of what other Mexican-Americans have told her, for
example:

21. Because I was speakin' to my baby... my ex-baby-sitter,
     and we were talkin' about the kids you know, an' I was
     tellin' her...uh, "Pero, como, you know...uh...la
     Estela y la Sandi...relistas en el telefon. Ya hablan
     mucho ingles." Dice, "Pos...si. Mira tu," dice,
     "Pos...el...las palabras del television. Yayu que
     me dice...ya me pide dinero pa'l 'ayscrin'y..." You
     know ? "Ya lue...y eso no es nada, esperate los
     chicharrones, you know, when they start school..."

     (BUT, HOW, YOU KNOW...UH..."ESTELA AND SANDI
     ARE VERY PRECOCIOUS ON THE TELEPHONE. THEY
     ALREADY SPEAK A LOT OF ENGLISH." SHE SAYS,

"WELL, YES, JUST IMAGINE" SHE SAYS, "WELL I
DON'T KNOW WHERE THEY GET IT FROM, " SHE
SAYS, "WELL, THE WORDS ON TELEVISION, AND
SHE ALREADY ASKS ME FOR MONEY FOR ICE CREAM
AND"... YOU KNOW ? "AND THEN... AND THAT ISN'T
ANYTHING, WAIT FOR THE CHICHARRONES, YOU
KNOW, WHEN THEY START SCHOOL"...)

Throughout the conversation Spanish is used in quoting
statements by individuals who chicano identity is emphasized. The
following passage in which Lola, who is of Mexican origin, is quoted
in English seemed to at first contradict this generalization.

22. An' Lola says, "Dixie has some, Dixie"... So Dixie
gave me a cigarette.

Lola, however, is in her late teens; and members of her age group,
although they know Spanish, tend to prefer English even in informal
interaction. Later on, however, if they marry within the chicano
community, they are quite likely to revert to the predominant usage
pattern. The use of English in her case reflects the fact that for
the present, at least, Lola identifies with the majority group of
English monolinguals with respect to language usage nouns.

The pattern of quoting chicanos in Spanish and talking about
them in English is reversed in the following passage in which M.
reports on the way she talks to her children:

23. Yea. Uh-huh. She'll get... "Linda, you don' do that,
mija...(DAUGHTER). Las vas...(YOU ARE GOING TO...)
you're going to get her... give her... a bad habit. "
Le pone el dedo pa 'que se lo muerda, (SHE GIVES HER
HER FINGER TO BITE), you know, "Iiya, she'll bite
the heck out of you. " "Ow!" La otra grita, (THE OTHER
ONE YELLS). So, una es sadist y la otra es masochist
(SO, ONE IS A SADIST AND THE OTHER IS A MASOCHIST).
(Laughter).

Further enquiry again reveals that in M.'s family children are ordinarily addressed in English.

Aside from direct quotes, Spanish occurs in several modifying phrases or sentences such as: those from Mexico, que tienen chamaquitos (Item 4). The effect here is to emphasize the ethnic identity of the referent. The use of si hay criaturas is particularly interesting in this respect. It is preceded by the following exchange:

24. M: There's no children. The Black Panthers next
        door. You know what I mean.
    E: Do they have kids?
    M: Just the two little girls.
    E: No, no. I mean, do some of the other people in
        the neighborhood have kids?
    M: They don't associate with no children... There's no
        children in the neighborhood. Well... si hay
        criaturas (THERE ARE CHILDREN, YES).

M. goes on to talk about the one other Mexican family in the building. The si hay criaturas here serves to single out Mexican children from others and in a sense modifies the there's no children several sentences above. The implication is that only the other chicano children are suitable playmates.

In the next group of examples the switch to Spanish signals the relative confidentiality or privateness of the message. The first example cited as Item 2 above is a case in point:

25. With each other. La senora trabaja en la caneria
    orita, you know. (THE MOTHER WORKS IN THE
    CANNERY.)

Here M.'s voice is lowered and the loudness decreases in somewhat the same way that confidentiality is signalled in English monolingual speech. Next consider the following:

26. E: An' how... about how about now?

M: Estos..me los halle...estos Pall Mall's me los
    hallaron (THESE...I FOUND...THESE PALL
    MALL'S...THEY WERE FOUND FOR ME...) No,
    I mean...

M. has been talking about the fact that she smokes very little, and
E. discovers some cigarettes on her desk. Her Spanish, punctuated
by an unusually large number of hesitation pauses, lends to the
statement an air of private confession. She is obviously slightly
embarrassed. Note the almost regular alternation between Spanish
and English in the next passage:

27. Mm-huh. Yeah. An'...an' they tell me "How did you
    quit, Mary ?" I di'n' quit. I...I just stopped. I mean
    it wasn' an effort I made que voy a dejar de fumar
    porque me hace dano o (THAT I'M GOING TO STOP
    SMOKING BECAUSE IT'S HARMFUL TO ME, OR...)
    this or that, uh-uh. It just...that...eh...I used to
    pull butts out of the...the...the wastepaper basket.
    Yeah. (Laughter). I used to go look in the...
    (Unclear)...se me acababan los cigarros en la noche.
    (MY CIGARETTES WOULD RUN OUT AT NIGHT.)
    I'd get desperate, y ahi voy al basurero a buscar, a
    sacar, you know? (Laughter) (AND THERE I GO TO THE
    WASTEBASKET TO LOOK FOR SOME, TO GET SOME).

The juxtaposition of the two codes here is used to great
stylistic effect in depicting the speaker's attitudes. The Spanish
phrases, partly by being associated with content like 'it is harmful
to me' or with references to events like 'cigarettes running out at
night' and through intonational and other suprasegmental clues,
convey a sense of personal feeling. The English phrases are more
neutral by contrast. The resulting effect of alternate personal
involvement and clinical detachment vividly reflects M.'s ambiguity
about her smoking.

A further example derives from a discussion session
recorded in Richmond, California, by a black community worker.

Participants include his wife and several teenage boys. Here we find alternation between speech features which are quite close to standard English and such typically black English features as lack of post-vocalic "r", double negation, and copula deletion.

28. You can tell me how your mother worked twenty hours a day and I can sit here and cry. I mean I can cry and I can feel for you. But as long as I don't get up and make certain that I and my children don't go through the same, I ain't did nothin' for you, brother. That's what I'm talking about.

29. Now Michael is making a point, where that everything that happens in that house affects all the kids. It does. And Michael and you makin' a point, too. Kids suppose' to learn how to avoid these things. But let me tell you. We're all in here. We talkin' but you see...

Note the underlined phrase in passage 28, with the typically black English phrase "ain't did nothin'" embedded in what is other-wise a normal standard English sequence. On our tape the shift is not preceded by a pause or marked off by special stress or intonation contours. The speaker is therefore not quoting from another code; his choice of form here lends emphasis to what he is saying. Passage 29 begins with a general statement addressed to the group as a whole. The speaker then turns to one person, Michael, and signals this change in focus by dropping the copula "is" and shifting to black phonology.

It seems clear that in all these cases, what the linguist sees merely as alternation between two systems, serves definite and clearly understandable communicative ends. The speakers do not merely switch from one variety to another, but they build on the coexistence of alternate forms to convey information.

It can be argued that language choice reflects the speaker's minority status within the English-speaking majority, and that selection of forms in particular cases,is related to such factors as ethnic identity, age, sex, degree of solidarity or confidentiality, etc. But the relationship of such social factors to speech form is quite different from what the sociologist means by correlation among variables. One could not take a rating of, for instance, ethnicity or degree of solidarity, as measured by the usual questionnaire techniques or other scaling devices, and expect this rating to predict the occurrence of Spanish or Black Dialect and Standard English in a text. Such ratings may determine the likelihood of a switch, but they do not tell when a switch will occur, nor do they predict its meaning. What seems to be involved here, rather, is a symbolic process akin to that by which words convey semantic information. Code switching, in other words, is meaningful in much the same way that lexical choice is meaningful.

To be sure, not all instances of code alternation convey meaning. Our tapes contain several instances where the shift into black English or the use of a Spanish word in an English sentence can only be interpreted as a slip of the tongue, frequently corrected in the next sentence, or where its use must be regarded merely as a sign of the speaker's lack of familiarity with the style he is employing. But, even though such errors do occur, it is neverthe- less true that code switching is also a communicative skill, which speakers use as a verbal strategy in much the same way that skillful writers switch styles in a short story.

How and by what devices does the speaker's selection of alternate forms communicate information? The process is a metaphoric process somewhat similar to what linguists interested in literary style have called foregrounding (Garvin, 1964). Fore- grounding in the most general sense of the term, relies on the fact that words are more than just names for things. Words also carry a host of culturally specific associations, attitudes, and values. These cultural values derive from the context in which words are usually used and from the activities with which they are associated. When a word is used in other than normal context, these associations become highlighted or foregrounded. Thus, to take an example made famous by Leonard Bloomfield (1936), the word "fox" when it refers to a man, as in "he is a fox", communicates

the notions of slyness and craftiness which our culture associates
with the activities of foxes.

    We assume that what holds true for individual lexical items
also holds true for phonological or syntactic alternates. Whenever a
speech variety is associated with a particular social category of
speakers or with certain activities, this variety comes to symbolize
the cultural values associated with these features of the non-linguistic
environment. In other words, speech varieties, like words, are
potentially meaningful and, in both cases, this is brought out by
re-interpreting meanings in relation to context. As long as the
variety in question is used in its normal environment, only its basic
referential sense is communicated. But when it is used in a new
context, it becomes socially marked, and the values associated with
the original context are mapped onto the new message.

    In any particular instance of code switching, speakers
deduce what is meant by an information processing procedure which
takes account of the speaker, the addressee, the social categories
to which they can be assigned in the context, the topic. etc. (Blom
and Gumperz, 1970). Depending on the nature of the above factors,
a wide variety of contextual meanings derive from the basic meaning
inclusion (we) versus exclusion (they). This underlying meaning is
then re-interpreted in the light of the co-occurring contextual
factors to indicate such things as degree of involvement (5), anger,
emphasis (7), change in focus (8), etc.

    We have chosen our examples from a number of languages
to highlight the fact that the meanings conveyed by code switching
are independent of the phonological shape or historical origin of the
alternates in question. The association between forms and meaning
is quite arbitrary. Any two alternates having the same referential
meaning can become carriers of social meaning.

    The ability to interpret a message is a direct function of the
listener's home background, his peer group experiences and his
education. Differences in background can lead to misinterpretation
of messages. The sentence "he is a Sikh" has little or no meaning

for an American audience. To anyone familiar with speech behavior in Northern India, however, it conveys a whole host of meanings, since Sikhs are stereotypically known as bumblers. Similarly, the statement "he is a fox" cited above, which conveys slyness to middle class whites, may be interpreted as a synonym for "he is handsome" by blacks. Communication thus requires both shared grammar and shared rules of language usage. Two speakers may speak closely related and, on the surface, mutually intelligible varieties of the same language, but they may nevertheless misunderstand each other because of differences in usage rules resulting from differences in background. We must know the speakers' normal usage pattern, i.e., which styles are associated as unmarked forms with which activities and relationships, as well as what alternates are possible in what context, and what cultural associations these carry.

Note that the view of culture that emerges from this type of analysis is quite different from the conventional one. Linguists attempting to incorporate cultural information into their descriptions tend to regard culture as a set of beliefs and attitudes which can be measured apart from communication. Even the recent work which utilizes actual speech samples by eliciting "subjective reactions" to these forms or evaluations, going considerably beyond earlier work, does not completely depart from this tradition, since it continues to rely on overt or conscious judgment. Our own material suggests that culture plays a role in communication which is somewhat similar to the role of syntactic knowledge in the decoding of referential meanings. Cultural differences, in other words, affect judgement both above and below the level of consciousness. A person may have every intention of avoiding cultural bias, yet by subconsciously superimposing his own interpretation on the verbal performance of others, he may, nevertheless, bias his judgment of their general ability, efficiency, etc.

Communication problems are compounded by the fact that we know very little about the distribution of usage rules in particular populations. For example, there seems to be no simple correlation with ethnic identity, nor is it always possible to predict usage rules on the basis of socio-economic indexes. While the majority of the speakers in a Puerto Rican block in Jersey City used Spanish in normal in-group communication and switched to English to indicate special affect, there are others residing among them, however, whose patterns differ significantly. A Puerto Rican college student took a tape recorder home and recorded informal family conversation over a period of several days. It is evident from his recording, and he himself confirms this in interviews, that in his family, English is the normal medium of informal conversation while Spanish is socially marked and serves to convey special connotations of intimacy and anger.

It follows that while the usual sociological measures of ethnic background, social class, educational achievements, etc., have some correlation with usage rules, they cannot be regarded as accurate predictors of performance in particular instances. On the contrary, social findings based on incomplete data or on populations different from those for which they were intended, may themselves contribute to cultural misunderstanding. The use of responses to formal tests and interviews to judge the verbal ability of lower class bilinguals is a case in point. Rosenthal has shown that teachers' expectations have a significant effect on learning (1969), and psychological experiments by Williams (1969) and Henrie (1969) point to the role that dialect plays in generating these expectations. When expectations created by dialect stereotypes are further reinforced by misapplied or inaccurate social science findings, education suffers.

Imagine a child in a classroom situation who in a moment of special excitement shifts to black speech. The teacher may have learned that black speech is systematic and normal for communication in Afro-American homes. Nevertheless, intent as she is upon helping the child to become fully bilingual, she may comment on the child's speech by saying, "We don't speak this way in the classroom," or she may ask the child to rephrase the sentence in standard English. No matter how the teacher expresses herself, the fact that she focuses on the form means that the teacher is not responding to the real meaning of the child's message. The child is most likely to interpret her remark as a rebuff and may feel frustrated in his

attempt at establishing a more personal relationship with the teacher.
In other words, by imposing her own monostylistic communicative
norms, the teacher may thwart her students' ability to express themselves fully. An incident from a taperecorded language session in
Black Language Arts will illustrate the point.

> Student: (reading from an autobiographical essay) This
> lady didn't have no sense.
>
> Teacher: What would be a standard English alternate for
> this sentence?
>
> Student: She didn't have any sense. But not this lady:
> she didn't have no sense.

Classroom observation of first-grade reading sessions in
a racially integrated California school district illustrates some of
the probems involved. Classes in the district include about 60
percent White and 40 percent Chicano, Black, and Oriental children.
College student observers find that most reading classes have a
tracking system such that children are assigned to fast or slow
reading groups and these groups are taught by different methods
and otherwise receive different treatment.

Even in first-grade reading periods, where presumably
all children are beginners, the slow reading groups tend to consist
of 90 percent Blacks and Chicanos. Does this situation reflect
real learning difficulties, or is it simply a function of our inability
to diagnose reading aptitude in culturally different children? Furthermore, given the need for some kind of ability grouping, how effective and how well adapted to cultural needs are the classroom devices
that are actually used to bridge the reading gap?

One reading class was divided into a slow reading group of
three children, and a second group of seven fast readers. The
teacher worked with one group at a time, keeping the others busy
with individual assignments. With the slow readers she concentrated
on the alphabet, on the spelling of individual words, and on

supposedly basic grammatical concepts such as the distinctions between questions and statements. She addressed the children in what White listeners would identify as pedagogical style. Her enunciation was deliberate and slow. Each word was clearly articulated with even stress and pitch, as if to avoid any verbal sign of emotion, approval or disapproval. Children were expected to speak only when called upon, and the teacher would insist that each question be answered before responding to further ideas. Unsolicited remarks were ignored even if they referred to the problem at hand. Pronunciation errors were corrected whenever they occurred, even if the reading task had to be interrupted. The children seemed distracted and inattentive. They were guessing at answers, 'psyching out' the teacher in the manner described by Holt (1965) rather than following her reasoning process. The following sequence symbolizes the artificiality of the situation:

> Teacher: Do you know what a question is? James, ask William a question.
>
> James: William, do you have a coat on?
>
> William: No, I do not have a coat on.

James asks his question and William answers in a style which approaches in artificiality that of the teacher, characterized by citation form pronunciation of [ey] rather than [ə] of the indefinite article, lack of contraction of 'do not', stress on the 'have', staccato enunciation as if to symbolize what they perceive to be the artificiality and incomprehensibility of the teacher's behavior.

With the advanced group, on the other hand, reading became much more of a group activity and the atmosphere was more relaxed. Words were treated in context, as part of a story. Children were allowed to volunteer answers. There was no correction of pronunciation, although some deviant forms were also heard. The children actually enjoyed competing with each other in reading, and the teacher responded by dropping her pedagogical monotone in favor of more animated natural speech. The activities around

the reading table were not lost on the slow readers, who were sitting
at their desks with instructions to practice reading on their own. They
kept looking at the group, neglecting their own books, obviously
wishing they could participate. After a while one boy picked up a
spelling game from a nearby table and began to work at it with the
other boy, and they began to argue in a style normal for black children.
When their voices were raised, the teachers turned and asked them
to go back to reading.

In private conversation, the teacher (who is very conscientious
and seemingly concerned with all her children's progress) justified
her ability grouping on the grounds that children in the slow group
lacked books in their homes and "did not speak proper English. " She
stated they needed practice in grammar and abstract thinking and
pronunciation and suggested that, given this type of training, they
would eventually be able to catch up with the advanced group. We
wonder how well she will succeed. Although clearly she has the
best motives and would probably be appalled if one were to suggest
that her ability grouping and her emphasis on the technical aspects
of reading and spelling with culturally different children is culturally
biased, her efforts are not so understood by the children themselves.
Our data indicate that the pedagogical style used with slow readers
carries different associations for low middle class and low income
groups. While whites identify it as normal teaching behavior,
blacks associate it with the questioning style of welfare investigators
and automatically react by not cooperating. In any case, attuned
as they are to see meaning in stylistic choice, the black children
in the slow reading group cannot fail to notice that they are being
treated quite differently and with less understanding than the
advanced readers.

What are the implications of this type of situation for our
understanding of the role of dialect differences on classroom learning? There is no question that the grammatical features of black
dialects discovered by urban dialectologists in recent years are of
considerable importance for the historical study of the origin of
these dialects and for linguistic theory in general, but this does not
necessarily mean that they constitute an impediment to learning.

Information on black dialect is often made known to educators in the form of simple lists of deviant features with the suggestion that these features might interfere with reading.   There is little if any experimental evidence, for example, that the pronunciations characteristic of urban Black English actually interfere with the reading process. Yet the teacher in our classroom spent considerable time attempting to teach her slow readers the distinction between pin and pen.   Lack of a vowel distinction in these two words is widespread among Blacks, but also quite common among Whites in Northern California.   In any case, there is no reason why homophony in this case should present more difficulty than homophony in such words as 'sea' and 'see' and 'know' and 'no' or that created by the midwestern dialect speaker's inability to distinguish 'Mary,' 'marry,' and 'merry.'

The problem of contextual relevance is not confined to contact with speakers of Black English. It also applies, for example, to the teaching of both English and Spanish in bilingual schools. When interviewed about their school experiences, Puerto Rican high school students in New York as well as Texas and California Chicano students uniformly complain about their lack of success in Spanish instruction. They resent the fact that their Spanish teachers single out their own native usages as sub-standard and inadmissable both in classroom speech and writing.

It is not enough simply to present the educator with the descriptive linguistic evidence on language or dialect differences. What we need is properly controlled work on reading as such, work which does not deal with grammar alone. Our data suggest that urban language differences, while they may or may not interfere with reading, do have a significant influence on a teacher's expectation, and hence on the learning environment. In other words, regardless of overtly expressed attitudes, the teachers are quite likely to be influenced by what they perceive as deviant speech and failure to respond to questions and will act accordingly, thus potentially inhibiting the students' desire to learn. Since bilinguals and bidialectals rely heavily on code-switching as a verbal strategy, they are especially sensitive to the relationship between language and context. It would seem that they learn best under conditions of maximal contextual reinforcement. Sole concentration on the technical aspects of reading, grammar and spelling may so adversely affect the learning environment as to outweigh any advantages to be gained.

Experience with a summar program in language arts for minority group members — mostly of Chicano origin — suggests a method for dealing with this problem (Waterhouse, 1969). Course attendance in this program was voluntary, and it soon became evident through group discussion that if the course were to be continued it could not start with the usual grammar and instruction. Several weeks of discussion were therefore devoted to achieving some agreement on the kind of communicative goals that would be relevant to students and that would require standard English. Once this agreement had been achieved, students then set out to enact such interaction sequences in the classroom using a role-play technique. Texts then produced in this way were discussed in relation to their communicative effectiveness; and in the course of this discussion, students soon began to correct their own and fellow students' grammar. The teacher's role was reduced to that of a discussion moderator, an arbiter of effectiveness, with the result that student motivation increased tremendously and learning improved dramatically.

It seems clear that progress in urban language instruction is not simply a matter of better teaching aids and improved textbooks. Middle class adults have to learn to appreciate differences in communicative strategies of the type discussed here. Teachers themselves must be given instruction in both the linguistic and ethnographic aspects of speech behavior. They must become acquainted with code selection rules in formal and informal settings as well as those themes of folk literature and folk art that form the input to these rules, so that they can diagnose their own communication problems and adapt methods to their children's background.

NOTES

Research reported on in this paper has been supported by grants from the Urban Crisis Program and the Institute of International

Studies, University of California, Berkeley. I am grateful to Eduardo Hernández and Louisa Lewis for assistance in field work and analysis.

The point of view expressed in this paper leans heavily on the work of Caludia Kernan (1969).

BIBLIOGRAPHY

Abrahams, Roger D. 1964. Deep Down in the Jungle. Hatboro, Pennsylvania: Folklore Associates.

Blom, Jan Petter and John J. Gumperz. 1971. "Social Meaning in Linguistic Structures: Code-Switching in Norway." In John J. Gumperz and Dell Hymes (Eds.), Directions in Sociolinguistics. New York: Holt, Rinehart and Winston. [In this volume, pp. 271-307.]

Bloomfield, Leonard. 1936. Language. New York.

Fishman, Joshua. 1965. "Who Speaks What Language to Whom and When. La Linguistique 2. 67-88.

Friedrich, Paul. 1966. Structural Implications of Russian Pronominal Usage. Sociolinguistics. Edited by William Bright, 214-253. The Hague: Mouton.

Garvin, Paul (Ed.). 1969. A Prague School Reader. Washington, D.C.: Georgetown University Press.

Gumperz, John J. and Edward Hernández. 1969. "Cognitive Aspects of Bilingual Communication." Working Paper No. 28, Language-Behavior Research Laboratory, University of California, Berkeley.

Hannerz, Ulf. 1968. Soulside. New York: Columbia University Press.

Henrie, Samuel N., Jr. 1969. "A Study of Verb Phrases Used by
    Five Year Old Non-standard Negro English Speaking Child-
    ren." Unpublished Ph.D. dissertation, University of Califor-
    nia, Berkeley.

Holt, John Caldwell. 1964. How Children Fail. New York: Pit-
    man. 1964.

Kernan, Claudia Mitchell. 1969. Language Behavior in a Black
    Urban Community. Working Paper No. 23, Language-
    Behavior Research Laboratory, University of California,
    Berkeley. October, 1969.

Kochman, Thomas. 1969. "'Rapping' in the Black Ghetto." Trans-
    action. February, 1969, pp. 26-34.

Labov, William. 1969. "The Logic of Non-Standard Negro English."
    In Linguistics and the Teaching of Standard English. Mono-
    graph Series on Languages and Linguistics, No. 22. Wash-
    ington, D.C.: Georgetown University Press.

Lance, Donald M. 1969. A Brief Study of Spanish-English Bilingual-
    ism. Research Report, Texas A & M University.

Mehan, B. 1970. Unpublished lecture on testing and bilingualism in
    the Chicano community delivered to the Kroeber Anthropolo-
    gical Society Meetings, April 25, 1970.

Rosenthal, Robert. 1968. Pygmalion in the Classroom. New York:
    Holt, Rinehart and Winston.

Sacks, Harvey. 1970. "On the Analyzability of Stories by Children."
    In John J. Gumperz and Dell Hymes (Eds.), Directions in
    Sociolinguistics. New York: Holt, Rinehart and Winston,
    in press.

Schegloff, Emanuel. 1970. "Sequencing in Conversational Openings."
    In John J. Gumperz and Dell Hymes (Eds.), Directions in
    Sociolinguistics. New York: Holt, Rinehart and Winston,
    in press.

Shuy, Roger W. 1964. Social Dialects and Language Learning.
    Champaign, Illinois: National Council of Teachers of
    English.

Stewart, W. 1968. "Continuity and Change in American Negro Dia-
    lects." The Florida FL Reporter. Spring, 1968.

Troike, Rudolph C. 1969. "Receptive Competence, Productive
    Competence and Performance." In James E. Alatais (Ed.),
    Linguistics and the Teaching of Standard English. Mono-
    graph Series on Languages and Linguistics No. 22. Wash-
    ington, D. C.: Georgetown University Press. pp. 63-75.

Waterhouse, John. 1969. Final Report, Comparative Literature 1A,
    Section 4, and Comparative Literature 1B, Section 5. Eng-
    lish for Foreign Students Program, University of California,
    Berkeley. Typescript.

Williams, Frederick. 1969. "Psychological Correlates of Speech
    Characteristics: on Sounding 'Disadvantaged.'" Unpubl. ms.,
    Institute for Research on Poverty, University of Wisconsin,
    Madison, March 1969.

18 | Author's Postscript

The essays in this volume span a period which saw many basic changes in our approaches to language and to speaking as a social activity. Linguistics has grown from a little known academic specialty into an established discipline, whose practitioners are in the vanguard of social science theory and whose advice is sought on a broad spectrum of practical problems ranging from computer technology, psychotherapy and cross-cultural communication to urban education and socio-economic development. Inevitably the scope of linguistics has changed, with the result that increasingly different types of data are becoming amenable to formal analysis. This volume reflects some of the theoretical issues arising from this expansion in scope.

The field work for these papers began at a time when information on speech behavior was largely limited to data from either the well known standardized-language societies such as France, Germany, Russia or China or from work on socially uniform tribal groups such as the American Indians. Given the information available then, most theorists tended to think of speech communities as consisting of speakers of one language, speaking grammatically alike, genetically related dialects. Grammatical analysis of a language seemed synonymous with studying the language behavior of human groups.

Work in Asia and Africa, along with the renewed studies of social dialects in the urban United States and England, has brought out the limitations of the notion of linguistically uniform speech communities. As detailed data become available, it can be shown that all but the very smallest speech communities are linguistically diverse and that this diversity serves important and necessary communicative

functions (chapter 8). Language varieties spoken within communities
moreover are by no means equally distinct and the degree of language
distance which separates them is not always a direct function of genetic affiliation. Many instances exist where, what are popularly
regarded as two distinct languages, are grammatically so alike as to
be almost indistinguishable in terms of the traditional analytical
categories (chapter 14). On the other hand, grammatically quite
distinct systems may be popularly regarded as part of the same language (see Ferguson's Diglossia, 1959). Clearly, the relationship
between the linguists' grammatical system and the speech behavior
of human groups is more complex than had been assumed. Empirical comparative study is required to investigate this relationship and
to this end new concepts are needed which enable us to separate the
study of speech distribution from other aspects of descriptive or historical linguistics and from the sociological study of language stereotypes, attitudes and values about language. The concepts of speech
community and linguistic repertoire, discussed in chapters 6 and 7,
attempt to meet this need.

The degree of grammatical diversity is not in itself the most
important sociolinguistic characteristic of linguistic repertoire.
Repertoires vary from bi- or multilingual systems to bidialectal and
grammatically homogeneous systems. What seems more important
socially is the way in which the grammatical options or variables in
the system co-occur in communicative situations. We can distinguish between compartmentalized systems, divisible into a number of
discrete speech varieties and fluid systems, where speech varieties
shade into one another as in a dialect continuum (chapter 9). It is
the linguistic relationship between varieties, as measured by co-
occurrence constraints (chapter 14) which are most sensitive to
social change. Compartmentalization seems to relate to social isolation of sub-groups while fluidity is connected with free occupational
mobility and lack of role segregation, such as are characteristic of
many rapidly changing societies.

A second major theme of this volume is the specification of
the relationship of sub-groups to the distribution of speech variants.
Until quite recently, our view of language and society was dominated

by Sapir who thought of languages as systems of signs having stable grammatical cores relatively impervious to social change. My earlier dissertation research on a German dialect spoken in the rural United States had shown that the present day distribution of dialect variants reflects the social and religious groupings formed after settlement in the nineteenth century United States and is not a direct function of dialect history. A South Asian village with its rigid caste stratification seemed an ideal test situation for examining the relationship between social stratification and dialect distribution in more detail. The hypothesis was that rigid caste boundaries should also be reflected by sharp intra-community dialect isoglosses.

Twenty months of field work in an Indian village provided only partial confirmation for this hypothesis. It was found that eighty percent of the local inhabitants, representing twenty-four indigenous castes spoke a single dialect while each of the remaining three, numerically small, untouchable groups showed distinct dialect features of its own. The anthropologist's categories of caste do not account for these findings nor can an explanation be based on such variables as wealth, education, social status or density of communication. The key explanatory factor seemed to be the norms governing the quality of social relations—norms which constrain friendship formation patterns and control the content of interpersonal communication (chapter 3).

We must conclude that the traditional practice of simply correlating the linguists' findings with independently collected social information is unsatisfactory for the study of ongoing social communication practices. What is needed is a model for sociolinguistic description which provides for ways of gathering linguistic and social information in terms of a single theoretical framework. Field work in Norway was concerned with this problem (chapters 6 and 16). The Norwegian community stands at the opposite end of the social spectrum from the Indian village. Local residents think of themselves as a community of equals, where differences in social rank are at a minimum and income differentials of little importance. Yet even in this apparently uniform group there were clearly detectable dialect differences and as in the Indian situation the norms governing interpersonal relations were again the determining factor. There are grounds, therefore, for postulating a new level of sociolinguistic analysis—the level of social communication. Ethnographic investigation of communication networks and communicative norms at this level is needed before we can specify in more detail how language usage relates to the macro-sociological categories of caste, class, role, and the like.

While the Indian fieldwork data had relied largely on the traditional linguist-informant elicitation procedures, the Norwegian linguistic data were supplemented by tape recorded experiments with natural friendship groups. Analysis of these discussion tapes called attention to the question of language usage rules, or rules by which speakers select among referentially equivalent forms within the repertoire. This problem has assumed major importance in modern sociolinguistics.

Much effort has been devoted to describing the use of linguistic variants in terms of the social environment, domain, setting, or speech event in which these variants occur. Our findings in Norway (chapter 16) along with the subsequent work in the urban United States (chapter 17) show that while there are some situations or speech events in which language use is predictable or narrowly prescribed there are always others which allow for the use of many alternates. Even in these latter less constrained cases, however, the occurrence of variants is not random. On the contrary, bilingual or bidialectal linguistic variants are used metaphorically in much the same way that choice between alternate forms of address intonation or stress patterns is used by monolinguals to communicate degrees of solidarity or distance. Thus, code-switching is not merely a case of grammatical variation, but can be regarded as a semantic process, a device for communicating social meaning.

Although the work described here deals largely with small groups, a number of issues emerge which have important implications for questions of politics and language planning. Much of the discussion in this latter area has focused on the growth of new standard languages in the developing countries. Linguists have been concerned with the creation of new technical vocabularies and with problems of standardizing grammar and spelling. The political and factional

strife that accompanies the standardization process has also evoked a
great deal of discussion. The ethnographic field work in India highlights the need for studies assessing the ways in which alternate
standardization policies affect internal communication. The social
mobilization processes that characterize political change in developing
countries require the opening of new channels of communication between governing elites and the rest of the population. The problem
here is not simply what language is to be chosen but how the standardization process is to be carried out. Linguistic analysis is required
to monitor the grammatical implications of the introduction of new
technical terminologies. If these new terminologies result in the
creation of new and obscure literary styles, the resulting compartmentalization of repertoire may favor certain elite groups and create
unnecessary problems for other groups, with the result that mobilization processes are impaired (chapters 2 and 8).

The final essay in this volume deals with the problem of language instruction in ethnically diverse schools, a problem which has
been at the center of sociolinguistic discussion in the United States
in recent years. In attempting to explain learning failure of ethnic
minority groups, linguists have tended to blame dialect differences.
The present analysis suggests that the dialect differences per se are
less important than miscommunication due to differences in communicative strategies, such strategies are signals of speakers' intent and
can crucially affect students' and teachers' ability to cooperate.

Taken together, the essays in this volume show a gradual
change of emphasis from dialect description to a focus on speaking as
a phenomenon of interest and as a manifestation of social order. To
the extent that criticism of work in modern linguistics is expressed,
the criticism is not directed toward linguistic theory per se, but at
the failure of linguists to deal adequately with the practical and sociological problems with which they are concerned. The goal is to raise
new issues for further research which, when properly investigated,
might lead to a theory of language behavior, which will make linguistic techniques more applicable to the study of social science problems.

Bibliography of
John J. Gumperz's Works

Compiled by Anwar S. Dil

List of Abbreviations:

AA	American Anthropologist
AnL	Anthropological Linguistics
IJAL	International Journal of American Linguistics
IL	Indian Linguistics
JASt	Journal of Asian Studies
Lg	Language
MSLL	Georgetown University Monograph Series on Languages and Linguistics
RPh	Romance Philology

1955 The phonology of a North Indian village dialect; the use of phonemic data in dialectology. IL [Chatterji Jubilee Volume] 16.283-95.

1957 a. Language problems in the rural development of North India. JASt 16.251-59. [Reprinted in Study of the role of second languages in Asia, Africa and Latin America, ed. by Frank A. Rice, 79-90. Washington, D.C.: Center for Applied Linguistics, 1962.]

   b. (With H.S. Bilgiri). Notes on the phonology of Mundari. IL [Taraporewala Memorial Volume] 17.6-15.

   c. Some remarks on regional and social language differences in India. Introduction to the Civilization of India: Changing Dimensions in Indian Society and Culture, ed. by M. Singer, 31-38. Chicago: The College, University of Chicago Syllabus Division.

1958 a. Dialect differences and social stratification in a North
Indian village. <u>AA</u> 60.668-81. [Bobbs-Merrill reprint
A-98.]

b. Linguistics and language teaching. <u>IL</u> [Supplement.
Proceedings of a Conference of Vice-Chancellors and
Linguists] 18.105-10.

c. Phonological differences in three Hindi dialects. <u>Lg</u>
34.212-24.

1960 a. (Ed. with Charles A. Ferguson). <u>Linguistic diversity in
South Asia.</u> <u>IJAL</u> 26:3, Part 3. = Publication 13 of the
Indiana University Research Center in Anthropology,
Folklore and Linguistics. viii, 118 p.

b. (With Charles A. Ferguson). Introduction. <u>Linguistic
diversity in South Asia</u>, ed. by C.A. Ferguson and J. J.
Gumperz, 1-18. <u>IJAL</u> 26:3, Part 3. [Reprinted in
<u>Language structure and language use: essays by Charles
A. Ferguson</u>, Selected and Introduced by Anwar S. Dil,
27-49. Stanford: Stanford University Press, 1971. Also
reprinted in <u>Readings in dialectology</u>, ed. by Wolfgang
Wolk. New York: Holt, Rinehart and Winston, in press.]

c. (With C.M. Naim). Formal and informal standards
in Hindi regional language area. <u>Linguistic diversity
in South Asia</u>, ed. by C.A. Ferguson and J.J. Gumperz,
92-118. <u>IJAL</u> 26:3, Part 3.

d. Munda languages. <u>Encyclopaedia Britannica</u> 15.991.
(-1971 edition).

e. The content of the first and second year language course.
<u>Resources for the study of South Asian languages</u>, ed. by
W. Norman Brown, 70-73. Philadelphia: University
of Pennsylvania Press.

f. <u>Hindi reader</u>, Vol. 1. Berkeley: Center for South
Asia Studies, University of California. iv, 207 p.

g. (With C.M. Naim). <u>Urdu reader</u>. Berkeley: Center
for South Asia Studies, University of California.
iv, 226 p.

1961 a. The language problem in South Asian studies. <u>Asian</u>
         <u>Survey</u> 1:2.28-31.
     b. Review of <u>The measurement of meaning</u>, by C.E. Osgood
         <u>et. al</u>. RPh 15.63-69.
     c. Speech variation and the study of Indian civilization.
         <u>AA</u> 63.976-88. [Reprinted in <u>Language in culture and</u>
         <u>society</u>, ed. by Dell Hymes, 416-28. New York:
         Harper and Row, 1964.]

1962 a. Means of increasing the student's use of vernacular in
         his area studies. <u>Conference on the strengthening and</u>
         <u>integration of South Asian language and area studies</u>,
         ed. by R. Lambert, 118-25. Philadelphia: University
         of Pennsylvania Press.
     b. Types of linguistic communities. <u>AL</u> 4:1.28-40.
         [Reprinted in <u>Readings in the sociology of language</u>,
         ed. by J.A. Fishman, 460-72. The Hague: Mouton,
         1968.] [Translated into Spanish and included in <u>Reader</u>
         <u>in ethno- and sociolinguistics</u>, ed. by P.L. Garvin and
         Y. Lastra, in preparation.]
     c. (With Ellen M. Gumperz). Naming practices in the
         Hindi speaking area. Washington, D.C.: Center for
         Applied Linguistics. Mimeographed.

1963 a. (With June Rumery). <u>Conversational Hindi-Urdu</u>.
         Vol. 1, Parts 1 and 2. Berkeley: University of Cali-
         fornia. xxx, 187; viii, 372 p.
     b. <u>Conversational Hindi-Urdu</u>. Vol. 2. Berkeley: ASUC
         Bookstore, University of California. xiv, 241 p.

1964 a. (Ed. with Dell Hymes). <u>The ethnography of communi-</u>
         <u>cation</u>. <u>AA</u> 66:6, Part 2. vi, 186 p.
     b. Linguistic and social interaction in two communities.
         <u>The ethnography of communication</u>, ed. by J.J. Gumperz
         and D. Hymes, 137-53. <u>AA</u> 66:6, Part 2. [Reprinted
         in <u>Man makes sense</u>, ed. by E.A. Hammel and W.S.

Simmons, 291-307. Boston: Little, Brown and Co.,
1970.]

c.   Hindi-Punjabi code switching in Delhi. Proceedings of
the ninth international congress of linguists, ed. by
H. Lunt, 1115-24. The Hague: Mouton and Co.
d.   Religion and social communication in village North India.
JASt 23.89-97.
e.   A brief Hindi reference grammar. Berkeley: Center
for South Asia Studies, University of California. 55 p.
Mimeographed.

1965 a.   Language. Biennial review of anthropology, ed. by B. J.
Siegal, 84-120. Stanford: Stanford University Press.
b.   The social group as a primary unit of analysis in dialect
study. Social dialects and language learning, ed. by R.
Shuy, 127-29. Champaign, Illinois: National Council
of Teachers of English.

1966 a.   Linguistic repertoires, grammars, and second language
instruction. MSLL 18.81-91.
b.   On the ethnology of linguistic change. Sociolinguistics,
ed. by W. Bright, 27-49. The Hague: Mouton and Co.
c.   Discussion. Sociolinguistics, ed. by W. Bright, 41,43,
44-47, 48, 69-70, 106, 161, 254, 275, 306, 307-308.

1967 a.   Language and communication. The Annals of the American Academy of Political and Social Science 373.219-31.
b.   Native informants, assistants, and interpreters. A
field manual for cross-cultural study of the acquisition
of communicative competence, ed. by D. I. Slobin,
84-92. Berkeley: ASUC Bookstore, University of
California.
c.   The relation of linguistic to social categories. A field
manual for cross-cultural study of the acquisition of
communicative competence, ed. by D. I. Slobin, 129-34.
d.   On the linguistic markers of bilingual communication.
Problems of bilingualism, ed. by J. MacNamara,
48-57. Journal of Social Issues [Special issue] 23:2.

1968 a. Some desiderata in South Asian areal linguistics. <u>Studies in Indian linguistics: M. B. Emeneau Felicitation Volume</u>, ed. by Bh. Krishnamurti, 118-23. Poona, India: Linguistic Society of India and Deccan College.

 b. The speech community. <u>International Encyclopedia of Social Sciences</u> 9. 381-86 (1968 edition).

 c. Language in social interaction. <u>Proceedings of the 8th international congress of anthropological and ethnological sciences</u>, 408-11. Tokyo: Science Council of Japan.

1969 a. Communication in multilingual societies. <u>Cognitive Anthropology</u>, ed. by S. Tyler, 435-49. New York: Holt, Rinehart and Winston.

 b. The measurement of bilingualism in social groups. <u>The description and measurement of bilingualism</u>, ed. by L. G. Kelly, 242-49. Toronto, Canada: University of Toronto Press.

 c. Sociolinguistics in South Asia. <u>Current trends in linguistics. V. linguistics in South Asia</u>, ed. by T. A. Sebeok, 597-606. The Hague: Mouton and Co.

 d. (With J. Das Gupta). Language, communication, and control in North India. <u>Language problems of developing nations</u>, ed. by J. A. Fishman, C. A. Ferguson, and J. Das Gupta, 151-66. New York: John Wiley and Sons. [Reprinted in <u>Reader in culture change</u>, ed. by J. Potter. New York: Harper and Row, in press.]

 e. (With Eduardo Hernández Ch.). Cognitive aspects of bilingual communication. Working paper 28, Language-Behavior Research Laboratory, University of California, Berkeley. [<u>Language use and social change</u>, ed. by W. H. Whitely, 111-25. London: Oxford University Press, 1971.]

1970 a. Sociolinguistics and communication in small groups. Working paper 33, Language-Behavior Research Laboratory, University of California, Berkeley. [Reprinted in <u>Readings in sociolinguistics</u>, ed. by

J.B. Pride. London: Penguin, in press. Also reprinted as: Sociolinguistics and problem solving.
Family problem solving: a symposium on theoretical,
methodological and substantive concerns, ed. by
Joan Aldous et al. New York: Dryden Press, in press.]

b.   Verbal strategies in multilingual communication.
Working paper 36, Language-Behavior Research Laboratory, University of California, Berkeley. [MSLL
23.129-47. Also to appear in Language, culture, and
education, ed. by R. Abrahams and R. Troike.
Englewood Cliffs, New Jersey: Prentice Hall, Inc.,
in preparation.]

c.   Comments. MSLL 23.22-23, 57, 145, 146-47.

1971 a.   Convergence and Creolization: a case from the Indo-
Ary.an/ Dravidian border in India. Pidginization and
creolization, ed. by D. Hymes, pp. 151-67. Cambridge:
Cambridge University Press.

b.   (With Jan-Petter Blom). Social meaning in linguistic
structures: code-switching in Norway. In this volume,
pp. 274-310. [To appear in Directions in sociolinguistics,
ed. by J. J. Gumperz and D. H. Hymes. New York: Holt,
Rinehart and Winston, in press.]

c.   (Ed. with Dell Hymes). Directions in sociolinguistics.
New York: Holt, Rinehart and Winston, in press.

d.   (With Eduardo Hernández Ch.). Bilingualism, bidialectalism, and classroom interaction. In this volume, pp. 311-
39. [To appear in Functions of language in the classroom,
ed. by C.B. Cazden, V.P. John, and D. Hymes. New York:
Teachers College Press, in press.]

e.   The communicative competence of bilinguals. Language in
in Society 1, in press.

f.   Author's postscript. In this volume, pp. 340-44.

g.   John J. Gumperz on language in social groups. Perspectives in linguistic education: conversations with language
scholars, by Anwar S. Dil. Abbottabad, West Pakistan:
Linguistic Research Group of Pakistan, in press.

Gumperz, John J   1922-
        Language in social groups:
essays by John J. Gumperz. Selected and   .
Introduced by Anwar S. Dil. Stanford, California:
Stanford University Press [1971]
            xvi, 348 p.   24cm.
(Language science and national development series,
Linguistic Research Group of Pakistan)
        Includes bibliography.

I. Dil, Anwar S. ,   1928-   ed.
II. (Series) III. Linguistic Research Group of Pakistan

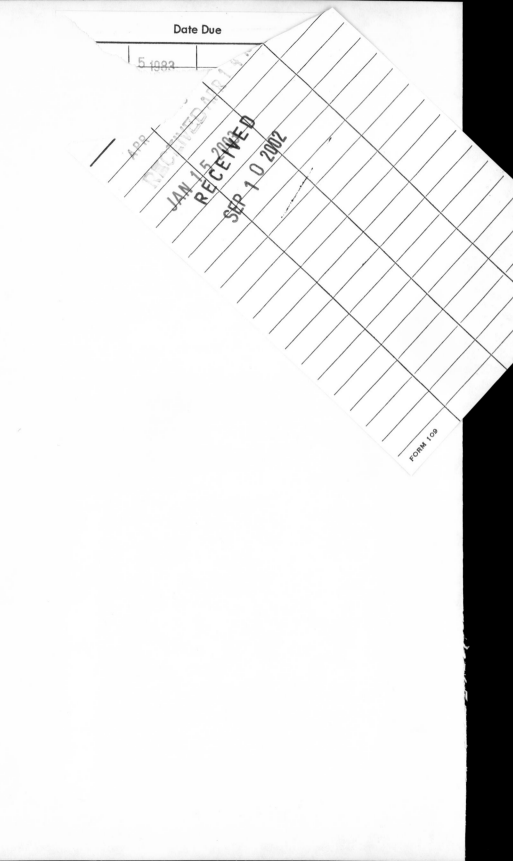